.EMOUNTAINS.CABRAMURRA.CARRAI.COBARGO.COLINTON.COLOHEIGH
.NJOLA.COOLUMBURRA.CORANG.DEU'
OROUGH.EMMAVILLE.FORBESRIVER.GI
LA.JOHNSRIVER.KANGAROOVALLEY.KC
RAJONGHEIGHTS.LAURELHILL.MALLAC
RICUMBENE.MORORO.MOUNTGEORGE.I
.NERRIGUNDAH.NEWNES.NIMBIN.NOV
TABULAM.TALBINGO.TOWAMBA.TOWO
Y.WYNDHAM.STANTHORPE.ARALUEN.I
ELLANGRY.BELLBROOK.BEMBOKA.BENDALONG.BERAMBING.BILPIN.BOBIN
GANNA.BOWENFELS.BOYDTOWN.BROULEE.BULGAFOREST.BULLIO.BUNDA
.BUNDOORA.BUNGAWALBIN.BLUEMOUNTAINS.CABRAMURRA.CARRAI.CO
COLINTON.COLOHEIGHTS.CONJOLA.COOLUMBURRA.CORANG.DEUAR
EY.DOYALSON.EBOR.ELLENBOROUGH.EMMAVILLE.FORBESRIVER.GLENR
'OP.JEOGLA.JERRAWANGALA.JOHNSRIVER.KANGAROOVALLEY.KOORA
CIUSZKO.KULNURA.KURRAJONGHEIGHTS.LAURELHILL.MALLACOO
^NGROVECREEK.MERRICUMBENE.MORORO.MOUNTGEORGE.MU
NERRIGUNDAH.NEWNES.NIMBIN.NOWRA
ABULAM.TALBINGO.TOWONG.TOWONG
NVALLEY.WYNDHAM.STANTHORPE
.HAVEN.BATLOW.BELLANGRY.BELLBROOK.P
J.BILPIN.BOBIN.BOORGANNA.BOWENFELS
.EST.BULLIO.BUNDANOON.BUNDOORA.BU^
ABRAMURRA.CARRAI.COBARGO.COLINTON
.MBURRA.CORANG.DEUARIVERVALLEY.DOY^
AVILLE.FORBESRIVER.GLENREAGHHILLTOP.'

EARTH CRIES

.KA.. ..ORAINGHAT.KOS(
.S.LAUREL....OOTA.MALUAB^
CROR.MOUNTGE.....MULLOON.NAB
H.NEWNES.NIMBIN.NOWRA.PADDYSRI'
INGO.TOWAMBA.TOWONG.WEROMBI.
ANTHORP.ARALUEN.BALMORAL.BAR(
OK.BEMBOKA.BENDALONG.BERAM.
OYDTOWN.BROULEE.BULGAFORE
BLUEMOUNTAINS.CABRAM(
NJOLA.COOLUMBURRA.C(
OUGH.EMMAVILLE.FORBES.
OHNSRIVER.KANGAROOVAL.
ONGHEIGHTS.LAURELHILL.MA
UMBENE.MORORO.MOUNTGEO!
RRIGUNDAH.NEWNES.NIMBIN.
' AM.TALBINGO.TOWAMBA.T(
HAM.STANTHORPE.ARAL'
BELLBROOK.BEMBOK
'FELS.BOYDTO'
NGAWALBI'
LOHEIGH
.EBOR.F
.JERR^
.KU'
RO'
N

Dedicated to a world burning.

First published in 2021 by the University of Sydney.

Funded by the University of Sydney Faculty of Arts and Social Sciences School of Literature, Art and Media.

Sydney University Press
Fischer Library F03
University of Sydney
NSW 2006 AUSTRALIA

Email: sup.info@sydney.edu.au
sydneyuniversitypress.com.au

 A catalogue record for this book is available from the National Library of Australia

ISBN: 978-1-74210-476-8 (paperback)
ISBN: 978-1-74210-477-5 (epub)
ISBN: 978-1-74210-478-2 (mobi)

Cover design: Emily Bronte Smith and Mary Stanley
Text layout: Melissa Snook

CONTENTS

CONTENTS

IMAGES

ACKNOWLEDGEMENTS

None of us could have imagined what this year had in store when we set out to create the 2020 University of Sydney Anthology. It has been a long and difficult journey, but seeing *Earth Cries* take shape has been unbelievably rewarding. There were so many people who helped us shape this spark of the imagination into a published work, and we'd like to take a moment to thank them.

To start things off, we would like to extend an extra special thanks to Agata Mrva-Montoya, who generously donated hours upon hours of her time to guide us through the development of this anthology. Your support and guidance throughout this project has been invaluable and we could not have done this without you.

Thank you to Dr Karl Kruszelnicki, for generously contributing the foreword to *Earth Cries*. Your expertise and insight are beyond anything we could have written ourselves and we cannot thank you enough.

To all of the students, staff and alumni of the University of Sydney who contributed to this year's anthology, without your incredible contributions there would be no *Earth Cries*. Whether through prose, poetry or artwork, each of you presented a unique and inspirational perspective on the climate crisis. Each and every one of you is incredibly talented in your field. Thank you all for allowing us to share your wonderful contributions.

We would like to specially thank Christine Dundas from the Sydney Environment Institute, and all of the University of Sydney's Marketing and Communication team, academic liaison librarians, and department staff for taking the time to advertise our call for submissions. For the first time, our submissions marketing had to be done entirely digitally and your support helped us gather an astounding range of talent from across the university community.

Thank you to Philip Glen and Marc Fernando from the Digital Media Unit for your continuing support with our website. Thank you to the Department of Media and Communications at Sydney University, without whose support and funding we would not be able to produce this anthology.

A very big thank you to the team at Sydney University Press, who continues each year to support the anthology through every stage of the publishing process.

Thank you to Dr Joëlle Gergis and the Australian Academy of Science for giving us permission to quote your work. Thank you to all our past writers and illustrators, for allowing us to share your contributions on our blog and social media.

We would like to thank Diana Chamma for creating our marketing material, and Emily Truman for giving her time during the beginning of this project.

And lastly, to the anthology team. All of you have been a joy to work with over the course of the past year. We've faced so many unexpected challenges this year, and yet you've all pulled through fantastically. From designing new awareness campaigns when we couldn't get on campus, to adapting to an entirely digital meeting process, all of you have exceeded expectations and I couldn't be prouder to call myself a part of our team. Thank you for creating an incredible 2020 anthology.

FOREWORD

Dr Karl Kruszelnicki

This anthology, *Earth Cries*, looks at our current and future planet – with Climate Change as a constant underlying thread.

Part of this anthology's strength is its broadness – poetry, photography, art, fiction and non-fiction. Using these different viewpoints, it ranges across modern-day bushfires and water shortages to apocalyptic visions of the future; from non-meat diets to the ecology of insects; from recycling waste to plastics and electric cars – and even the environmental cost of clothing and emails.

So I will take a different viewpoint, and look at climate change in five simple steps.

Step 1 – The propaganda machine

Big Fossil Fuel knows that the climate is changing due to the burning of fossil fuels. In fact, they did much research on this, beginning in the early 1970s. But around 1990, they reversed tack and started running a propaganda campaign, denying the science of climate change. By the year 2013, they were spending $1 billion a year on disinformation.

One of the first known scientists to think about climate change was Joseph Fourier, back in 1824. He realised that the surface temperature of the earth was due to heat from three sources – the sun, deep space and the interior of the planet. He also recognised that without an atmosphere, our earth would be a lot colder. Around 1856, Eunice Newton Foote did the first experiments showing that carbon dioxide could trap the heat of the sun.

Around 1895, Svante Arrhenius had calculated that 'Any doubling of the percentage of carbon dioxide in the air would raise the temperature of the earth's surface of 4°C.'

By 1961, Charles David Keeling had enough measurements from his station in Hawaii to show that there was a steady annual overall rise in carbon dioxide. In the year 1958, carbon dioxide was at 317 parts per million (ppm). By early 2021, it had reached 415 ppm.

The cost is already high – and not just in physical terms of droughts, floods, heat waves and coral reef bleaching. In 2017, subsidies of fossil fuels were about USD $5.2 trillion (about 6.5 percent of global Gross Domestic Product, or GDP), according to the International Monetary Fund (IMF).

But surely these subsidies, while bad for the environment, were good for the global economy?

No, according to the IMF.

These subsidies have depressed economic growth by 3.8 percent since 2015, and additionally, are directly harming people's health (3.6 million people die each year from fossil fuel air pollution).

Why would Big Fossil Fuel do this? As the saying goes, *It's nothing personal, it's strictly business.'*

Step 2 – Ten years labour & 400,000 Hiroshima bombs per day

The great appeal of carbon-based fuels is the colossal amount of energy they carry. A barrel of oil (about US$50) carries as much energy as a labourer can deliver in ten years of hard work (about $500,000). (A barrel of oil – 159 litres – carries the same amount of energy as 200 kilograms of coal.) But the direct result of that convenience is that greenhouse gases add about 400,000 Hiroshima bombs of heat to our atmosphere each day.

Let's start at the beginning.

When the Sun is directly overhead and there's a clear sky, it dumps about 500 watts of heat onto each square metre of the Earth's surface. The waste heat from the decay of radioactive elements in the Earth's core adds another 0.1 watts per square metre. The waste heat from combustion of carbon, air conditioning, etc, adds another 0.028 watts per square metre. But the greenhouse gases (mostly carbon dioxide, but also methane and others) we've added to the atmosphere add an extra 3.1 watts per square metre. The surface of Earth has many square metres. This 400,000 Hiroshima-bombs-of-heat-per-day is just heat from the Sun that previously would have escaped to space after heating the ground – but now it's trapped in our biosphere (lower atmosphere, upper oceans).

Incoming sunlight is made up of about half heat (short wavelength or near infra-red), a bit less than half visible light, with the rest being ultraviolet. On the way down from the Sun, this short wavelength heat passes through the carbon dioxide without interacting with it. The heat warms up the surface (land and water), which then radiates the heat upwards at a longer wavelength (3,000-70,000 nm, or far infra-red).

Here's where global warming happens – on the upward path. This longer wavelength heat does interact with the carbon dioxide. Some of it does not go out into space, but is trapped in the atmosphere.

How much? 400,000 Hiroshima bombs per day. You can get away with doing this for a day, or a week, or a month, or a year, or even a decade. But when you do it for many decades, you can change the climate.

Step 3 – Where did/do greenhouse gases come from?

There were no carbon atoms in the very early universe, once it cooled down after the Big Bang (about 13.8 billion years ago). Carbon atoms were manufactured inside stars, beginning about 280 million years after the Big Bang. These carbon atoms were then incorporated into later generations of stars, and their planets.

On Earth, we had the Carboniferous Period about 300–360 million years ago. The carbon dioxide level back then was about eight times higher than it is today (yes, the biosphere was much hotter), and the trees grabbed this gas and turned it into cellulose. The trees were buried and turned into hydrocarbons underground. Land-based carbon life was turned into coal, while ocean-based carbon life went to oil. If you do the conversion from coal to oil, seventy litres of petrol is equivalent to 1640 tonnes of vegetation (covering 1.13 square kilometres of land) that has been processed for millions of years. Yes, fossil fuels are truly Buried Sunshine.

Since the beginning of the Industrial Revolution (about 1750), we have dumped about 1600 billion tonnes of carbon dioxide into the atmosphere.

Our 2018 emissions were about 37 billion tonnes.

In 2018, the biggest single emitter was China, with the USA and Europe close behind. Between them, China, the USA and Europe accounted for about sixty-five percent of global carbon dioxide emissions. Another twenty-three percent came from 'Other Asia', six percent from South America and Africa, two–three percent from shipping emissions. Australia, with 0.3 percent of the world's population, emitted domestically 1.1 percent of global carbon dioxide – but when you include our international fossil fuel exports, that rises to about five percent.

You get a different picture when you look at not just a single year, but all the cumulative emissions from 1750 to 2018.

As you would expect, because the Industrial Revolution began in the UK, the location of 'All Europe – including the UK' accounts for thirty-three percent of that 1600 billion tonnes. Coming close behind are North America (at twenty-nine percent) and 'China and Other Asia' (also at twenty-nine percent). All the nations in the Southern Hemisphere (Africa, South America and Oceania) account for just seven percent.

Step 4 – Effects of climate change – tip Earth off its spin axis

Global warming has given us the first Antarctic heatwaves (up to 18.2 degrees), killed 50,000 people in a European heat wave, and made Sydney the hottest place on Earth (4 January 2020, Penrith, almost fifty degrees). The Australian Bureau of Meteorology has had to introduce a new colour (purple, for 'extra hot'), while a new Bushfire Category of 'Catastrophic' has had to be created.

Over the last twenty years, some twenty disasters (caused and/or worsened by climate change) have inflicted damage to countries at a cost of more than ten percent of their annual GDP. Dominica in the Caribbean was especially hard hit. In 2015, Tropical Storm Erika caused devastation costing about ninty percent of their GDP, but in 2017 Hurricane Maria caused damage worth about 260 percent of their GDP.

Other nasty (and very costly) effects of climate change include unpreceded rainfalls (not snowfalls) in Alaska, Amazon rainforest dieback, Siberian heatwaves and fires, unprecedented glacial melting in Greenland, unexpected changes to tropical monsoon rains, unexpected spreading of diseases of plants, animals and humans – and much more.

But another effect of global warming is that it has tipped the earth off its spin axis (but only by a tiny, tiny amount).

By itself, the tipping of the Earth's axis is tiny, and won't change anything. But it is amazing that we humans (who could all fit very uncomfortably into a cube with sides one kilometre long) can affect the spin of a planet some 12,700 kilometres in diameter.

Until 2005, the Geographic North Pole (the spin axis) was migrating slowly towards the equator at six–seven centimetres per year. But in 2005, it suddenly both changed direction (to migrate parallel to the equator) and accelerated (to more twenty-six centimetres per year). This has been linked to the melting of vast quantities of ice (mostly in polar and mountain regions) that turns into liquid water at sea level, and then migrates towards the equator. In 2020, this melting amounted to about 750 billion tonnes of ice. Think of a bicycle wheel that is spinning perfectly true – and then place a small weight anywhere on its rim. The wheel will settle into a new rhythm.

Step 5 – Not only can we stop local warming with today's technologies, we can even reverse it

That headline is correct – we can stop, and reverse global warming, within a few decades. The only thing stopping us is the massive disinformation campaign funded by Big Fossil Fuel (see Step 1 above).

Two excellent starting points are the websites drawdown.org and bze. org.au. This is (of course) such a huge field that I can barely touch upon it.

One simplistic way is to look at individual sectors, worldwide.

Heat and electricity account for about thirty percent of greenhouse emissions. If we went onto a war footing (think USA, Pearl Harbour, 7 December 1941), we could be totally renewable within ten years.

Transport is about sixteen percent. Electrics and batteries are already good enough for short-haul. For long-haul (shipping and planes) we need to go to hydrogen. Let's say fifteen years.

Manufacture and construction accounts for twelve percent (ten years).

Agriculture is about eleven percent, and will take a few decades. It's alive, and will resist our efforts. But something as simple as adding one percent seaweed to cattle feed reduces methane emissions by eighty percent.

Changing land usage and deforestation is about six percent, as are fugitive emissions. Coming in at five percent each are industrial processes and building upkeep and maintenance (all doable in ten years).

To stop, and then reverse, climate change we don't need any new technologies or scientific breakthroughs. We already have everything we need. However, these breakthroughs will happen, and will only make the job easier.

We can do it. Just remember the motto of Big Business, *It's not personal. It's strictly business.'*

.EMOUNTAINS.CABRAMURRA.CARRAI.COBARGO.COLINTON.COLOHEIG
/NJOLA.COOLUMBURRA.CORANG.DEUARIVERVALLEY.DOYALSON.EBOR.EL
OROUGH.EMMAVILLE.FORBESRIVER.GLENREAGHHILLTOP.JEOGLA.JERRAW
LA.JOHNSRIVER.KANGAROOVALLEY.KOORAINGHAT.KOSCIUSZKO.KULNUR
RAJONGHEIGHTS.LAURELHILL.MALLACOOTA.MALUABAY.MANGROVECREEK
RICUMBENE.MORORO.MOUNTGEORGE.MULLOON.NABIAC.NANAGLEN.NELL
.NERRIGUNDAH.NEWNES.NIMBIN.NOWRA.PADDYSRIVER.RAPPVILLE.ROSE
TABULAM.TALBINGO.TOWAMBA.TOWONG.WEROMBI.WINGELLO.WOLGAN
Y.WYNDHAM.STANTHORPE.ARALUEN.BALMORAL.BARGO.BATEHAVEN.BAT
ELLANGRY.BELLBROOK.BEMBOKA.BENDALONG.BERAMBING.BILPIN.BOBIN
GANNA.BOWENFELS.BOYDTOWN.BROULEE.BULGAFOREST.BULLIO.BUND
.BUNDOORA.BUNGAWALBIN.BLUEMOUNTAINS.CABRAMURRA.CARRAI.CC
COLINTON.COLOHEIGHTS.CONJOLA.COOLUMBURRA.CORANG.DEUAR
EY.DOYALSON.EBOR.ELLENBOROUGH.EMMAVILLE.FORBESRIVER.GLENR
'OP.JEOGLA.JERRAWANGALA.JOHNSRIVER.KANGAROOVALLEY.KOORA
'IUSZKO.KULNURA.KURRAJONGHEIGHTS.LAURELHILL.MALLACOO
^NGROVECREEK.MERRICUMBENE.MORORO.MOUNTGEORGE.MU
'NERRIGUNDAH.NEWNES.NIMBIN.NOWRA
,BULAM.TALBINGO.TOWAMBA.TOWONG
,NVALLEY.WYNDHAM.STANTHORPE
.HAVEN.BATLOW.BELLANGRY.BELLBROOK.P
,.BILPIN.BOBIN.BOORGANNA.BOWENFELS
,EST.BULLIO.BUNDANOON.BUNDOORA.BU'
,BRAMURRA.CARRAI.COBARGO.COLINTON
,MBURRA.CORANG.DEUARIVERVALLEY.DOY/
,AVILLE.FORBESRIVER.GLENREAGHHILLTOP.'
.KA   ORAINGHAT.KOS'
S.   OOTA.MALUAB/
ORORO   MULLOON.NAB

EARTH CRIES

,H.NEWNES.NIMBIN.NOWRA.PADDYSRI'
INGO.TOWAMBA.TOWONG.WEROMBI.
,NTHORP.ARALUEN.BALMORAL.BAR(
'OK.BEMBOKA.BENDALONG.BERAM,
'OYDTOWN.BROULEE.BULGAFORE
'LUEMOUNTAINS.CABRAM,
'IJOLA.COOLUMBURRA.CC
OUGH.EMMAVILLE.FORBES.
OHNSRIVER.KANGAROOVAL,
ONGHEIGHTS.LAURELHILL.MA
UMBENE.MORORO.MOUNTGEO,
RRIGUNDAH.NEWNES.NIMBIN.
'AM.TALBINGO.TOWAMBA.T(
'HAM.STANTHORPE.ARAL'
'' BELLBROOK.BEMBOK
'FELS.BOYDTO'
A Climate Change Anthology   NGAWALBI'
LOHEIGH
.EBOR.F
.JERR/
).KU'
,BRO'
,N

2100 – A TRUE STORY

Vivienne Reiner

> We are already committed to dangerous levels of climate change,
> and Australia is the most vulnerable nation in the developed world.
>
> *Dr Joëlle Gergis, Australian author and scientist on IPCC's Sixth*
> *Assessment Report underway*

Preamble

Leading Australian climate scientist Joëlle Gergis' book, *Sunburnt country: the history and future of climate change in Australia* (2018), highlights what can be expected if we limit global warming to 1.5-2 degrees this century – in line with the Paris Accord aimed at preventing runaway climate change – as well as higher-emission scenarios that are not the focus of this story.
This futuristic story relies largely on Gergis' research to make the unimaginable imaginable – what do these facts and figures look like – a day in the life of a two-degree warmed world.

Sunrise

The day breaks – sunrise being one of the few natural cycles that still seems to remain intact – but the sky is a white blanket of smoke, impermeable, as the sound of a single bird, like a warning, wakes and calls out from afar.
The earth is vibrant. Like a chameleon playing a cruel trick of remembrance, grasping at sounds of the waves. But no, this cannot be so in the city – is it wind, or cars – the echoed vibration is strangely comforting. Like a dying patient, the sea sound is a memory from the past – a flashback to its former glory.

An apricot orange spreads gingerly across the white distance, which quickly becomes red, a now familiar backdrop to a number of small, black birds going about their business. It is already hot. The smell of smoke; fine particulate matter from bushfires connects with the back of the throat and like an addict, we breathe our collective cigarette for the morning, a compulsion to inhale even as it brings us closer to death. Recovery between bushfire seasons is all-too-short, the catastrophic bushfires of the 2020s having faded into insignificance – with wildfires much more likely than what we used to think would be the 'new normal'.[1] And things could have been so much worse.

The *ABC 702* Sydney morning news predicts another day of fifty degrees[2] and announces renowned activist Greta Thunberg has just died a few years shy of becoming a centenarian. 'At the funeral were her child Harlem who is now seventy; grand-daughter Belle, middle-aged; and her great grand-daughter Elke, fifteen – these are the children dubbed the "climate babies" as they are living through an era where the only certainty is change.'

Turning down the radio, Sheila, also middle-aged, downloads the weekend newspapers on her tablet before the enforced blackout that will save energy as the day kicks in. If only they had understood when there was time that there would not really be any such thing as 'resilience' – not now – muses Sheila as she attempts some semblance of a routine in her newspaper-reading ritual, hard as it is. Sheila, whose great-grandfather had been in the same year at school as the man who went on to be Australia's former Prime Minister at the time of the first Great Fires, Scott Morrison, suddenly wondered if things might have been different. What if the so-called quiet Australians and the 'technological optimists',[3] who held onto their belief somehow in a better future, had ignored his

---

1 See, e.g. Readfearn 2020.

2 Temperatures reached forty-seven degrees in the western Sydney suburb of Richmond in 2016–17 and Gergis argued if we do too little too late it is very possible that Sydney temperatures will soar past fifty degrees 'in years to come'. Worldwide, with dramatic reductions in greenhouse gas emissions, about half the population will likely still face at least twenty days annually when extreme heat can kill – up from less than one in three currently. See Mora et al. 2017.

3 In 1987, Costanza and Daly recommend prudent pessimism over technological optimism because disaster would be the outcome in a worst-case scenario of irreversible damage to Earth's life-support systems, where technological fixes would no longer be possible.

joke not to be 'scared' of fossil fuels and stopped treating the Earth like a business in liquidation.[4]

In fact, ordinary folk did mobilise eventually and ensured we met our Paris Agreement aimed at limiting warming to 1.5-2 degrees above pre-industrial levels – which is why things are only so bad. So bad – there are still trees left to burn. Some said at the time that even this lower level – 1.5 degrees – would still lock in unacceptable, dangerous climate change; time and again, credible science revealed the past projections were too conservative, that things were deteriorating faster than anticipated;[5] already the temperature had risen by one degree when for a moment, the world blinked and saw that global warming was literally burning our planet.

Such small degrees with a huge difference! Rising global temperature averages means more in some places than others but the effects are felt everywhere.[6] Globally, greenhouse gases already released into the atmosphere were leading to flow-on effects and tipping points.[7] The rate of change is too fast for the Earth to heal: its deterioration revealing the true value of freely offered ecosystem services for which human capital is no substitute.[8]

Remembering what it used to be like, Sheila thinks to a time when Darwin was a bucket-list destination. Now increasingly inhospitable.[9] And the nearby renowned biodiverse Kakadu with its wetlands – vulnerable.[10]

---

4 See Morrison 2017 and Daly 1977, 248.

5 Linden 2019.

6 NASA n.d.

7 According to Gergis, even if greenhouse gas emissions were stopped immediately, the Earth is locked in to further warming as the climate system establishes a new equilibrium over centuries to millennia. Furthermore, Rockström et al. (2009) argued that we have already crossed the threshold of three of the nine interlinked planetary boundaries.

8 Costanza et al. (1997) reported that the value of the world's ecosystem services and natural capital was an average of US$33 trillion annually, or about double gross national product, and this was considered a conservative estimate.

9 Gergis (2018, 225) argues that if we do too little too late to reduce greenhouse gas emissions, much of inland Australia will be increasingly unliveable and Darwin will not resemble any part of modern-day Australia under a high-emission scenario.

10 Predicted collapse of many vulnerable ecosystems including iconic wetland areas like Kakadu if highly disruptive climate feedbacks are triggered (Gergis 2018, 253).

Holidays are becoming harder to find – with neighbouring island nations like Kiribati destroyed,[11] the colours of the Great Barrier Reef, which made it one of the Seven Wonders of the World, bleached[12] and the ski seasons across Victoria and some of New South Wales halved from what they used to be;[13] is it any wonder, when already one formerly constant polar extreme, the Arctic, no longer supports ice in the summer?[14]

The page leads in *The Sydney Morning Herald* provide some distraction: For school children, reading and writing has improved markedly, the economic and regulatory restrictions on energy-fuelled digital entertainment making way for traditional pastimes. In the cities, suicide is down because much of the nation, on a war-like footing fighting disasters, is focused on survival. But in country areas the reverse is true. Reporting on the spring just passed, the newspaper notes more farmer deaths in the state, as the 'broken promise' of winter rains weighed too heavy – the main chance for a break in the drought another year denied.[15] New South Wales farmers also have to fear the southern-moving front of Queensland's heat-loving fruit fly.[16] The reverberation of unemployment, from shrinking family farms to once-booming tourism[17] is felt across country areas and the young everywhere suffer climate anxiety, as truth – the traditional antidote – is rendered impotent.

Australia is no longer seen as a lucky country, but in other parts of the world tensions are heightening, with twenty-five percent more

11 Tong (2019) predicts that Kiribati may be under water in twenty years, maybe fifty years and likely in 100 years; what is known is that it is inevitable, says former Kiribati president.

12 Gergis (2019) noted a staggering ninety-nine percent of tropical coral reefs will disappear: 'An entire component of the Earth's biosphere – our planetary life support system – would be eliminated'.

13 Gergis (2018, 198) explains that according to the CSIRO, the 112-day season will be twenty–fifty-five days shorter.

14 There is a thirty-five percent chance the Arctic will be ice-free in summer by 2100. See IPCC 2019b.

15 Gergis argues that rural suicides in NSW tend to peak in spring when it emerges that drought-breaking rains during winter have not occurred; droughts will become longer and areas hotter, radically transforming rural economies.

16 Gergis 2018, 222.

17 Leading up to 2020, tourism was significant. When Gergis wrote in 2018, it employed one in twelve Australians.

asylum seekers each year entering the European Union alone – the new 'climate' refugees.[18]

Midday

Lost in time reminiscing, as she is increasingly wont to do, Sheila realises it is time to meet her friend Jo for brunch in Parramatta (not far from her home in Richmond), sandwiched between Sydney's sister cities in the East and the Aerotropolis far out West. Sheila's hometown is truly Sydney's demographic centre, but much muggier than the exclusive beach-side eastern suburbs.

After covering herself with sunscreen, she squirts on some DEET before heading out. After all, it's just a matter of time before the dangerous dengue fever comes to the fast-developing 'southern tropics' as Sheila likes to joke about Sydney, so best to be prepared for the mosquito's migration from the traditional home of South-East Asia and far north Queensland.[19] Because, although they say climate change has been stopped at two degrees, Sheila has her doubts.

Some said the maximum increase in temperature about the two degree mark agreed by compromise at the United Nations' Conference of Parties might in fact already be putting climate change beyond the realm in which it could be controlled.[20] Scientists are conservative and do not as a rule want to predict the end of everything, their work framed in a world of possibilities and probabilities. And did anyone think to ask them: what is the chance that the end of life as we know it might come sooner? When there had still been hope, we all pointed, look: we still have time to waste; only *just so many* animals, plants, life-support systems of the Earth will perish. Maybe, Sheila thinks, she's lucky she is even here today!

As if on autopilot, Sheila takes precautions every day to protect herself, although she can't predict chance disasters like flying storm debris or parched falling tree branches that could end her life in a moment. Today,

---

18 Harvey 2017.

19 Modelling shows if no global action is taken to reduce greenhouse gas emissions, dengue fever could spread as far south as northern NSW or even Sydney. See Gergis 2018, 230–1.

20 Renowned NASA climate scientist James Hansen, quoted by McKibben (2012) said 'two degrees of warming is actually a prescription for long-term disaster.'

Sheila steps over an ant-ridden bird on the footpath – even hardy ravens are dropping dead, from fire or heat.[21]

'You would have made a great mother,' Sheila's friend Jo has told her many times. But who has children now? It seems a cruel twist of fate that the predicted overpopulation problem has been resolved. But it is not by swift starvation as predicted by Malthus so long ago, but by Nature's fury. Even in poor countries young adults brace for a future they can't hope to turn back.

Sheila turns off all the power (including air conditioning) except for the fridge at the flick of a smart switch and escapes what will be a literal oven by midday. This is a good day, as Sheila is fortunate to make it to the light rail on time (early in the day is good before extreme conditions can send the prolific public transport into a meltdown of endless cancellations and confusion).

Now the government has stepped in and cars are not allowed, save for police, firefighters and the like; despite the strange feeling that comes with living in a benevolent autocracy of sorts, Sheila finds the ruling has come as some relief because traffic had made commuting a daily dread. She is happy for small mercies though, such as not having grown up in Brisbane, where even days of thirty-five degrees have jumped since the time they averaged just a dozen a year around 2020, mixing with the growing humidity in summer to create a steaming, sticky dampness.[22]

Arriving at her stop, Sheila walks the street alone; the area, as is often the case these days, is strangely silent, as if people are uncomfortable lingering outdoors. Are they afraid, or waiting? What are they waiting for?

Generally of optimistic character, Sheila has excelled in her effort today to wear bright colours that set against the at-times dull and dusty city. She can do this without too much cost, finding treasures in the second-hand shops that have again become popular ('Reduce, Reuse, Recycle' being one of the government mantras, supported by various cash incentives and fines).

'Jo, you look lovely today,' Sheila calls out approvingly as she spots her best friend at Café 2021 – it is a cute, nostalgic eatery that tries to present things as they had been, before. You don't pay extra for the decor

---

21 According to Ward (2020), dying birds were an issue in the summer of 2020.

22 In a high-emissions scenario, Gergis (2018, 221) shows that Brisbane days of more than thirty-five degrees will number fifty-five annually, making the southern Queensland climate in summer's wet seasons excruciating.

– plastic, petroleum-derived seats, as if anyone can afford that now, nor electric-powered lights, especially in the middle of the day!

No, what is really expensive is the food (but that's not unusual).[23] What *is* novel is the produce they try to source. It is a bit of a luxury, but Café 2021 seeks food and drink that is hard to come by – like dairy and meat. Ironic that veganism was trendy in the twenties but now is like breathing is to living.[24] Those were the days when if you went fishing, you were told not to eat the babies so they could grow up, but now there are barely enough fish to feed and grow future schools.

Sheila scans the Specials insert in the menu to confirm what is still not available today: beef burgers and milkshakes are crossed off. She sighs and opts for the reliable beverage, juice – thirty dollars reconstituted, not fresh of course, but much better than desalinated water;[25] she can pick it even in the expensive carbonated varieties. Jo asks after a coffee – almost past its peak but, 'Still cheaper than gold,' Jo shrugs.

Ever a popular Sydney pastime, talk moves to real estate, which has become somewhat of an extreme sport. 'You know Hornsby? Up near Ku-ring-gai National Park? I heard that thousands of homes there backing onto the bush will become uninsurable,' Jo muses.[26]

Sheila rejoins: 'They say that one of the things that convinced Prime Minister Morrison to do his bit to limit warming to two degrees was the fact that, in addition to Sydney's well-heeled suburb of Rose Bay at threat of being inundated, were parts of Sydney's CBD!'

'And what about coastal towns,' Jo adds. 'Some of Newcastle and "sea-change" towns like Port Macquarie, Ballina and Byron Bay, would

---

23 Gergis cites CSIRO and Bureau of Meteorology projections showing that winter and spring rainfall in southern Australia is expected to continue to decrease in agriculturally intensive areas like Australia's largest food bowl, the Murray-Darling.

24 In a United Nations report cited by Abrams (2019), a dramatic shift towards plant-based diets would help combat the devastating impacts of climate change.

25 Desalination plants will be increasingly relied on for water security in Australia's capital cities, says Gergis.

26 Gergis shows that in and around Sydney extreme heat will render 100,000 households classified as having a high risk of bushfire, with a possiblility that in Hornsby, 20,000 homes within 100 metres of the bush will become uninsurable under businesss as usual.

have been among the most heavily hit; settlements retreating from rising sea levels and storm surges.'

'Yes, along with airports like Sydney that would have been largely under water, although flying is already virtually impossible these days anyway; almost no escape ...'[27]

Sunset

Hours later, the friends arrive at their next destination, the beach – '*a bit of a schlep*' – but a good way to cool down during the hottest parts of the day into late afternoon. As they step off the Metro at Collaroy the sea breeze hits them, a good few degrees cooler. The sound of hungry seagulls are a welcome intrusion from what is at this time an extension of the strangely silent spring – wildlife pretending to hibernate and Nature's beauty wilting under an angry sun.

Like checking one's watch to feel some semblance of control over the time of day, Sheila and Jo cannot help but appraise the beleaguered coastline. 'Would you live in those?' Jo asks, pointing to the last mansions on the frontline that no longer have a sandy beach at their doorstep but rather, a cliff of sorts.

'I wouldn't buy one, if that's what you mean,' Sheila replies. 'It's literally living on the edge.'

Like a science fiction fantasy unimaginable when these luxury houses were built, another home recently toppled into the sea. Of those still standing Sheila and Jo can see more than twenty metres of their backyards have washed away, hit by huge waves riding king tides[28] – not such a surprise when once-in-a-decade or rarer extreme sea-level events are now happening every few weeks.[29]

---

27 Gergis cites Coastal Risk Australia mapping indicating that, under a high-emissions scenario, two metre sea-level rise, some of Australia's most densely populated suburbs, major cities and crucial pieces of infrastructure could be underwater by 2100 (2018, 226).

28 Gergis (2018) wrote some Northern Beaches waterfront houses had twenty metres of backyards washed away in 2016, and McPhee (2020) reported that a number of houses started collapsing into the sea after storms.

29 Gergis references a study which found that for a sea-level rise of just fifty centimetres (as opposed to one to two metres predicted under high emissions), extreme sea-level events that used to happen rarer than every ten years are likely to occur every ten days by 2100 (2018, 212).

Sheila is able to enjoy ocean swimming frequently these days – thanks to increasing sea temperatures – but she wonders when the deadly box jellyfish might hit Sydney.[30] Overhead, as if they have always been there, dark clouds gather and grumble, and the friends realise they do not have much time to get home before the rain comes.

On the way home, it feels like something more than light rail is needed, as the all-too-common hail the size of golf balls pop off the roof and gathers on the ground, like rough snow. Fortunately, by the time Sheila reaches her stop, the hail has abated, only to be followed by bucketing rain lashing about, this way and that, like a mini tornado. 'Here we go again,' Sheila glares suspiciously about her, senses sharp. The strongest storms resulting in inundation are happening now perhaps several times a year, when before they had been every century.[31]

As she makes her way around fallen trees, some on cars and houses, Sheila again reflects without surprise on the fact that Australia today is averaging a 300-fold increase in inundation,[32] with the Sydney region most affected by regular coastal flooding – at over 2000 times more than at the turn of the century – yes this was predicted and reported in 2012 in Rupert Murdoch's conservative newspaper *The Australian!*[33] Disbelief, then denial, then doubt enflamed by professional 'gas lighters' ensured no-one was listening. Deafening now, the streets jerk alive with sirens, horns and flashing lights of red and blue. Emergency services are always at the alert to respond to such events, as expected. Though not long-lasting, the rain disappears – imagining its job done;[34] at least it may have slowed down the bushfires, which seem to strike more often at night these days. One can only hope.

---

30 Philp 2018.

31 Gergis argues that even with sea level rise of fifty centimetres on average, places inundated in Australia once a century will be flooded several times a year.

32 Gergis 2018.

33 In Sydney, inundation will increase 2200-fold. This is from a 2012 report by the Antarctic Climate and Ecosystems Co-operative Research Centre, what the authors referred to as conservative interpretations of IPCC projections for sea-level rise, as reported in *The Australian* by Denholm 2012.

34 Gergis cites CSIRO projections in 2015 that show global warming will result in an increase in extreme rainfall, even in areas where average rainfall declines.

Back at home, the Parramatta River has also burst its banks,[35] the smart electricity system, besieged, does not kick in – another night without cooked dinner for Sheila, and likely another shopping expedition in the coming day or so to replace soiled food from the fridge that can no longer be relied on. Another night without her husband, Frank, who now likely needs to work around the clock for weeks, merely sleeping at home before setting off again to attend to the latest disaster. She leaves him a note: 'Wish you were here.'

Fortunately, Sheila has planned a special cold entrée in what was a sturdy home that so far had no leakages or cracked tiles, unlike what so many neighbours have experienced over the years. The previous evening, Sheila had somehow nabbed a couple of oysters – akin to eating pearls going by the cost, she muses.[36] As well, she selects some fresh vegetables for herself. Though rising in price and of variable availability, they are still preferable, although canned food is more reliable, but who can stand that?[37]

Wine – another luxury these days, which Sheila knows from government announcements is equivalent to 120 litres of water per glass – but she wants to savour the moment. She pours a glass of Fiano (Chardonnay long gone from the continent), props up her mobile on the dinner table and live streams the evening television news.

The news reader blares ...

From Sydney floods – to drought and famine in the African continent, where conflict over essentials is prompting another war.[38] The World Health Organisation chief Akin Bhuto says a flashpoint over a lack of drinking water in South Africa is adding to stresses in the region from increasing famine following the devastation of

---

35 Arup (2010) reported on how sea level rise will affect Australia's cities.
36 Oysters and other shellfish are at grave risk from climate change according to the ABC (2017).
37 For the vulnerable worldwide, above two degrees global warming could add another 100 million people or more at risk of hunger. See IPCC 2019a.
38 It had been warned that a globally sanctioned two degrees warming would be a 'suicide pact' for drought-stricken Africa, with delegates from developing nations at the 2009 Copenhagen climate summit chanting: 'One degree, one Africa,' recalled McKibben (2012).

crops in Somalia and Ethiopia, posing an imminent threat to global security and presenting an ethical challenge.[39]

… Looking further afield, a human settlement on Mars is nearing the end of construction – it might not be long until the prediction by scientist Stephen Hawking a century ago, that humans might need to relocate from Earth, could be closer to fact than fiction.[40]

… Now to sport, and the Australian Open grand slam will be moved again, from March into the winter months, because of fears players could die of a heart attack from bushfire smoke inhalation or extreme heat.[41] It comes on the back of a wide-ranging report into heat and the outdoors, with solutions including blanketing dry, cracked sports grounds with 'AstroTurf' to retraining many blue-collar workers for inside-only occupations.

There is not a lot to do in the dark and, keen to save her phone and computer charge in the event of an emergency, Sheila decides to turn in early. She's going to have a big day tomorrow, so after gathering some essentials, including clothes to protect her from water, wind, heat and fire, she goes to bed.

Unable to sleep at first because of the dulled white smoky sky that rarely goes dark, Sheila eventually lulls into a state of seemingly semi-consciousness, images of the past flashing by, her mind's farewell to this land. She sees:

A lush, deep green forest live with the sound of life – yes, a rainforest drunk on an abundance of water and space just to be, no longer a museum

---

39 The University of Sydney 2019 and McPhedran 2015.

40 In 2017 popular scientist Stephen Hawking warned that people would need to colonise another planet within 100 years or face extinction.

41 As reported in *Financial Review* (2020), experts recommended in January 2020 the Australian Open be moved from summer to November or March because of extreme heat.

piece,[42] she is skipping through, koalas[43] on the trees (abundant – like she's seen in the wildlife hospitals), she looks up, and the sky between the trees is a sharp blue (the thick blanket of bushfire smoke no more). She reaches out … laughs, is this real … her husband, Frank, by her side, smiling. All around them, life is pulsating, the air as one with the soil, seeming to move to the beat of the crickets (or frogs?) in their mating call, alive, Frank pulls her into an embrace, his lips press against hers as if they have not a care in the world.

The final sunrise

Sheila hastily packs her bags by the gentle light of dawn and stumbles outdoors, as if still in a dream, remembering what was once, or could be …?

Australia, naturally a land of droughts and flooding rains, has become too extreme from climate change.[44] Once beautiful, its uniqueness has turned foul, its resilience destroyed.

'All aboard,' comes the sea-man's rousing cry and Sheila shuffles, along with many others, onto a small boat with room only for single-ticket-holders and one suitcase each.

---

42 According to Gergis (2018, 238), rates of extinction of species are likely to increase as temperatures rise by 1.5 degrees and should accelerate sharply as the temperature rises beyond two degrees, placing many of our most species-rich areas at risk. Species that could become extinct include those living near the upper limit of their temperature range, species with restricted climatic niches, those that cannot migrate to new habitats because of habitat fragmentation, areas with high fire risks or those living in areas inundated by rising sea levels. This means many of Australia's most valued, iconic areas including the Queensland tropics and the World Heritage Gondwana Rainforests of Australia that extend from NSW to Queensland, formerly called the Central Eastern Rainforest Reserves and home to 200 rare or threatened plant and animal species.

43 As observed by Arlington (2017), koalas, which once derived all their nourishment requirements from leaves, have been observed seeking drinking water, while, according to Hannam (2020), a Parliamentary inquiry found that habitat loss threatened NSW koalas with extinction by 2050 in the absence of urgent intervention.

44 Gergis (2018) cites economist Ross Garnaut's claim that Australia is the most vulnerable country in the developed world; recently the Asia-Pacific, which includes Australia, was dubbed 'Disaster Alley' by experts. Climate change will affect different countries in different ways; in Australia, whose climate is variable, we can expect even greater extremes.

As they race away from the shore, Sheila tries not to look back, but invariably can already see in her mind's eye the redness – or is it flames – almost choking on the smoke, tears burning her eyes. 'Where the bloody hell are you,' she whispers, imagining Frank on the frontline, unwilling to turn around.

Acknowledgements and postscript

This is dedicated to my mother Mimi, who always sees the emergency long before others, and to my children, Veronika and Hannah, whose families will live through 2100.

With the world actually on track for roughly three to five degrees warming or more,[45] many scientists agree the low-emissions scenario of 1.5–2 degrees is overly optimistic, even if all countries honour their Paris pledges.[46] In fact, from 2020, in order to meet the target of 1.5–2 degrees we would now require greenhouse gas emissions reductions of between 7.6 percent and 2.7 percent every year for a decade,[47] or at least half the reductions that were achieved in the first months of COVID-19, year-on-year to 2030.[48]

These conservative, consensus-science projections to meet the Paris targets are dependent on some degree of carbon-dioxide removal (CDR) or 'negative emissions' – in other words, technologies such as carbon sequestration, which despite years of investment have failed. Even so, the United Nations Environment Program gap report provides only a probability of meeting the less ambitious target of limiting warming to below about two degrees of some sixty-six percent.[49]

Gergis concludes: 'This suggests that the Paris Agreement's upper end of two degrees warming – the benchmark recognised as the threshold of "dangerous" climate change – is a best-case scenario.'[50]

---

45 Gergis 2019, Australian Academy of Science 2015.
46 UNEPb 2019.
47 UNEPa 2019.
48 Lenzen et al. 2020.
49 UNEPb 2019, 21–22.
50 Gergis 2018, 248.

References

ABC. "Scientists searching for the 'Goldilocks' oyster which best adapts to climate change." *ABC News*, August 15 2017. https://www.abc.net.au/news/2017-08-15/scientists-studying-how-oysters-adapt-to-climate-change/8804502.

Abrams, A. "How eating less meat could help protect the planet from climate change." *Time*, 8 August 2019. https://time.com/5648082/un-climate-report-less-meat/.

Arlington, K. "Researchers investigate koalas' need for drinking water as climate change bites." *The Sydney Morning Herald*, 3 March 2017. https://www.smh.com.au/national/nsw/researchers-investigate-koalas-need-for-drinking-water-as-climate-change-bites-20170302-gup55b.html.

Arup, T. "Rising sea levels will swamp parts of Sydney." *The Sydney Morning Herald*, 16 December 2010. https://www.smh.com.au/environment/climate-change/rising-sea-levels-will-swamp-parts-of-sydney-20101215-18yak.html.

Australian Academy of Science. 2015. "The science of climate change: Questions and Answers [brochure]." Australian Academy of Science, February 2015. https://www.science.org.au/files/userfiles/learning/documents/climate-change-wr.pdf.

Costanza, R., and Herman Daly. "Toward an ecological economics." *Ecological Modelling* 38 (1987): 1–7. doi:10.1016/0304-3800(87)90041-X.

Costanza, R., Ralph d'Arge, Rudolf de Groot, Stephen Farber, Monica Grasso, Bruce Hannon, Karin Limburg, Shahid Naeem, Robert V. O'Neill., J Paruelo et al. "The value of the world's ecosystem services and natural capital." *Nature* 387 (1997): 253–260. doi:10.1038/387253a0.

Daly, Herman E. *Steady-state economics*. 2nd ed. Island Press, 1977. https://islandpress.org/books/steady-state-economics.

Denholm, M. "Coastal flooding may rise 2000-fold." *The Australian*, 4 July 2012. https://www.theaustralian.com.au/news/health-science/coastal-flooding-may-rise-2000-fold/news-story/86169211501ff2d0e5a951d4f08473c2.

Financial Review. "Australian Open should be moved because of extreme heat: researchers." *Financial Review*, 20 January 2020. https://www.afr.com/companies/sport/australian-open-should-be-moved-because-of-extreme-heat-researchers-20200120-p53sxz.

Gergis, J. *Sunburnt country: the history and future of climate change in Australia*. Carlton, Victoria: Melbourne University Press, 2018.

Gergis, J. "The terrible truth of climate change." *The Monthly*,
August 2019. https://www.themonthly.com.au/issue/2019/
august/1566136800/jo-lle-gergis/terrible-truth-climate-change.
Hannam, P. "NSW koalas on course to be extinct in the wild before 2050,
inquiry finds." *The Sydney Morning Herald*, 30 June 2020. https://
www.smh.com.au/environment/conservation/nsw-koalas-on-course-
to-be-extinct-in-the-wild-by-2050-inquiry-finds-20200630-p557j2.
html.
Harvey, F. "Devastating climate change could lead to 1m migrants a year
entering EU by 2100." *The Guardian*, 22 December 2017. https://
www.theguardian.com/environment/2017/dec/21/devastating-
climate-change-could-see-one-million-migrants-a-year-entering-eu-
by-2100.
IPCCa. *Climate change and land.* Intergovernmental Panel on Climate
Change, 2019a. https://www.ipcc.ch/srccl/.
IPCCb. *The ocean and cryosphere in a changing climate.* UN Environment
Programme, 2019b. https://www.unenvironment.org/resources/
report/ipcc-special-report-ocean-and-cryosphere-changing-climate.
Lenzen, M., Mengyu Li, Arunima Malik, Francesco Pomponi, Ya-Yen
Sun, Thomas Wiedmann, Futu Faturay, Jacob Fry, Blanca Gallego,
Arne Geschke ... Moslem Yousefzadeh. "Global socio-economic
losses and environmental gains from the Coronavirus pandemic."
PLoS One 15, no. 7 (2020). doi:10.1371/journal.pone.0235654.
Linden, Eugene. "How scientists got climate change so wrong." *The New
York Times*, 8 November 2019. https://www.nytimes.com/2019/11/08/
opinion/sunday/science-climate-change.html.
McKibben, B. "Global warming's terrifying new math." *Rolling Stone*,
12 July 2012. https://www.rollingstone.com/politics/politics-news/
global-warmings-terrifying-new-math-188550/.
McPhedran, I. "Climate change is a major security threat for Australian
Defence Force." *News.com.au*, 22 September 2015. https://www.news.
com.au/technology/environment/climate-change/climate-change-is-
a-major-security-threat-for-australian-defence-force/news-story/000
4ff65f764649400889ab59f7c26ce.
McPhee, S. "Wamberal Beach, NSW erosion: beach homes 'partially
collapse'." *News.com.au*, 18 July 2020. https://www.news.com.au/
technology/environment/wamberal-beach-nsw-erosion-significant-
risk-of-structural-collapse/news-story/9224260482749b5271e27b13
6d98028d.
Mora, C., Bénédicte Dousset, Iain R. Caldwell, Farrah E. Powell, Rollan
C. Geronimo, Coral R. Bielecki, Chelsie W. W. Counsell, Bonnie
S. Dietrich, Emily T. Johnston, Leo V. Louis et al. "Global risk of
deadly heat." *Nature Climate Change* 7 (2017): 501–506. doi:10.1038/
nclimate3322.

Morrison, S. "Scott Morrison brings a chunk of coal into parliament." *The Guardian*, 9 February 2017. Video. https://www.theguardian.com/global/video/2017/feb/09/scott-morrison-brings-a-chunk-of-coal-into-parliament-video.

NASA. "GLOBAL Land-Ocean Temperature Index in 0.01 degrees Celsius base period: 1951–1980." *NASA*, n.d. https://data.giss.nasa.gov/gistemp/tabledata_v4/GLB.Ts+dSST.txt.

Philp, Jude, Michael Kingsford, Will Figueira, Killian Quigley and Maria Byrne. "Jellyfish behaving badly?" *The University of Sydney*, 2018. Podcast. https://www.sydney.edu.au/engage/events-sponsorships/sydney-ideas/2018/jellyfish-behaving-badly.html.

Readfearn, G. "Bushfire crisis conditions eight times more likely under 2C warming, analysis shows." *The Guardian*, 5 March 2020. https://www.theguardian.com/australia-news/2020/mar/05/bushfire-crisis-conditions-eight-times-more-likely-under-2c-warming-analysis-shows.

Rockström, J., Will Steffen, Kevin Noone, Åsa Persson, F. Stuart Chapin III, Eric F. Lambin, Timothy M. Lenton, Marten Scheffer, Carl Folke, Hans Joachim Schellnhuber et al. "A safe operating space for humanity." *Nature* 461 (2009): 472–475. doi:10.1038/461472a.

The Climate Institute. "A brewing storm: the climate change risks to coffee." *Fairtrade Australia & New Zealand*, 2016. https://www.fairtrade.net/library/a-brewing-storm-the-climate-change-risks-to-coffee.

The University of Sydney. "Hope vs fear: climate change as a security issue." *Sydney Ideas*, 2019. Podcast. https://soundcloud.com/sydney-ideas/hope-vs-fear-climate-change-as-a-security-issue.

Tong, A. "Why island nations' isolation on the climate change threat must end." *The University of Sydney*, 2019. Podcast. https://soundcloud.com/sei_sydney/why-island-nations-isolation-on-the-climate-change-threat-must-end.

UNEPa. "Cut global emissions by 7.6 percent every year for next decade to meet 1.5°C Paris target – UN report." *UN Environment Programme*, 26 November 2019. Media release. https://www.unenvironment.org/news-and-stories/press-release/cut-global-emissions-76-percent-every-year-next-decade-meet-15degc.

UNEPb. "Emissions gap report 2019." *UN Environment Programme*, 26 November 2019. https://www.unenvironment.org/resources/emissions-gap-report-2019.

Ward, A. "Hundreds of birds dead in SA's Gluepot Reserve during scorching summer." *ABC*, 5 March 2020. https://www.abc.net.au/news/2020-03-05/bird-kills-over-summer-highlights-south-australias-climate/12018060.

FIRE AND SAND

Isla Scott

Flames lick and dance from tree to tree to tree,
in soaring colours of agony and heat,
and swirling flashes of blood and buttercups,
a sickening rainbow of yellow, and orange, and dead.

It'd be dangerously beautiful
if I weren't so damn afraid.
The entrancing inferno draws near.
Golden embers and ashes rise up
in a hazy, tragic ballet.

And when I look out to the ocean
all I see is a glistening reflection of hell.
Fragments of fire flicker warnings in the waves.
We sit on the beach and face away from the pyre,
the heat burning up our backs.

But the flames grow ever closer,
and the panic flares within.
There's no more shoreline left to flee to,
no more ships left in the sea, so
as the fire eats up life
and chokes out char across the land,
I'm stranded on a beach of people
sticking their heads in the sand.

TRY, TRY AGAIN

Johanna Ellersdorfer

It began over summer in the studio at work, during the bushfires that now seem oddly distant. I sat in front of a painting, my colleagues either side of me, each encased in their own experience of the world through a set of headphones. A list of podcast recommendations was open on my phone and I skipped from one to another, until I stumbled across the series, *How to fail with Elizabeth Day*. Recognising the name of one of her guests, the writer Olivia Laing, I clicked play, and for forty-five minutes I allowed myself to inhabit her story. I listened as she talked about dropping out of university, about losing her way and being made redundant from a job she had loved – a list of failures that culminated in her becoming a celebrated writer. *This is nice*, I thought, and over the next few weeks I listened to more episodes. Then, some time in December as I rode my bike home from work, that eerie red sun hovering in the sky, I wondered what, precisely, was so 'nice' about failing.

* * *

Failure, insomuch as I've thought about it, is a descriptor applied more to people than circumstance. However, this understanding of failure is a relatively recent construct. Scott A. Sandage, cultural historian and author of *Born losers: the history of failure in America*, writes that failure was, up until the nineteenth century, a term applied to circumstances, not people, and it was almost exclusively associated with finance and economics. People 'made a failure' if they experienced economic hardship, they did not *become* a failure. By the mid-twentieth century, however, this had shifted and the success or failure of any person, as Sandage writes, 'often depended on the story a man could tell about his own life'.[1] The stories I listened to on the *How to fail* podcast were just that: narratives told in such a way that the success of Day's guests became the sum of their failures.

* * *

When I first started listening to *How to fail*, I had been working as a paintings conservator in a small studio in Sydney for about eight months. The studio was sequestered in an industrial complex neighboured by a scrap metal yard and a concrete plant. The closest bus stop was a twenty-minute walk away and the closest train station was thirty minutes away. Most days, this made the forty-minute bike ride from home the most appealing commute option. The streets around the studio were perpetually covered in dust. Lorries and cement mixers would hurtle down them at all times of day, oblivious to the handful of pedestrian commuters and cyclists wanting to cross the road.

Over the summer, as I dismounted my bike and waited patiently for the trucks to pass, the heat emanating from their slipstreams would create small pockets of warm air that mingled with dust, and the smell of petrol fumes would exacerbate the dry heat of the day. For weeks at a time, in the midst of the fires, the entire area looked bleak and arid, the heavy yellow-grey sky amplifying the strangeness of the industrial landscape. It was vastly removed from the studios I'd previously worked in – sterile spaces tucked away in museums or old houses. *It's just different,* I thought to myself, then dashed across the road.

* * *

Inside the studio I felt completely disconnected from the world outside. It was a windowless space enclosed by towering white walls with a constant supply of filtered air, climate controlled to 'cardigan weather'. Aside from occasional screeches and crashes from the scrap metal yard up the road, life in the studio was silent. I worked alongside my colleagues, but not with them, each of us wearing headphones, listening to music or podcasts for most of the day. Sitting at my easel, I'd inevitably find myself listening to another episode of *How to fail.*

---

1   Sandage 2005, 11.

At first I was a tentative listener, rationing episodes between helpings of true crime and documentaries. When I ran out of guests whose names I recognised, I began listening to the stories of those I didn't, all confirming that same narrative of failure breeding success. As I listened, a knot of discomfort began to grow in my stomach. I willed myself to feel buoyed by the possibilities that failure could present. Perhaps these feelings of discomfort were a quiet call to arms, alerting me to my own personal inadequacies so that I might find the courage to somehow change my circumstances, even though I couldn't quite articulate what was wrong.

Then, the fires began to worsen and the city streets came to be constantly engulfed in clouds of smoke. As my decision to ride or walk or catch the train to work each morning was dictated by the air quality index that I would check with great regularity on my phone, I began to consume them even more obsessively.

* * *

Attitudes towards failure cultivated in the realms of entrepreneurship have increasingly seeped through the walls of Silicon Valley and into the wider world. The oft-repeated mantra 'fail fast, fail often', has its roots in the lean startup methodology, a philosophy that privileges the incremental development of products and services. It posits that every failure is an opportunity to improve a product, and if these failures are addressed quickly and consistently, the 'sunk cost effect', that idea of investing too much in an idea that simply won't work, might be avoided.

How to fail aligns with this idea, translating something of this process of gradual improvement to individual lives, rather than the life of a business. Each episode follows the same formula. Elizabeth Day introduces her guest in her soft British accent, emphasising their success. Then she gently guides them through a discussion of three failures. Her guests are sincere, honest and vulnerable, and provide moving accounts of some of the worst moments in their lives, from heartbreak to mental illness, career failures and losing loved ones.

Since 2018, Day has recorded seven seasons with high profile guests including actress Phoebe Waller-Bridge and philosopher Alain de Botton. In 2019 she published a book inspired by the conversations from the podcast, called *How to fail: everything I've ever learned from things going wrong*. It's a format that clearly resonates with the masses, and in many ways, it resonates with me too. Hearing her guests frame success as the sum of their failures reinforces that failure shouldn't be feared. Even now, when I listen to her voice, its friendliness and warmth, I can't help but sometimes think, *yes, failing isn't so bad.*

* * *

By midsummer it was too smoky to ride to work. I would catch a train and then a bus, walking the last twenty-minute leg of the journey. When I arrived at the studio, I would put on a heavy smock over my light summer dress, pulling the long sleeves down over my arms. Then I would sit at my easel and plug in my headphones. At lunch time my colleagues and I would eat together in the stuffy tea room, but I was mostly quiet as they talked around me.

As the fires began to dominate our conversations, I found myself contributing more. We compared maps on our phones, monitoring the shifting of flame icons, and shared links to crafting groups for animal rescuers and letter templates to send to our MPs. When I left in the evenings, I noticed how the twilight air felt on my bare skin. Sometimes it was comfortably warm and clear, other times my eyes watered from the smoke. Most days, I would feel a dull ache in my throat. It was as though there was something deeply wrong that I just couldn't articulate, and I began to wonder whether, despite the increased connection with my colleagues, my job was the problem, if *different* was actually *not a good fit.*

According to the most recent Houshold, Income and Labour Dynamics in Australia (HILDA) survey, seventeen percent of Australian workers are not satisfied with their jobs. This number increases for Generations X and Y.[2] *How to fail* gently urged me to both question how satisfied I was in a career that was okay, but maybe not great, whilst reminding me that I could change things incrementally, slowly working towards something that felt more like success. It was a consolation that I clung to fiercely, but the tighter I held on, the more discomfort I felt, until I was quite aware that the loop of failure narratives I was using to help me through the day were actually part of the problem.

* * *

By mid-January, my walks to and from the studio were less a welcome relief than something else to be endured, and my colleagues and I began

---

2 Cassells 2017, 7.

to discuss wearing masks to filter out the worst of the smoke. There was genuine concern and camaraderie in those conversations, even if we often came up blank, unsure whether any of us were taking sufficient precautions. Yet during this period, the knot of discomfort in my stomach intensified. Every morning when I arrived at the studio, I would look out over the cracked cement of the carpark and a voice in my head would whisper, *surely there's more than this*. Then, as the door clicked closed behind me, a quiet sense of unease would settle in.

Although we often shared podcast recommendations, I never mentioned *How to fail* to my colleagues. Initially I put this down to embarrassment. It was a kind of self-help and I felt ashamed to be such a willing listener. Increasingly though, I was also frustrated by the guests. They all made it sound too easy, as though each failure could be turned around by simply being in the right place at the right time or adopting a positive attitude. I wanted to hear about failures that were huge, life changing and irreversible. Failures that had ruined everything, stories of people having *been* failed in ways that no neat narrative could contain. I also wanted to know about failures that had occurred so incrementally that the exact point at which things went wrong was impossible to locate, like a small series of ruptures that went by unnoticed until suddenly there was a gaping hole that no one could easily explain.

* * *

The queer theorist Jack Halberstam provides one such alternative in his book, *The queer art of failure*. In it, he writes about a series of seascape paintings by the Californian artist Judie Bamber. When I searched for them online, I found a series of small painted squares, cut at the horizontal midpoint, depicting the sky meeting the ocean. Each image was as blank as it was beautiful and even mediated through a screen, I couldn't help but stare at them.

Halberstam argues that 'failure appears in these paintings within visuality itself, as a line or threshold beyond which you cannot see, a horizon that marks the place of the failure of vision and visibility itself'.[3] They depict a space in which time is suspended, defiantly resisting that sense of movement towards a defined goal. Perhaps the discussions on *How to fail* were neglecting to consider failure as a place to linger. As

---

3   Halberstam 2011, 105.

something that could occur in and of itself, rather than a transitory state between two binary experiences. Yet as I looked at these paintings, I thought of that eerie red sun outside, and I knew this permission for passivity only extended so far.

* * *

Looking back, there is a certain resonance between Bamber's paintings and the photos that began to proliferate amidst the fires. But in the photos, their backgrounds flattened by smoke refracting shades of red and sickly grey, there is also something menacing about this space in which to linger. Perhaps this menace lies in the human element, as these flat backgrounds are punctuated by people. People in boats, people standing knee-deep in the ocean. Closer to home, there were photos of people wearing suits, masks wrapped around their faces, the ghostly shadow of buildings behind them. These images captured moments in time, beyond which it was difficult to see. Each photo was evidence of a kind of stasis, of waiting for policy and action, and even quite simply acknowledgment, to catch up with what was happening in real time. Yet while we waited, preparing to try, try again, inconceivably large tracts of land burned, wildlife and flora were decimated, properties were lost, and people died.

I wonder now if *How to fail* was, for me, just another kind of enclosure. If I was constructing a cocoon to block out the world beyond myself and my problems, which, if the podcasts were to be believed, could all be fixed quite easily with a combination of patience, soul-searching and luck. Perhaps the lingering doubt was never to do with my own perceptions of failure and success. Whether my job made me miserable, or whether I could accept failure and stay there for a while, was inconsequential in the broader scheme of things. I was surrounded by failures that were much more permanent and damaging and inherently difficult to rationalise. Perhaps the source of my discomfort was quite simply the ease by which I could turn inwards, when the world around me was burning.

References

Cassells, Rebecca. *Happy workers: how satisfied are Australians at work?*. Bentley: Curtin Business School, Curtin University, 2017.

Halberstam, Jack. *The queer art of failure*. Durham: Duke University Press, 2011.

Sandage, Scott, A. *Born losers: a history of failure in America*. Cambridge: Harvard University Press, 2005.

CLEARING THE AIR: CHILDFREE BY CHOICE

Charlotte Lim

My boots crunch through what's left of the snow as I make my way to class when I smell it: smoke. It's almost as if I'm being pre-haunted about my upcoming return to Sydney, following a year-long exchange in Sweden. Normally the lingering residue of burnt wood would be a comforting, pleasant scent that I'd inhale happily – but now, on this crisp January morning, it conjures up this guttural fear, coalesced with the unpleasant anticipation of having to fly back home to a place that for many, has become a living hell.

Although I'm fine physically (at least for now), every day I wake with a dreaded curiosity and tune into the news about Australia's bushfires. Sixteen people have died.[1] Over 250 million tonnes of CO_2 have been emitted into the atmosphere; more than half of Australia's annual greenhouse gas emissions.[2] Sydney is experiencing the worst air quality it's ever seen.[3] And I fear the smoke is here to stay.[4]

The rampaging assault from the bushfires is what tipped the scale of moral conscience beyond any sense of balance; sealing my decision to remain childfree by choice. It's a decision mostly fuelled by my own climate anxiety, backed by the enormous ecological impact of each human on Earth.[5] But also I believe that any child would suffer in a world wracked by climate change. The science speaks for itself; the carbon footprint

---

1 Gorrey 2020.
2 Readfearn 2019.
3 Cockburn 2019.
4 Zhou 2019.
5 Mason 2016.

reduction of having one less child is more than double that of living car free.[6] We just need to break our collective cognitive dissonance, and act.

I'm all too aware of the privilege that comes with the ability to make the choice to be childfree, but I also believe that those who have privilege should use it in a way that minimises harm wherever possible. I've come to the conclusion that I could never, in good conscience, bring a child into the world who will have to suffer through the existence of human-induced climate change.

Let's be real here, the world isn't just fraught with dangers of the impending climate disaster; it's *fucked*.

Even after the Paris Agreement, global greenhouse gas emissions have risen by four percent.[7] And, in a completely non-suicidal way, I wish I'd never been born, because without existing I wouldn't have contributed to screwing up the planet. This feeling I thought only I felt is far more common than I realised, and is actually referred to by psychologists as 'eco-despair', a sane and normal reaction to the climate crisis.[8]

My first brush with mass existential depression occurred after being taught about human-induced climate change in high school science. It still brings me anxiety to reflect just briefly on my teenage self's climate panic, and it's even more unfathomable to imagine what it would be like to be a child at school in ten or fifteen years, feeling the same shame and guilt simply because of their existence, and having to just keep on living, despite the total collapse of the world as we know it.

I wouldn't want to be born today and eventually realise that previous generations *could* have done something but didn't. Or they did, but it wasn't enough.

I do admit to being somewhat isolated from the mass rallies calling for climate action in Sydney, but I still head out every Friday in Sweden and strike, joined by a handful of youths and some thirty woke retired people.[9] It's a pitifully small, but nonetheless loyal group of strikers. However, despite the global collective effort, the pessimism I have for my future – let alone the future of the generations who come after me – persists.

Some days I find myself mourning a very specific version of parenthood that I'll miss out on. But then I remember: I have friends, the capacity

---

6   Wynes and Nicholas 2017.
7   Thunberg 2018.
8   Buckley 2019.
9   Siriniwasa 2019.

to have pets, relatives who have children and there's always the option to adopt an already existing child. There is so much more to living a rich and fulfilling life *without* biological kids. Plus, I firmly believe that people need to start making sacrifices now.

'We already have all the facts,' says Greta Thunberg, 'all we have to do is to wake up and change.'[10]

*

This article was originally published by *Honi Soit*.

References

Buckley, Cara. "Apocalypse got you down? Maybe this will help." *New York Times*, 15 November 2019. https://www.nytimes.com/2019/11/15/sunday-review/depression-climate-change.html.

Cockburn, Paige. "Sydney smoke at its 'worst ever' with air pollution in some areas 12 times 'hazardous' threshold." *ABC News*, 10 December 2019. https://www.abc.net.au/news/2019-12-10/sydney-smoke-returns-to-worst-ever-levels/11782892.

Gorrey, Megan. "Man confirmed dead on South Coast as NSW bushfire death toll rises." *Sydney Morning Herald*, 3 January 2020. https://www.smh.com.au/national/nsw/man-confirmed-dead-on-south-coast-as-nsw-bushfire-death-toll-rises-to-eight-20200103-p53oii.html.

Mason, Betsy. "Maps Show Humans' Growing Impact on the Planet." *National Geographic*, 23 August 2016. https://www.nationalgeographic.com/news/2016/08/human-footprint-map-ecological-impact/.

Readfearn, Graham. "Australia's bushfires have emitted 250m tonnes of CO_2, almost half of country's annual emissions." *The Guardian*, 13 December 2019. https://www.theguardian.com/environment/2019/dec/13/australias-bushfires-have-emitted-250m-tonnes-of-co2-almost-half-of-countrys-annual-emissions.

Siriniwasa, Himath. "'Sydney is choking': 20,000 rally for climate action." *Honi Soit*, 11 December 2019. https://honisoit.com/2019/12/sydney-is-choking-20000-rally-for-climate-action/.

Thunberg, Greta. "School strike for climate - save the world by changing the rules." Filmed November 2018 at TEDxStockholm, Stockholm.

---

10 Thunberg 2018.

Video. https://www.ted.com/talks/greta_thunberg_school_strike_for_
climate_save_the_world_by_changing_the_rules/transcript.

Wynes, Seth, and Kimberly Nicholas. "The climate mitigation gap:
education and government recommendations miss the most effective
individual actions." *Environmental Research Letters* 12, no. 7 (2017).
doi: DOI: 10.1088/1748-9326/aa7541.

Zhou, Naaman. "Australia's bushfire crisis: how long are the fires and
smoke expected to last?" *The Guardian*, 13 December 2019. https://
www.theguardian.com/australia-news/2019/dec/13/australias-
bushfire-crisis-how-long-are-the-fires-and-smoke-expected-to-last.

THE CHILDREN KNOW BETTER

Bianca Yeung

He points out how
they've mucked up the back burning
the trunks are scorched black
at their base but
untarnished skin
and naked branches
lie higher up
where inexpert hands with
flames at their fingertips
chose not to reach.

I ask him how he knows this
he tells me
of an elder, and
I wonder how
much longer the loudest voices
in this country
will proclaim
they know
what's best for a land
they do not know,
like stone-set parents
speaking for children
with ten times their wisdom.

For I know several
children
with bare feet that skip through dewy grass
with fingertips outstretched as butterfly landing pads
with eyes turned skyward to paint pictures with clouds

they splash, giggling hysterically
bicycle through muddy puddles,
throw tea parties with leaves for plates
and gumnuts to tip the waiter with

laughter fills the air

then smoke fills the sky
fills their lungs

and they turn around
to go back inside.

THE FIRES THAT BURNT THROUGH US ALL

Raz Badiyan

My moon has changed colour and
    I haven't been myself.
The trees have turned black and I can
        no
          longer
             breathe.
I drove north to the sky
   and there were clouds upon clouds
     of ash
    and pillows of smoky bark.
Remnants of the vast
         lands.
  Remnants
  of us.

There was a time
   when I saw through you
   to the other side;
Had you figured out
   from your hands
     to your stride.

Saw how you
   came to be and
  what you loved and
  how you lied;

Trying your best
                        to run
        but you
    couldn't hide.

Now, the signals
        are weak
    from smoke
        wind
    and haze,
Blurring the line
    between
new
    current and
old ways.

WALKING, SKETCHING AND DOGS: AUTOETHNOGRAPHY IN THE TIME OF FIRE AND RONA

Jakelin Troy

The year 2020 has been a catastrophic, even dystopian, year for most of the world's human and non-human population. For me, it became increasingly important to find a way to manage the trauma and anxiety response I felt rising in me as I understood we were trapped on this island and my university island looked to be sinking, socially and economically. An island I love, but I hate to be trapped anywhere – maybe it is the nomad in me developing a kind of 'cabin fever'. It has been an even more difficult year for me as I have been locked out of my Ngarigu Country, the Snowy Mountains of South-Eastern Australia. I watched from a distance as my Country and its plants and animals burnt; deeply burnt, massively burnt. More than a million animals and 12.6 million hectares burnt.[1] I drove from Namadgi to the alps recently, and it is still a fire ground, huge burnt trees trying to regrow leaves, small pathetic trees just charcoal sticks, the ground grey and black.

My incinerated Country and the looming menace of COVID-19, 'the Rona' as it has come to be known in Australia, drove me to engage with one of my core personal and professional practices: 'journaling', particularly visual capture of my experiences in photographs and small paintings in a little sketchbook, as a record of all my feelings. I turned to 'autoethnography', described by Carolyn Ellis, pioneer in the field, as 'research, writing, and story, and method that connects the autobiographical

---

1   Werner and Lyons 2020.

and personal to the cultural, social, and political'.[2] Bochner explains that 'narrative inquiry and autoethnography – the kind of qualitative research that Carolyn [Ellis] and I are interested in – pulls away from that obsession with science' of the academies and gives voice to the personal and the emotional.[3] This time of quiet reflection has led me to explore my growing interest in my own responses to my experiences in Country using techniques of Indigenous research methodologies: observation, reflection, yarning and engagement with narrative and stories.

I walked on Country, looking and thinking, documenting and sharing my experiences. Walking is a way to develop thinking, a 'peripatetic practice' employed by philosophers since Aristotle, and journaling focuses that thinking. I also began a Facebook page, you can find me under Prof: JakelinTroy @ProfessorTroy, with my friend and research colleague, Mujahid, from the Torwali community in Swat, North Pakistan, as part of this journaling. It really began as a collaboration, the two of us Indigenous people thinking about walking and talking on Country. Mujahid shares pictures of his mountains of Kohistan, the Hindu Kush, and I share pictures of dogs I meet while walking kuyu (Torwali) and mirrigan (Ngarigu).

I walk with Shadow, my little companion, my long-haired Chihuahua, whose life partner died in the last couple of months. His lonely soul is also nourished by walking. He has become Shadow of the Mountain, a strong outdoor dog, no longer the lap companion, looking for his walk every day, impatient to get out and join me in reverie as I paint my sketches from whatever rock or grassy knoll we choose as our seat.

The dogs I meet are posted on the Facebook page as Ngunawal Country (Canberra, or any other Country I am walking in), Dogs of Mount Rogers (or another place). My daily walks have been around this mountain in Canberra. I also encounter many interesting habitations made by people using the materials they find on the mountain.

Sometimes I ride my horses with my daughter through the grasslands and share a livestream on Facebook. I talk about the Country, the grasslands and the Ngunawal cultural practices associated with the land, plants, animals and geography. It helps me think about my own Ngarigu community and the Ngunawal as our neighbours, creating a story in my

---

2   Ellis 2004, xix.
3   Ellis and Bochner 2004, 8.

Pages from my sketchbook 2020, Jakelin Troy.

mind that reaches out to how it was and still is for us to be living in our Countries as the Aboriginal owners of these places and sharing this region.

My sketchbook is filling. They are rough but satisfying. Each image evokes a memory of where I sat and what I thought. Some look out from Mount Rogers to the High Country, now with snow on the peaks visible from my vantage points. I can see right through to the heart of my Country, Kiandra. The book is a visual journal recording my moods, through the moods of the landscape. Sometimes it is dark, dramatic and foreboding, contrasted with days when it is light, optimistic, saturated with possibilities and the promise of spring.

In addition to my wanderings and sketchings, I wrote the following piece as a sort of blog as we reached the middle of the shutdown period in May. It is part of an, as yet unpublished, collective writing effort with my colleagues in the Sydney Indigenous Research Hub and is another element to my autoethnograhy of life in the Rona.

Lost and found in the time of rona

In many ways the COVID-19 (the Rona) working from home arrangements came at a good time for me. I have spent five years working

Pages from my sketchbook 2020, Jakelin Troy.

in Sydney and living in Canberra. While I enjoy being a nomad, it has meant that I left my daughter for days at a time and I had never previously had such a sustained separation. It had a worse effect on me than on her, she often told me that she was very proud that I am a professor at a top university. She was pleased that the weekends we now shared were devoted to her and she was seeing more of me than she did when I was at home and working in my office until late at night and all Saturday and Sunday. I hadn't realised I had become such an absentee mother.

The Rona came hot on the heels of the bushfire emergency in south eastern Australia, irony intended. I almost choked to death on the smoke and I am unsure whether I have had Rona or not. I certainly had a bad time with my lungs and a very sore throat. I tried to get tested but was sent away. Now I am healthy and don't need to be tested. I am walking and riding my horse and eating well, mostly – with a bit of sugar when I am zoomed out!

I am sustained by my colleagues and friends through our online forums. The Sydney Indigenous Research Network has steady attendance and membership is growing. We support each other with increasingly pithy discussions about ethics, research methodologies and the value of research to Indigenous communities. I am learning about Indigenous researchers doing 'non-Indigenous' research and non-Indigenous researchers doing Indigenous research. My PhD student is working with me on how to take social research completely online, keeping the human in an inhuman world where we only have community through stop-start internet connections and pixelated images. Machines are taking over.

I am editing a book with my friend and colleague in another time zone. He is at the top of the Northern Hemisphere, while I am at the bottom of the Southern Hemisphere. He keeps in touch with people in all time zones and regions, as he has always done, through social media channels. He is used to social distancing because he lives in a country where economic and social hardships naturally impose isolation. I am not so accustomed to this; I am usually free to go wherever and do more or less whatever I want without scrutiny.

Rona is a very levelling experience. We are all equals in the online world. Maybe some are more equal because it has always been their world. I hope it doesn't continue. I like to see people. This is something I have discovered about myself. I am not the socially awkward introvert I have always believed myself to be. I miss people.

References

Ellis, Carolyn. *The ethnographic I: a methodological novel about autoethnography.* Walnut Creek, California: AltaMira Press, 2004.

Ellis, Carolyn and Art Bochner. "Building connections in qualitative research: Carolyn Ellis and Art Bochner in conversation with Stacy Holman Jones." *Forum: Qualitative Social Research* 5, no. 3 Article 28 (September 2004).

Werner, Joel and Suzannah Lyons. "The size of Australia's bushfire crisis captured in five big numbers." ABC Science: Sum of All Parts. 5 March 2020. https://www.abc.net.au/news/science/2020-03-05/bushfire-crisis-five-big-numbers/12007716.

THE COLD FIRESTORM OF DIGITAL BUSHFIRE PHOTOGRAPHY

Victor Zhou

Looking back to the 2019–20 Australian bushfires, my social media feed was set on flames by the digital images of catastrophic bushfires that were caused by the climate crisis.[1] Flesh, wood, scales, guts, shells, feathers and s(kin) all became one within a sublime flame. Red flames and smoke, so large and high, ignited and hazed these digital images, making it hard to see through to the environment, Country, human and non-humans within them. And even then, with an upward flick of my finger on the cold screen, the images disappeared from my view. As the bushfires continued to roar, the digital photographs continued to spark higher and higher, fuelling an ever-growing firestorm. This whirling blizzard of digital bushfire images became blurred and indistinguishable, interfering with our eyes, glitching and stunning them with their sheer mass and numbers.[2] My eyes were not fast or powerful enough to register any punctum that would pierce me and help me feel.[3] As I sat behind the white-blue screen, rapidly scrolling away at the endless drone of bushfire images, it barely singed me – it became a cold firestorm. As the grand, transcendental flames grew taller, I teetered towards sublime indifference.

Although the transparency of the screen allowed me to see to faraway places, its solid materiality prevented me from touching, smelling and feeling. Head tilted, mouth open, I was spellbound by the images' red radiance. And on the same screen, I read an update in January 2020 that

---

1   van Oldenborgh et al. 2020.
2   Kracauer 2016.
3   Barthes 1981.

800 million animals were killed and more than one billion animals were affected.[4]

My eyes could not read these deaths fast enough. They accelerated at dizzying speeds – *a blue-tongued lizard's death, a koala's death, a kangaroo's death, an ant's death, a magpie's death, a gumtree's death, a child's death.* Although I could not see them, they haunt these images, leaving ghostly traces. The intense crackling of the flames may have eclipsed their voices – but they are not mute. They are muffled and quiet. We should, as Tina Campt suggests, listen and feel the affective frequencies of the images, rather than simply looking at them.[5] Similarly, for David Banggal Mowaljarlai, the world is not a static NASA globe photograph from out of space.[6] Mowaljarlai's being spills over and beyond the skin of their body, pouring, overlapping and continually feeling; becoming one with Country and land.

By feeling, instead of looking, we can attend to the ghostly traces of living-kin whose flesh now exists as hot shimmers and ash, flowing with the voracious fires and smoke. Although the ashes have now settled into the soil, they can still reach out to warm our flesh. They can tend to our cold burns of sublime indifference. They can help us feel e(motion), motivate us, move us. They can slowly pull us out of the present-as-of-now and into a future-imagined-otherwise. These ashes sway, swish, rustle and interweave. I can remember the smell of smoke; I can feel them in my lungs and through my being. I am becoming more-than-flesh. Scattered non-human-particles slowly suffuse into molecular receptacle flesh-systems, becoming-with-beings and then reliving-with-world. We may act for them as they act through and with us. They remind us, and through this collective memory they sustain, prompt us to response-ability.[7] They stick, shred, (re)order, (re)wire and are buzzing by degrees. The ashes of feelings slowly hum within me, and their hot intensities fuel my frustration, actioning me to change forevermore.

4 Dickman 2020.
5 Campt 2017.
6 Powerhouse Museum 2020.
7 Haraway 2016.

References

Barthes, Roland. *Camera lucida: reflections on photography*. Hill & Wang, 1981.

Campt, Tina. *Listening to images*. Duke University Press, 2017.

Dickman, Christopher. "A statement about the 480 million animals killed in NSW bushfires since September." 8 January 2020. https://www.sydney.edu.au/news-opinion/news/2020/01/03/a-statement-about-the-480-million-animals-killed-in-nsw-bushfire.html

Haraway, Donna. *Staying with the trouble: making kin in the Chthulucene*. Duke University Press, 2016.

Kracauer, Siegfried. *Photography*, trans. Thomas Y. Levin. 19, no. 3 (2016).

Powerhouse Museum. *Linear*. Sydney: Powerhouse Museum, 15 November 2019–20. June 2020. Exhibition catalogue.

van Oldenborgh, G. J., Krikken, F., Lewis, S., Leach, N. J., Lehner, F., Saunders, K. R., van Weele, M., Haustein, K., Li, S., Wallom, D. et al. "Attribution of the Australian bushfire risk to anthropogenic climate change." *Natural Hazards and Earth System Sciences* Discuss. (2020): 1–46. https://doi.org/10.5194/nhess-2020-69, in review, 2020.

SIREN SUMMER

Gabrielle Platt

To the summer that broke our heart,
we are used to burnt skin and burnt land
but this is a different kind of flame.
The land, the living lie together in pain
with every day a new reason to weep,
their damaged lungs and throats choked in the cities
while lives and homes are gutted in the bush.
Mates lost, two-legged,
wiped off the Earth, four-legged.
Another siren sounds.
A country staggering with weary limbs and thinner skin,
but still standing.

THE WOLF

Francesca Edwards Rentsch

The bulldozers ate the mountains before she was born, but mother is poor – father is dead – so they live on the dust-plains where the forest clings to what hills are left. The girl can't see the cities in the distance, as high as they thrust into the sky, only their glows at night, which brighten the horizon like a dozen suns all rising at once. Scattered over the scarred plains are the huts of other backcountry folk, built by their grandparents out of the sheets of tin that blow in from the city slums on the backs of summer tornadoes. The huts crouch in small dells; their windows blink shockingly, as though woken from a fitful sleep. The forest claws at the plains, but the roots of the trees rip slowly from the ashy soil. Their anorexic branches rend the sky; their leaves lie rotting. The forest buries itself beneath its own dead. And passing between the trees are red tongues and desperate claws, grey fur mottled from the acid rains; the wolf, who is the rage of the forest, and can never listen to reason.

Grandmother tells the girl stories of trees so tall that not even her father could see over them, and trunks so thick that she couldn't wrap her arms around them. Engorged vines wove between the trees into a web that would snatch you right off the path. And once you leave the path you would never find it again, and then the wolves would eat you. She laughs, because grandmother tickles her, and she squirms on the withered lap that she is getting too big for.

When grandmother was not much bigger than the girl is now, the forest came right up to the door. She used to sneak out under the gate to play in the forest, but she would never leave the path. Once she found a robin's nest and was teasing the mother bird as she slurped up the yolks (how precious was that gold, but the girl has never seen an egg), when a beautiful woman called to her from the forest; she was lost, and needed to take grandmother's hand and be guided back to safety. But grandmother refused, and when the woman turned her back it was as hollow and rotten as a log. Once, near the clearing where their father was cutting wood, she saw a troll climb out of his swamp, and she threw stones at him until he climbed back in. Once, she built a trap and caught a rabbit in it, but as she broke its neck she felt eyes on her, and then she turned and ran back up the path like the devil himself was after her, for she knew that only the eyes of a wolf could mean to do her such grievous harm.

When grandmother was not much bigger than the girl is now, she saw the mother of her friend Tommie wade naked into a stream to bathe and on her belly was the third nipple she used to suckle the devil. Grandmother told her brothers and they chased the woman out of her house and stripped her, and then they drowned her. That winter, grandmother's mother gave birth to a baby that her father gave to the forest; but grandmother saw it before he wrapped it in a blanket and took it away, and she saw that it had wings, and a wrinkled nose like a bat.

When grandmother was not much bigger than the girl is now, a pack of wolves got into the hen house and tore the creatures apart. The next night, they ate her father when he stepped outside to relieve himself, and the night after that, they ate her mother when she walked out into the forest because it was her duty to follow her husband. The fourth night, the wolves came to sit around the house and howl. The howl of the wolf is more terrible than the claws that follow it, for all the melancholy and rapaciousness of the forest lives in its howl. When grandmother opened the door to throw the shells from the beans out into the yard (she had forgotten the hens were dead) the wolves seized her by the ankles and dragged her towards the forest – she was too frightened to scream, so she heard their abominable snorting – but the brothers were waiting and they shot the wolf holding her, and shot two more before the pack could get over the fence and away. This is the girl's favourite story, because grandmother pretends to be the wolf and chases her around the room, waggling her tongue, and then she shows the girl the wolf skin with bullet holes in it. His swollen tongue had been as long as grandmother's two hands, and it dripped red with grandmother's blood; and his black lips still streamed with bloody slaver for days after he was dead.

The girl's mother says, 'Here, your grandmother has been sick; take her this basket, with the last of the tinned beans, and the oat cakes, and some Panadol.'

The girl puts her knife into the basket; it is half as big as she is, and she sharpens it every day. She puts on her cape that grandmother made for her. She is careful to close the gate behind her; they have a goat this year for mother to milk (sometimes it comes out grey, and sometimes with swirls of pink, and they drink it even though grandmother has told her that milk should be white), and there are many hungry things in the forest.

The trees thrust bony fingers across the path – they hope to scratch out her eyes – but the girl is not afraid; she often takes the path to grandmother's. She listens to the little creaks and groans; the tortured roots are always slowly ripping from the soil, but she doesn't know whether they are clinging to the earth or trying to free themselves from it. She passes piles of dead leaves before she notices they are moving; when she looks more closely, they are swarming insects with bulging heads and clicking jaws, and underneath their hairy legs she thinks she can see the bleached white of dry bones.

She has not gone far when – there, just off the path, only a few small steps. In amongst the skeletal trees, a carpet of sonorous bluebells; a last breath of air, a final effort at fecundity. She has never seen anything so beautiful. She steps off the path.

Their stems are as thick as her baby brother's arms. She bends down and breaks them. Sap stains her fingers.

When she stands the wolf is waiting for her. He is a huge one, and grey. She can count every rib that cuts through his chest. She can see lice seething in his matted coat. His paws – *huge*, as large as her head – are blistered and scabby, and his claws are splintered. There are welts on his muzzle; when he snarls, they crack and bleed pus. He has lost the tip of his tail. His eyes are red as a wound; red as her cape; red as her menses. His tongue lolls over slavering chops. He pants; he can hear her heart beating beneath her soft breasts. It is a stronger beat than his own. Out darts a dainty, pointed tongue; she licks her lips, and the spittle makes them shine. She drops her basket; her knife is in her hand.

The ghosts of older battles rise to watch this next encounter. The palimpsest of the forest awaits a new addition. She is a woodcutter's daughter. He is a wolf. They are opposites, the epitome of both their breeds, and neither can reject their own nature. How can a girl be anything but civilised? How can a wolf be anything but beastly? They stand as champions, in the tradition of a long line of champions, since the day that man awoke to himself and stood apart for the first time.

They come together. His guts are red on the bleeding bluebells.

She prospers.

IN OUR PURSUIT

Rosalin Xie

The Lion has come far.
His bones are forged
from stone, bronze and iron.
His mind has journeyed
with Homer, Dante and Melville.
But the stars he aims for are far,
too far from reach.

Donning his suit and tie,
The Lion surges forward
past the skyscrapers and cars,
above the cement and smoke,
wielding his briefcase against
all that lies in his path.

His presence encroaches the land,
spindly arms, reaching, grasping
everything and nothing –
to swallow the whole world
for enough is never enough.

The factories huff angrier,
the waters creep higher.
From the pandas in the east
to the minks in the west,
his animal kingdom withers.

'They'll applaud once I'm done',
he thinks as he wades, waist deep,
through his riches toward the stars.
For in the stars lay his throne;
the throne that is his alone.

He plunders till the day
his footprints stain the sky.
The weight of his endeavours
crush a weeping daffodil –
he pays no mind to weeds.

He looms over the stars.
Has the Lion not come far?
He expects applause, cheers,
a celebration of glory and success,
but looks back to find
that the Earth is far,
too far from his reach.

PRIMAVERAL

C.L. Crozier

His wife's side of the bed was empty.

He was used to this. His wife had an unusually close relationship with her mother. When they married she'd made it very clear that she would go back home often and, so far, she'd kept to that promise. They marked the calendar together so that he would always know when it was time for her to leave. But there was still a month to go before her next departure and the bed was empty. She was gone.

He tried to ignore her absence. Their home was icy without her. All through winter she was the only thing that provided him with warmth. And now she was gone. He fed the dog without her. It was three times happier than any other dog at the prospect of being fed, but the selfish brute couldn't seem to share any of that happiness with him. He tried to focus on his work without her, his depressing job that tore husbands from wives and left countless empty beds in its wake.

She should have told him she was leaving.

She should have given him the chance to make things right.

In times like these, there was no one else to turn to but his brother, Sid. He didn't like Sid. As his wife was always quick to tease – he didn't like anyone except for her. Only ever her. But recently the teasing that had once lit up their dreary home had turned malicious and as cold as the bed left empty in her absence. So he turned to Sid, the elder of his younger brothers and the one he disliked the least.

He would never ask his youngest brother for advice.

Over the course of the morning he drafted and penned a long, meandering electronic letter, begging audience with his brother. Moments after he worked up the courage to hit send came the reply: '*k. Sea u @ 1*' which was meaningless to him. He decided the best thing to do was to wait at their usual meeting place on the off chance his brother actually showed up. If he was going to stew in his loneliness he might as well do so while enjoying the unseasonably warm weather.

He always met Sid at the same spot. Sid was a man of the sea and always seemed deeply uncomfortable anywhere other than his own boats. They would meet on the rocks at a certain beach: a secluded cove at the mouth of a cave known only by the birds, the fish and the truly desperate. He found a place in the shade to stand and stare at the lazy ebb and flow of the ocean, keeping an eye out for his brother's boat.

A family of seagulls meandered past, the chicks still bristling with the fluffy down that made them look like tiny marbles rolling around his feet. They didn't notice him. Didn't care that they were walking in his shadow. The young and healthy never noticed him, and those that did were too tragic to even speak of. And even though they were so small, so fragile, and shouldn't have survived in the harsh cold of January, they didn't notice him.

Judging by the position of the sun, it was nearing three o'clock when Sid's boat appeared on the horizon. He didn't recognise it at first. The tiny fishing vessel was heaped high with something that distorted its silhouette. As it came closer, he spotted Sid at its helm and he realised the shape was rubbish. A mountain of waste scooped from the sea and heaved into a dingy that ought to have sunk under its weight. The boat drifted towards the rocks and pulled in closer than any less experienced seaman would dare.

'Alright get in,' Sid grunted.

He stared at his brother, then let his eyes drift over the heaving mountain of garbage littering the boat. There was no smell; nothing on the boat could decompose, at least not within a millennium or two. It didn't make it any less revolting.

'You are joking.'

'Look mate, I don't shit on you when you're trying to sweep your Mc-fucking-mansion. Either get in or don't. I don't have time to sit around waiting.'

He thought he did a good job of hiding his disgust as he stepped into his brother's floating mountain of landfill. He kicked aside a plastic bag, then struggled to shake it off as it wrapped around his ankle.

'So this is your new hobby,' he remarked, peeling the bag from his leg as Sid started up the engine. It was a clever little design, solar powered and so silent it felt like they were gliding. The maker's mark on the side told him it had been made by their cousin Lio, who'd been in the solar power game for longer than there had been a solar power game. He also apparently liked to counteract any good he might have achieved by breeding cattle and chartering his own aircraft every day. But in the great diplomatic spirit that seemed to run in their family, he'd managed to spin that as a good thing.

'Someone's gotta do it. Fish eat this crap you know.'

He knew. They washed up on his own shore. Gulls, fish, sometimes dolphins. Nothing was immune.

'Can't you get one of your nymphs to do it for you?'

'They hate it when you call them that. And I am, obviously, they're all giving it a shot, but there's a lotta ground to cover. Huge domain, the sea.'

It was a jab. He tried not to rise to it.

'I was hoping to talk to you about something else,' he said. He found an old beach chair that seemed sturdy enough and perched unsteadily on the end of it.

'About Seffy right?'

'She hates it when you call her that.'

Sid huffed a laugh through his nose. 'She hates a lot of things. Guess you don't know that, since you're here.'

He didn't reply straight away. For a long while there was nothing but the gentle lapping of the waves.

'I didn't tell you why I wanted to meet.'

'No, but I have a pretty good idea,' Sid said. 'The birds have started migrating.'

'I don't see what that has to do with –'

'She left you, didn't she?'

'She's visiting her mother.'

'It's January and I'm wearing a bloody t-shirt. She left you, Dee.'

It's never easy to stare the truth in the face. The gulls were birthing chicks, the sun was beating delirious heat on the world and, of course, his marriage bed was still empty. It was January. And it was spring.

Persephone had left him.

'Perhaps it's time to just let her go.' The words barely slipped out, so faint they were almost lost to the wind. He felt himself slipping into the depths of his thoughts, and suddenly longed to be back in the safety of the Underworld, not pootling along the ocean surface in a garbage barge.

'Can't you just kidnap her again?'

'For the last time I never abducted her. That was a complete fabrication.'

'Well you'd better do something. You know little brother likes his mortals. I wouldn't want to be the guy who wiped them out just because he couldn't keep his wife satisfied. Oh hello, what've we got over there?'

There was a formless shape floating some way in the distance. As they drifted closer it took shape. 'One of your lot,' Sid said as he scooped it into the boat. It was a seal, or had been a seal once. Sid crouched and slit it open from end to end and wrenched out a stomach filled with what he termed 'undigestible human shit'. When he was done, he heaved the carcass back into the sea and tossed the stomach onto the pile. His movements were smooth, practised, with the finesse that can only come from muscle memory.

'You want my honest opinion?' Sid asked as they watched the seal sink beneath surface.

'That's why I'm here.'

'It's not you. Well, not just you. I mean it probably wouldn't hurt if you "redecorated the Underworld" if you get my meaning, but that's only half of it. For Gaia's sake, she *loves* this world but look at it,' he gesticulated at the mountain, the seal's stomach glistening on top like a jewel from the sea. 'It's dying. And instead of making the most of its final years she has to spend half of it cooped up inside with Mister Morose.'

'You expect me to undo the damage of seven billion humans?'

'You're the god of the bloody underworld. You should know better than anyone the impact one person can have.'

It was true. His domain was testament to what one powerful human could do to the world. He couldn't count how many times a change of power meant more work for him. If it was so easy to inspire people to kill, how hard could it be to inspire them to save themselves?

Sid was right. To restore his world, he had to help save hers. True, he couldn't shape the elements like his siblings, or force nature to obey his call, but he could speak, he could inspire. Money was no object; he and Charon had been splitting the profits from their ferry service for centuries. He could do very little. And yet, with what little ability he had, he could do anything.

'And what if I fail?'

'Then you'd best find Prometheus and ask for some tips on pain tolerance,' Poseidon said. 'And if you happen to survive whatever little brother has in store for you,' he pretended to raise a glass to the heavens, squinting at the clear sky, 'we'll just have to usher in the reign of Persephone.'

TEMPORAL CONFLICT

Lauren Poole

Museology and heritage studies – my disciplines – have, at their heart, a temporal conflict: they don't know which way to look.

Do they look backwards at material culture and focus on the past in its many forms?

Do they look around at the present day and ask what material culture is called to do, is responsible for, at this contemporary moment?

Do they look forward and steward these pasts, these presents, into the future?

Do any of these directions matter when the foundations on which we make sense of time – the structures, strictures, assumptions and expectations – are quaking beneath our Corinthian-columned feet?

Ozymandias' ruin porn

And on the pedestal these words appear:
'My name is Ozymandias, king of kings:
Look on my works, ye Mighty, and despair!'
Nothing beside remains. Round the decay
Of that colossal wreck, boundless and bare
The lone and level sands stretch far away.[1]

* * *

'Ruin porn' is a divisive term. Coined by James Griffioen to describe photographers picking over Detroit, like vultures in search of a decaying

---

1   Shelley 1818, Lines 9–14.

subject, it has become a point of conflict between academic and artistic interests and the lives of those they are interested in.

The word 'porn' has been criticised as inappropriate, but makes blatant that ruin porn is voyeuristic, visceral, and at times exploitative in nature. This is not a fascination with what once was or might have been; this is the thrill of the apocalypse unleashed, the schadenfreude of decay, watched from a place and life which is conserved.

There must be distance between observer and ruin; to admire ruins as aesthetic and existential landscapes, you need the privilege and ability to step back.

* * *

'Here' and 'there' imply 'now' and 'then'. Here is now, and there is then, and then means either a time in the past or in the future. There implies here and then implies now, but the reverse is not necessarily true. I am here now doing what I have to do and am absorbed in doing. There need be no thought of a there or a then.[2]

Ruins are 'over there' and – we hope – never here, now. We are comforted being spatially, circumstantially and temporally distant from them; a false sense of security in returning to a home that is not ruined.

Yet.

To feel this thrill, to observe and paint and write, we also hold at a distance all future ruins, and the possibilities and processes of ruination that may or will create them. Be they erosion by sand and wind or capitalistic destruction, we hope that those processes will not visit upon us, not now, not here, not ever.

* * *

The persistence of Shelley's poetic depiction – one of the most cited quotations in ruins literature – a tale of a traveller, told to a poet, told to an audience – bolsters a further belief that even if ruins are gone, their poetic depictions survive; we remember those secondary memories and stories. We take comfort from Shelley's permanence just as we take warning from Ozymandias' impermanence. By conquering the loss of time and place in word, we hope to fend off the possibility of more loss.

---

2   Tuan 1978, 11–12.

Do I need to recollect Shelley's traveller's recollections? Is it easier to see these 'trunkless legs of stone'[3] as something beautiful and worthy of memorialisation, when I know that they are distant in time and word?

* * *

I wrote an essay about ruins but they were antiquated ruins, or mystical ruins, or capitalist ruins. I did not write an essay about the sites I spent days and energies and lives studying, and which will turn to ruins before my eyes and under my pen.

The futures of Anne Boyer

In *Garments against women*, the piece titled 'Not writing' begins:
'When I am not writing I am not writing a novel called *1994* about a young woman in an office park in a provincial town who has a job cutting and pasting time.'[4]
And ends:
'I am not writing a history of these times or of past times or of any future times and not even the history of these visions which are with me all day and all of the night.'[5]
The piece details mundane and imaginary things which Boyer is not writing. Not that she *cannot* write them, but that she *is not*. Among these are memoirs ('not writing about a memoir about the prohibitions of memoirs.'[6]), poems and legislation ('not writing a new constitution for the republic of no history.'[7]).
Although imaginary works are mentioned, it is not until the concluding 'visions' that the piece moves from speculative to hallucinogenic. We come to question all we have read so far, reassessing them less as brainstormed to-do lists, and more as alternate timelines, versions of lives and outputs that are inaccessible but have leeched through in prophecy and lingering unease.

---

3   Shelley 1818, Line 2.
4   Boyer 2016, 41.
5   Boyer 2016, 43.
6   Boyer 2016, 41.
7   Boyer 2016, 42.

By opening with the image of time as 'cut and pasted' and closing with layered histories which co-exist outside of any possible historiography, I am left with the sinking feeling that these future times may not be written, and if they are, they will bear more resemblance to visions than to anything written before.

How am I to record these visions, these futures; how am I to conceptualise them now – and in an unrecognisable climate-ravaged world, where is the place for them at all? Should I not write these histories? Will these not-histories come to pass? Writings that will not be written; and not writings which will appear as closer to reality than fiction?

Ruin porosity

In 1962, a British scheme (inspired by film producer William MacQuitty, and drawn up by architects Jane Drew and Maxwell Fry and engineer Ted Happold) proposed to encase the Temples of Abu Simbel in Upper Egypt in bubbles, sealing them off from the contaminated waters of the rising Aswan High Dam. The scheme proposed creating a labyrinth of shells and passages to simultaneously preserve the stone in filtered, nuclear-powered water and allow visitors to flock to viewing platforms and underwater elevators.[8]

Instead, the Egyptian government and UNESCO went with Swedish firm Vattenbyggnadsbyrán's plan whereby the temples, carved out of the solid rock mountain face, were cut into 7047 pieces, removed, transported and reassembled – supported by internal concrete domes and artificial hills.

As gifts for their assistance, four countries, Spain, the Netherlands, Italy and the United States were offered other temples – also in the dam's path – to be taken apart and reassembled in institutions of their choice. In the competition that followed, the Metropolitan Museum of Art won the Temple of Dendur and built the Sackler Wing to contain it.

MacQuitty's vision and the architect's plans were deemed impractical amidst scores of impractical schemes. Were bubbles worse than inserting jacks under the mountain, opening them and slowly filling the gaps with cement? Worse than placing the temples on a concrete barge and letting the rising waters carry it to safety?

The issue was that any scheme accepted must retain the shaft of light which enters the larger temple twice a year, illuminating three statues in

---

8   Allais 2013, 19.

the innermost chamber – Ramesses II, as well as sun gods Re-Horakhte and Amon-Re – and leaving the fourth, Ptah, god of darkness, always in shadow.

Light can't pass through water as it passes through air.

Light can't pass through glass and concrete as it passes through air.

So, they cut the temples into pieces and carried them away.

* * *

There is something deeply appealing about encasing a site in a glass bubble. I imagine water creeping around the bubble's exterior, waves bobbing and rising against the curve as the dam slowly fills. It feels futuristic and ancient: let us live under glass roofs in colonies on Mars, and wear helmets as we search for Atlantis below.

The temples, dragged ashore – pulled apart, reconfigured, resuscitated.

How sweat was wiped from brows; muscle and machine working against the tide, a few more inches, a few more inches.

How much effort to stay afloat, to stay out of reach? How much were we willing to expend to save these temples, to trade others in its stead? How many repetitions before we run out of shore and strength? How long before we decide we cannot expend time and energy saving one fragment of one past, when there are so many others calling for us?

* * *

I find myself experiencing preemptive survivors guilt for anything safely above the predicted sea-level rise for this century. I fixate on sites on mountains and hilltops and try not to get attached to the coastline, cutting myself off from the beach and the cliffs.

I try to picture those low-lying sites as MacQuitty might have: cocooned in shining glass bubbles. I focus on the tourists' faces, on the ex-local guide showing them 'round, on the interpretation and transformation, and the site not as static but alive.

I want the glass to shine, but in my mind it is always battered and shattered by storms; floating in red algae and reeking of decomposing fish; deserted but for bilge water and carrion birds.

I don't know what to say to these imaginary tourists: they didn't build the bubbles here; they built them elsewhere, where governments or individuals could spare the money; or where they couldn't spare the loss to national pride.

I gesture to the interpretation panels and explain: the people who lived here, who created this significance; they have moved, and I don't have a word for how to carry tangible history inside an intangible memory.

* * *

'Ruination presents the possibility of renegotiating the porous border between the social and ecological ontological ordering.'[9]

Ruins are fluid.

They leak.

They leak into your thoughts, and they leak into your essays, and they leak into all the things that aren't ruins yet.

Ruins are somewhere between alive and dead – stuck in a moment of undying; not known and not forgotten; monumental and monumentalised.

There isn't an exact point when you designate something 'ruined' or 'is now a ruin'. It's a process – but the reason we keep a distance between us and it, is that *it is still moving*.

Are the Abu Simbel temples – as they exist now – ruinous?

Are they – having been rescued from certain drowning, quartered and reanimated – un-ruinous?

Faced with climate-fueled destruction of cultural heritage, do we jump for glass bubbles to enclose our favourites? Do we plan a careful retreat, carrying what we can? Do we take the winding road along the sea, and see that the line where the ruin starts and the yet-to-be-ruined world ends is blurry and dripping?

[R]uins … often defy attempts at ordering, signifying ruptures in narratives of political, cultural, or economic progress … there may be much value in keeping such wounds open, in order to not forget or accept as inevitable the decisions and mistakes that have led to rampant ruination.[10]

* * *

9   DeSilvey and Edensor 2013, 477.
10 Gasky 2014, 120.

Heritage is ninety percent 'this dust is historic' and ten percent 'move the bloody mountain'.

The end of perpetuity

'[O]ne feature of Western modernity that is truly distinctive: its enormous intellectual commitment to the promotion of its supposed singularity.'[11]

In *The great derangement*, Amitav Ghosh argues that part of our difficulties in fighting or even acknowledging climate breakdown is that we do not have narrative patterns, particularly in the West, that can accommodate the breadth and pace of the crisis; that climate breakdown is so immense, events multiplying so improbably, lives and stories altered so deeply in creation and retelling, that literature and climate are simultaneously entwined and repelled.[12] The singularity to which Western modernity clings can be the accelerator of climate breakdown and also jam the brakes on efforts to stop it.

To put it another way: we don't know how to conceptualise or narrate stories about or in climate change.

To put it a way back: we don't know how to conceptualise or narrate time-scales which incorporate the individual (as in literary fiction); civilisational systems (as they cannibalistically accelerate); and planetary scales at all.

Faced with these enormities, and reeling from our inability to comprehend them, it can feel easier to focus on singular losses, singular deaths, in a simplistic and inaccurate attempt to comprehend a continuous rolling disaster.

* * *

It would not be wrong for me to call 2020 'a long year'; 'the long 2020'; 'the end of the future and the return of the present'. Reduced to today, this hour, this moment, we are trying to shut off what might come next.

As someone with multiple severe illnesses (and a generally uncertain lifespan), the feeling of a voided future is familiar. In the viral hellscape that is 2020, I have heard loved ones and academic peers express how time and their place within it has warped; stuck in an eternal contemporary

---

11 Ghosh 2016, 103.
12 Ghosh 2016, 1–84.

moment. They vocalise that they no longer know what may happen; that their plans make no sense; that they close down thoughts of future times because they might as well be prophecies as solid projections. Their lives are turning on a dime, over and over, until they are temporally exhausted. They want out of this singularity; want out of this perpetual present.

What then does it mean to feel this temporal angst, live in a Western singularity, and work in a discipline oriented around the material past? What happens when the future presented to you is not only incomparable to that past, but threatens to eviscerate the timeline your work is based on and lived within?

* * *

Museums and heritage work are on a time frame of 'in perpetuity'; there is no real end point – beyond the inevitable heat death of the universe. To hold simultaneously historical objects and places, and their unlimited future potential, leaves little room in the present. Each decision is weighed against the long term, and immediate challenges and paradigm shifts can get lost amidst duties and inheritances.

Enormity is built into these disciplines. But all historians live through historic times, and there are growing calls in museology and elsewhere to reorientate institutions towards the present and the roles they can take, because silence is not an option.

With this temporal reorientation, and the closing down of a recognisable future, how does the perpetual archivist deal with the end of perpetuity?

* * *

In being so large, so overwhelmingly singular as to permeate everything, climate breakdown threatens to remove perpetuity itself. There is a clash between our disciplinary responsibility to conserve and remember for the future, and the need to take drastic action (uncharacteristically fast and severe) in the present to *give* a future in which we have the luxury to conserve and remember. If we cling to the image of a reassured outcome, of the work being someone else's, of letting history unfold without our input, we risk abandoning the very histories we hold dear and preserving in their stead ever-shrinking insular disciplines – built on a shoreline which is underwater, written in books abandoned, busying itself with its own a-historicity.

* * *

'The future ain't what it used to be.'[13]

Hodder's things

> Once humans have invested in things, they became trapped in maintaining those investments and the benefits that they produced. There is a long-term trend towards greater human-thing entanglement that is a product of the fact that human 'being' depends on things and the fact that things depends on other things and on humans. Things are unstable and finite, so that change within entanglements is continually produced.[14]

Ian Hodder's reconceptualisation of the 'thingly relations of things'[15] not as entanglement but entrapment is a malevolent interpretation of human-thing relationships; one which seeks to understand that objects are not neutral, self-sustaining or self-contained, and that humans are not the non-partisan, controlling object-holders that we imagine ourselves to be.

Having discussed the long trajectory of these relationships, Hodder concludes with climate and ecological breakdown as, if not an end point, then, an opportunity for dealing with entrapment – even if it means reassessing the very objects which we base our humanity around.

If '[t]he whole environment (in the Anthropocene) is itself an artifact needing care, fixing, and manipulation',[16] is our collective atmosphere a 'thing'? Can anything be a 'thing' in the age of entrapment? And what does that mean if we task museology and heritage with caring for and conserving the history and existence of all human 'things'? Will such a task – trying to curate an atmosphere – reinforce our collective uncertainty about whether to intercede in its trajectory, as we try to remain objective?

---

13 Berra 1998, 154.
14 Hodder 2014, 32.
15 Hodder 2014, 33.
16 Hodder 2014, 33.

* * *

Even in orientating towards – around, besides, away from – climate breakdown, I see in myself and others a tendency to place the survival of things, be they objects or sites, above the lived human cost. In efforts to save the corporeal, it feels easier to work with the practicalities of moving tangible heritage; even though this reinforces old-fashioned notions that dismiss the importance of intangible heritage.

It feels easier to build a bureaucracy around moving boxes of old books, than it does to realise that not all books are written down.

I suspect much of this is to do with the boundedness of tangible heritage: saving an object is manageable, discrete, achievable. It can make you feel as if you've 'done your bit'; that you have proof of your own self-determined helpfulness.

But there is a cognitive dissonance in preserving, conserving and consigning things which we insist will continue in the present – while ignoring the processes of and possibilities for their destruction, irrelevance and abandonment in the near future.

Why are we building storehouses on floodplains and wrapping things in acid-free paper when we no longer have an assurance that they will float and stay alkaline? Is there an argument that some energy be invested away from near-sighted object preservation and shifted towards climate and ecological work, whose mitigation may save many more objects?

* * *

'To work at the world of objects was to labour at the earliest grief.'[17]
And yet this is a preoccupation with things. Where are the bodies?

The bodies of Sven Lindqvist

… history is still living even in the bodies of those who took part in it. History is lying in wait till finally it kills them. When you open the dead body you will find history in the form of silvery fibres.[18]

---

17 Boyer 2018, 145.
18 Lindqvist 1979, 28.

I first encountered Lindqvist's seminal work on working class history in 2019. Of the assigned readings across my masters and extra-curricular academics, it was one of the first to jolt me out of my 'thing-ly' preoccupation – that is, to place bodies beyond my own in the creation, discourse(s) and use of history. To speak about history not merely as cultural, social, even architectural, but as visceral.

This viscerality, this embedded em-body-ment, is uncomfortable for scholars and practitioners alike. When we weld ourselves new forms of thinking, of understanding, of relating to physical things and communities, I sense a deep unease in looking beyond those epistemological ideas to recognising museological and historical work in relation to and within physical bodies.

Living bodies.

Dying bodies.

Dead bodies.

After all, human material culture has to come from humans.

There is something comforting in looking after things which are able to exist seemingly on their own; to see continuity across time outside of ourselves, which then becomes imbued with immortality. They might outlive us, and thus their existence (to finite mortals) feels much larger.

The idea of an even wider crisis which might subsume such immortality is thus doubly terrifying.

How do we grapple with our own impermanence, if we have previously comforted ourselves with the thought that things will outlive us?

And if we are to look beyond things, see that we also have a duty and debt to the bodies that produced these objects and in whom history lives on, then *when* are the bodies we are concerned with? Do we confine ourselves to bodies alive now, as I write these words; as they are printed; as they are read?

Or are we seeking to draw a line around history, around what it is or can be, and pre-emptively calculate our losses?

No?

* * *

[T]he history of Swedish industry is still thought of as the history of its owners and directors. Practically every factory history has been written for them, by writers selected by them, and paid by them to produce results that would then be approved by them.[19]

What does it mean when the people writing about bodies are themselves bodily safe? When those writing about loss are the ones who will lose least? How do we as a discipline orient ourselves around not ourselves?

I have a fear that in talking about loss of heritage, sites, landscapes and museums, I am simply reinforcing an idea of loss which only encompasses such things and places already deemed 'valuable'. That the foundations upon which I see loss are ones which ignore, pave over, whole chunks of culture and history, focusing the eye on a speck of dust on a diamond, rather than the blood mine from which it came, the hands from which it was stolen, and the voices calling even now for its just return.

Are we presupposing that we even have an acceptable status quo against which to measure our losses?

No?

What does this mean for those who have already lost or been lost from climate disruption? What does it mean for the multitudes of peoples, cultures, histories, places, significances, which are not valued by our current system but who are losing far more than the system itself ever will?

What then?

* * *

There are many modes through which Lindqvist's ideas can be extended to climate change: the lifecycles of carbon emissions from those in the Global North; the unequal effects of that carbon, as those same high-emitting countries and peoples are also the ones most protected and able to protect themselves; the future burdens (geo-engineering, negative emissions technology, water and food shortages, foreshortened lives) that we place in the bodies of the young today and going forward; the wet bulb temperatures which will render entire regions uninhabitable; the idea that we can choose which bodies we wish to remember, and which we don't; the idea that our bodies, as academics, as holders of what we deem heritage – even as it is held by others – are separated from much of the turmoil we are witnessing or foreshadowing.

I can write about these things from the safety of an air-conditioned, carefully ventilated room on a hill – and know that my bemoaning,

---

19 Lindqvist 1979, 24.

however much it swells in my gut and leaks from my eyes, means almost nothing compared to those on the climate coal-face. That I may study what histories and heritages are being lost, and that my study may be held up, horrifically, honorifically, as somehow more worthy of grief and attention than the lives and bodies of those that heritage belongs to, and from whom it is being stolen.

* * *

Lindqvist shouts:
'NO AREA OF MODERN HISTORY HAS BEEN MORE DISTORTED BY ONE-SIDED TREATMENT THAN THE HISTORY OF BUSINESS.'[20]
In this statement, and others capitalised throughout his essay, Lindqvist not only challenges the way we create, understand and do history, but also the way we literally read it.

In jolting the reader into a higher register, insisting on the importance of volume in a work already reevaluating historiography, Lindqvist questions the academic frameworks we place over the lives and stories of others. This is no jargonised abstract – by being direct, out of line with traditional formats, Lindqvist reinforces his ideas of inseparable bodily experience and the necessity of workers' investigation of their histories.

Did you read the capital letters as shouting in your head? Did it make you uncomfortable? Did it jolt you out of some neutral tone? Did you realise that the bodies he spoke of, the people he mentioned, were all people who might shout at you as well?

No?

Nothingness

'Nothing besides remains.'[21]

'This place is not a place of honor ... no highly esteemed deed is commemorated here ... nothing valued is here.'[22]

Appendix F of the infamous 1992 report by Sandia National Laboratories on warnings for future societies about nuclear waste includes

---

20 Lindqvist 1979, 24.
21 Shelley 1818, Line 12.
22 Trauth et al. 1992, F-49.

a full print of Shelley's *Ozymandias*; the first block of text in italics.[23] The proposed written warnings are similarly italicised, such that – skimming the dense document – these passages appear almost as continuations of Shelley's prose.

Where Shelley is preoccupied with the fragments left and great nothingness they have been subsumed by, these new warnings attempt to convey that the appearance of nothingness can be deceiving and dangerous. Further, that remains are not always grand or poetic, but physically and culturally repulsive.

Shelley attempts to reach back into a bygone era; Sandia attempts to warn their whatever-future of a danger from our present-now-passed.

* * *

Climate breakdown comes within in-built loss. No matter how you tweak the charts and build up the buffers, museology and heritage will have to come to terms with the fact that the histories handed down to us, the ones we thought would carry on into perpetuity, can no longer exist in a form we recognise. Even if we reframe some of this loss as transformation – as there is good reason to do, heritage being processual not static; even if we look beyond the tangible – we are still losing things just as we cling more dearly to them.

I think we should take an interest in the nothingness left behind from this processual loss; that the absence of what we understand as markers of the need to remember are themselves things we can engage with.

What do we look like in a period characterised by destruction? What do we do when potential future destruction relies on us just continuing as we always have?

Or are we faffing with time and words when there are actions to be taken?

Even as I write, I cannot help wavering; falling between text and tense, past and present, remembrance and ruin; leaking into each other, refusing to unhand me.

Wobbling between we and they and you and I – because I am still fighting twin urges which cry 'the individual has been held falsely culpable' and 'every action taken is, at the most basic level, only possible to take by oneself'.

---

23 Trauth et al. 1992, F-10.

I am wafting between visions of collapse – Ozymandias in the sand, pharaoh in his temple, Shelley on the page, the un-written bodies and myself in the lived moment – and trying to come to terms with personal and professional conceptions of time which breakdown with each passing molecule. Unlike history, collapse cannot be separated onto pages or behind scenes. It is not an absolute binary but a living matter of degrees.

I struggle to incorporate these visions and futures into disciplinary understanding and present participation.

How do I come to terms with the fact that the things I study, vowed to protect, see before me now, may or will be immeasurably transformed or lost?

What do I do?

Do I not write?

Do I cling to here and now, build my own bubble?

Am I talking about what has already happened; what is already happening; what is readily approaching – when I am not ready? How do I put down these thoughts in a formal abstract; how do I explain my methodology while Ramesses II haunts my writing; the winds are hot, and the oceans are high …

References

Allais, Lucia. "Integrities: the salvage of Abu Simbel." *Grey Room* 50 (2013): 6–45.

Berra, Yogi. *The Yogi Book: I really didn't say everything I said*. New York: Workman Publishing, 1998.

Boyer, Anne. *A handbook of disappointed fate*. USA: Ugly Duckling Press, 2018.

Boyer, Anne. *Garments against women*. London: Mute Books, 2016.

DeSilvey, Caitlin and Tim Edensor. "Reckoning with Ruins." *Progress in Human Geography* 37, no. 4 (2013): 465–85.

Gasky, Andrew Emil. "'Ruin porn' and the ambivalence of decline: Andrew Moore's photographs of Detroit." *Photography and Culture* 7, no. 2 (2014): 119–39.

Ghosh, Amitav. *The great derangement*. USA: University of Chicago Press, 2016.

Hodder, Ian. "The entanglements of humans and things: a long-term view." *New Literary History* 45, no. 1 (2014): 19–36.

Lindqvist, Sven. "Dig where you stand." *Oral History* 7, no. 2 (1979): 24–30.

Shelley, Percy Bysshe. "Ozymandias." *The Examiner*, 1818.

Trauth, Kathleen M. Stephen C. Hora and Robert V. Guzowski, "Expert judgment on markers to deter inadvertent human intrusion into the waste isolation pilot plant." Sandia National Laboratories, USA: Sandia National Laboratories, 1992.

Tuan, Yi-Fu. "Space, time, place: a humanistic frame," in *Making Sense of Time*, eds. Tommy Carlstein, Don Parkes and Nigel Thrift. New York: John Wiley and Sons, 1978.

RENAISSANCE

Ashleigh Cuthill

I floated underwater, consciously repressing the mild panic I always felt when fully submerged. Breathe in, breathe out, steady, hold your nerve. Breathe too fast and the oxygen supply runs out before you reach open air – not a thought designed to calm the anxiety hammering at the walls of the mental box I keep it firmly locked in.

Although I have held this position at the museum for many years, diving has only recently become a necessary skill and it is not one I could have ever foreseen. Every dive I take is carefully planned with plenty of error margins to placate even the most persistent worry; I have my system and methods to cope. I stopped to take a reading and reassure myself that I was where I thought I would be. Everything looks different underwater, even though I had passed through these halls when it was still possible to walk through them. It was disorienting to no longer be able to count your steps. I floated along at head height, steady so as not to disturb the silt at the bottom. Not that there was much sediment there yet, but in time there would be and good habits once broken are hard to re-establish. I knew my younger colleagues enjoyed going by at knee height as though they were flying in a dream, but they had joined us after the flood and understood that, at least in Venice, 'archaeologist' was synonymous with 'diver'. For me, the entire situation was too far removed from my origins to enjoy this as they did with their carefree explorations.

I clung to my wayward thoughts and drifted on.

These halls had once held great works of art, and even now, less valuable works could still be seen at intervals along the passage, too unimportant to engender the panic in archivists as they struggled to move the larger works up to the ground floor and out into the boats departing frantically from shore. I say ground floor, but that has never really been accurate here in Venice, nor was shore if I'm to be completely honest.

I recalled the efforts of all staff members, janitors and professors alike, wading through knee high water to load the barges as quickly as they could before they left, never to return. An act of great unity in the immediacy of purpose. But there is only so much history that can be removed; many of the artefacts, small and large, were loaded onto the barges in such a haphazard way that some were damaged as there was no time to undertake proper procedures to ensure their safety. And yet they were saved. It was not the same for many of the buildings where so much of recorded history had passed through the halls.

That was what had attracted me to this role when I first began my career, to work in an environment that had witnessed the passage of time. I had a summer job as a waitress in a hotel in Venice, the money had been okay for a student like me and I had enjoyed working on the fringes of the elite, in a stunning venue rich with history and artefacts.

While completing my studies, I had cut my teeth, cataloguing the collection, ascertaining what value, if any, there was in a town replete with such items. I'd been young then and could never have imagined the twists and turns of life. I prefer academia over physical work, had always preferred to converse with my customers rather than race back and forward from kitchen to table; preferred cataloguing collections to being in the dust and heat of a dig site, content to forgo notoriety as long as I was left alone in the cool shade with the artefacts imagining the foibles that caused these items to be brought into being. While I sat in my office and daydreamed of the conversations from long ago between artist and subject as one studied the other and committed it to paper for all posterity and the reverse was lost to time; I missed the warnings. My head buried in paper, my thoughts surrounded by dreams and the water slowly rising. With every turn of the tide, slowly rising, until the trickle became a gush and then an unstoppable flood.

Like the tide at Mont St Michel, you could see the flood water advance, a foot higher than the lagoon beneath and rushing ever forward. Spilling first over the embankments and streets and then down into lower levels of the buildings. The warning bells were the first indication of the oncoming sea, no longer kept at bay by the ever present MoSE system installed to prevent such a happening and at their tolling leapt into dreaded action to save what could be saved.

It became clearer in the calm that followed the first rush of immediate action that my skills were not of value in other positions, and so I bowed to the inevitable and at my advanced age I learnt the skills required to continue my life's work albeit underwater. I took the classes, excelled at them really, even though I never liked the physical. Even now, fate finds ways to shock me, to remind me of the lesson I never seemed to learn. At the end of the passage, I turned left along the gallery and came to the piece furthest from the entrance. I came to study the effects of the brackish water on paintings centuries old and to see if it was possible to raise them from the water. A 'renaissance' as it were, not the first these masterpieces had seen in their lifetime. A shame really, to see them in such a state, I knew where every piece was located when I shared the air around them. Now I breathed from the tank a carefully mixed concoction of gas, while they stagnated with the petrified logs that supported the buildings above.

Do paintings petrify? I guess we'd find out if we couldn't raise them. A difficult task physically, made more difficult by the necessity of finding support for the project to begin. Not a prospect I relished at the best of times and there were greater concerns of the times than forgotten masterpieces. The scarcity of employment was far more important to many, as well as the settling of displaced populations. There was no room in the worries of other people for the images of gentry from long ago.

Once again, they'd be left behind to rot and whither along with the remnants of the city above and the livelihoods of the people who worked there. A persistent tone drew me from my thoughts as the alarm signalled that my time here was drawing to a close. Reluctantly, I said my goodbyes to the subjects, caressed the signature and committed their final resting place to memory. I was sure that was where it would remain, forgotten by mankind as easily as the wisdom of experience is dismissed by the idealism of the young.

WHO IS THE LAW FOR? DRINKING WATER GOVERNANCE AND CLIMATE JUSTICE IN NORTHERN AUSTRALIA

Kirsty Howey and Liam Grealy

On 5–6 March 2020 in Mparntwe (Alice Springs), on the unceded traditional lands of the Central Arrernte people, a coalition of First Nations people and organisations, activists, researchers, health professionals and social justice workers met to discuss climate justice for Northern Territory communities and to workshop possible solutions.

A climate justice lens focuses attention on the historical and social genesis of climate change, examines its unevenly distributed impacts and attempts to engage solutions that support those who have been traditionally marginalised and most affected.[1] The Housing for Health Incubator at the University of Sydney was honoured to present recent research which frames the drinking water legal regime in the Northern Territory – one that privileges certain populations over others – as a climate justice issue.

That safe and adequate drinking water is essential for life is a given. Yet Indigenous residents of remote Northern Territory communities have long been aware of the growing precarity of drinking water where they live. The Northern Territory has suffered through two of its hottest and driest wet seasons on record, with aquifers running close to dry in some areas. A number of remote Indigenous communities, including Yuelamu, Yuendumu, Yarralin, Borroloola and Kakadu's largest homeland of Mudginberri, have experienced water contamination or supply problems in recent years. These impacts may be exacerbated as temperatures rise and rainfall patterns become more erratic.

---

1   See Schlosberg and Collins 2014.

Liam Grealy, Surprise Creek.

Such events are typically narrated through their immediate causes – drying aquifers, algal blooms, failing treatment equipment and corroding infrastructures – and prospective techno-fixes – sinking new bores, new water treatment facilities, groundwater surveys and so on. Such explanations give little consideration to major forces that set the stage for water insecurity, including competing 'consumptive uses', such as by pastoralism and the extractive industries.

While some attention has been given to water security through recent reforms to the *Water Act 1992* (NT), prompted by the Scientific Inquiry into Hydraulic Fracturing in the Northern Territory, and the State Government's ongoing Water Regulatory Reform consultation process, this legislation has very limited geographic application in relation to drinking water. These discussions have also given little consideration to who is responsible for the provision of drinking water.

We therefore asked the question: if you live in a remote community, who is legally accountable for supplying you with safe and adequate drinking water? And if something goes wrong: who does the law say is responsible and must take action to fix it? The answer to this question led us to a quite different diagnosis of the problem, and to laws that do not tend to feature prominently in discussions about water justice.

The *Water Supply and Sewerage Services Act 2000* (NT) (*WSSSA*) regulates the provision of public water supply in the Northern Territory, and requires that the provision of 'water supply services' in 'water supply licence areas' be licensed by the Utilities Commission, a government-established regulator which oversees essential services provision in the Northern Territory.[2] Power and Water Corporation (PAWC) is the current and sole licensee, and is subject to a range of provisions regarding asset management plans, license compliance reports and service plans. In contrast with many other Australian jurisdictions, however, the Northern Territory has not set minimum standards for water supply (including water quality). Instead, the Department of Health and PAWC have entered into a Memorandum of Understanding (MOU) that says that the Australian Drinking Water Guidelines 'will be used as the peak reference' regarding drinking water quality.[3] Further, this legislation only applies in eighteen gazetted towns in the Northern Territory, including Darwin, Alice Springs, Katherine and Tennant Creek, where the vast majority of the state's non-Indigenous population lives.

Outside these towns, specifically in the seventy-two Indigenous communities, and roughly 500 remote outstations generally located on Aboriginal-owned land, water supply is neither licensed nor indeed regulated at all. A regime of water testing, incident reporting and response and public reporting of drinking water quality in some of these places is outlined in the MOU referenced above – although in strict legal terms, this regime is unenforceable. In the vast majority of outstations or homelands, there is no systematised regime of water testing conducted by the authorities. The absence of legal requirements outside of towns in the Northern Territory means that failures to test and report water quality are often discovered in moments of crisis, where local residents have no alternatives.

We call this fragmented system of water governance 'archipelagic' following Canadian geographer Karen Bakker.[4] The Northern Territory is fragmented into multiple governance islands that are hierarchically differentiated.

Yet the challenges of infrastructural and service provision in remote places has not precluded other jurisdictions from establishing

---

2   *Water Supply and Sewerage Services Act 2000* (NT).
3   Australian Drinking Water Guidelines 2011.
4   Bakker 2003.

protections. South Australia's *Safe Drinking Water Act 2011*, administered by the Department of Health, requires all suppliers of drinking water to be registered, to have approved risk management plans (including monitoring programs and incident protocols), to be subjected to regular audits, to report results and to comply with the minimum water quality standards in the Australian Drinking Water Guidelines.[5] In short, it makes drinking water providers legally accountable, uniformly, across South Australia.

When the next incident of water contamination surfaces, it is important that there are clear public standards for testing, reporting and remediation with direct lines of legal accountability to residents. As a matter of climate justice, such legislated standards are one important means to protect drinking water for all Northern Territory residents, wherever they live.

*

This article was originally published by the Sydney Environment Institute, 12 March 2020.

References

Australian Drinking Water Guidelines 2011, https://www.nhmrc.gov.au/about-us/publications/australian-drinking-water-guidelines.
Bakker, Karen. "Archipelagos and networks: urbanization and water privatization in the south." *The Geographical Journal* 169, no. 4 (2003): 328–41.
Safe Drinking Water Act 2011 (SA).
Schlosberg, David and Lisette B. Collins. "From environmental to climate justice: climate change and the discourse of environmental justice." *Wires Climate Change* 5, no. 3 (2014): 359–74.
Water Supply and Sewerage Services Act 2000 (NT).

---

5   *Safe Drinking Water Act 2011* (SA).

DROWNED

Jennifer Sacks

The city sits still, a blanket of grime covering the landscape like dusty sheets over forgotten furniture. Quinn walks slowly up her street, holding her bag of groceries close to her chest – she managed to grab the last two precious water bottles at the store. She skirts around the bright patches of sun that highlight the pavement, clinging to the slivers of shade offered by the barren tree branches in an attempt not to sweat in the heat; she knows she can't shower today. The sun bakes thick, brown dust onto parked cars, which were long ago sacrificed to the dirt. Quinn thinks they look like oversized chocolate cakes with a powdered cocoa coating. Well, she likes to think that. The reality is too depressing. Brittle grass breaks below her feet like shards of glass – crisp, sharp, *snap*. The plants that used to decorate the neatly manicured gardens have been dried out by the unforgiving sun, parched past the point of wilting. Quinn feels like those plants: sapped of all moisture, wrung out, ancient.

Her house is at the end of the street, completing the matching set of once-quaint townhouses that have lost the game of time. They look as though they've absorbed the brownish glaze that covers the city, speckled with ash-like dust. The hinges of the front door squeak their protest as Quinn pushes it open, only to be greeted by an alarming sound: the faint but definitive beat of trickling water. She's sure Jamie forgot to check the roster, and set the timer for that matter. She dumps the groceries on the small kitchen island and leaps up the stairs, rapping her knuckles sharply on the bathroom door.

'Jamie! Time's up, you're going to get us cut off!'

'It's fine, Mu– shit!' The trickle of water stops abruptly. Quinn secretly hopes Jamie still has conditioner in her hair, sticky strands to punish her for the next week.

Quinn tries to remind herself of Jamie's age; selfishness is normal in a teenager. Granted, it used to be selfishness over not wanting to help wash the dishes, but the reality is that the dishes are rarely washed nowadays, just wiped down with a crusty rag. So, long unscheduled showers it is. Quinn feels calmer, until she returns to the kitchen to cook dinner. With the water shut off, there's nothing left to boil the pasta with, even if it was going to be too little for their big pot anyway. She turns the TV on to distract her from her anger. Pasta is the only staple that is always available and always cheap – it needs water to prepare, and most people avoid that if they have the luxury of money. Quinn opens the bare kitchen cupboards, trying to scavenge dinner as the steady voice of the news anchor floods her mind.

> In a major breakthrough, a new study by the Institute of Natural Resources has overturned the previous theory that it was inadequate urban planning and an exponentially growing population that caused the water crisis. Instead, new data suggests that rapidly worsening global warming figures placed us on a trajectory to our current predicament years ago. The government is now issuing warnings not to drink tap water, and rather to use it for household necessities like showering and flushing the toilet. This comes as we have started using the last twenty percent of our water reservoir, a section usually left untouched due to the debris that gathers there.

At the sound of Jamie's footfalls descending the stairs, Quinn quickly turns the TV off. As Jamie appears in the kitchen, Quinn can see the telltale matts in her hair from the leftover, half-dry conditioner. She tries not to let her smug smirk show. They sit down at the dilapidated kitchen table, precariously balanced with folded paper slid under the wobbly legs. They have toast for dinner. It scratches their throats as they swallow, getting stuck on the way down: sandpaper in their mouths. Still, they eat the entire slice and end their meal by splitting the half a bottle of water that they had been saving.

'I'm going to have to go to Roseburg tomorrow, to the stream,' Quinn says, voice gruff with scratchiness.

'Mum, you know we don't have permission until next month. It's too dangerous, they'll arrest you.' Jamie's smooth forehead creases; she knows she shouldn't have taken that long shower, she didn't even use a bucket to catch the excess water. Quinn studies her daughter's face, feeling bad herself. No teenager should have to deal with what she does. The anxiety shows. Her glowing skin is dulled from lack of hydration, and her once full, glossy brown hair has lost its lustre. She doesn't want to add to Jamie's worries.

'Okay, hun. We'll figure something else out.'

It's still dark when Quinn gets out of bed. Her eyes sting as she pulls them open, dry as though she's just won a staring contest. She quickly pulls on a grey hoodie; it'll camouflage her in the darkness of pre-dawn but won't be as stark as black against the stream when the sun starts to rise. Creeping downstairs, she rifles around carefully in the kitchen trying to find water bottles to take with her. She thought they had more, but then again it's been a long time since bottles of water were a normal item on the shopping list. Stuffing what she can find in a backpack, she quietly tiptoes outside, careful not to wake Jamie.

The sound of rushing water is like flipping the pillow over to the cold side on a hot summer's night: refreshing, comforting, reassuring. Creeping through the dense brush – she had avoided the visitor's trail into the forest – Quinn arrives at the edge of the trees. Their coarse, spiky leaves threaten to cut her, but still she pushes forward to see past them. A line has already started to form at the stream's edge along one of the only spots that isn't fenced off with barbed wire. Tired looking people line up to show the machine-gun armed soldiers their passes. The rising sun breaks through the dense canopy, casting a grey hue over the clearing. The soldiers stand over each person and watch as they fill their bottles: no more than a litre each. The gushing water flows downstream – a gift from Mother Nature that is gratefully scooped up by those who are permitted.

The third woman in line looks nothing like everyone else: radiant skin, silky hair, and she takes at least five litres worth of water. She must work for one of the government families. She has no fear of the soldiers, her shoulders are back and her head is raised. Her long black hair shines in the light that manages to catch it, and she looks youthful – smooth, clean, carefree. Unlike Quinn, there are no harsh cracks that mar her face like the desert ground splitting. The woman rises from the banks of the river and turns around to leave, at which point Quinn realises she is straining her neck past the line of bushes. The woman's green eyes widen as they catch Quinn's, her mouth opening to alert the soldiers. A dash of black emerges from the trees a few metres down from Quinn. The soldiers immediately spring into action. Quinn allows a slow sigh of relief to escape her mouth as the woman is swallowed up in shouts and the confusion of people dispersing as the soldiers draw their weapons. Quinn takes it as her opportunity to run upstream.

Soon the clearing fades and she begins to climb over slippery, moss-covered rocks, disappearing from the soldiers' line of sight as the stream bends around the tree line. The embankment here is rocky and a wrong step could mean a broken bone, or worse. No one had bothered to extend the barbed wire this far; most people agree the hazardous path isn't worth the risk. But Quinn has no other choice.

Her hands shake and her breathing is heavy, the pounding of her heart almost drowning out the rushing of the stream as she starts filling the water bottles. She barely registers how the water gets murky after passing over her hands – she never has time to get the grime out from under her nails or the creases of her knuckles in the rare few minutes she gets to shower. She shakily replaces the cap of the last bottle as a gunshot resounds through the forest, reverberating from branches to rocks to water and seeming to bounce around in Quinn's head. *Poor thing*, she thinks of the black blur she had seen earlier, while silently counting her lucky stars that it wasn't her.

The bag is heavy as she swings it back over her shoulder, and she has to creep across the rocks much more carefully, avoiding the slimy patches of moss. She crouches low behind the rocks as she approaches the clearing. The soldiers are crowded around the crumpled black figure and the leaking bottles of stolen water that surround it. All Quinn can see is the top of the head – brown hair matted with what looks like the start of a pool of blood. She doesn't stay to watch, slipping back into the forest where rocks give way to the solid ground of the clearing, and running off to freedom.

The pinks and purples of the sunrise have been pushed out of the sky and replaced with the usual grey smog by the time Quinn arrives home. She ignores the creaking of the door as she swings it open, elated that she has secured drinking water for Jamie and herself.

'Jamie!' Even Quinn is surprised by the tone of happiness in her voice; it's an unfamiliar emotion. As she opens the cupboard to replace the now-full water bottles, the silence of the house seems to press down on her.

'Jamie?' She calls again, rising slowly. She speeds up as she gets to the stairs, taking them two at a time. Jamie's bed is unmade, but there is no sign of her daughter. She checks all the rooms in their small house, her footsteps reverberating like gunshots. The laundry by the washing machine has been messed; Jamie's black hoodie is missing. Quinn's stomach convulses as though she has been punched. She starts to retch.

The clearing. A black blur wearing Jamie's hoodie.

Water bottles scattered. The very ones that Quinn was sure had been in their kitchen.

Bloody brown hair. Not blood. Greasy conditioner in brown hair.

Her lungs refuse to accept her breaths, and she runs outside in an effort to get fresh air. The unfamiliar wetness of a tear trails its way down the papery skin of her cheek. She didn't know she could still cry. She feels the tears everywhere. Her face is flooded with them, rivers of tears in the wrinkles of her skin. When she feels her hair getting wet, she realises that she is not crying at all. It's raining.

She lays down on the spiky grass, it sticks through her t-shirt and pokes at her back. The rain pelts down heavier, the first they've seen in a year. The faded grass turns a muddy brown as the water mixes with the parched soil. Her clothes soak through, rivers of brown run down the side of the street as dirt is washed off the cars and houses. Quinn lets the makeshift tears of raindrops fall down the sides of her cheeks, pooling in her ears, drenching her hair. She opens her mouth.

Maybe the rain will satiate her thirst.

Maybe it will drown her.

THE CLOUD CATCHERS

Isla Scott

The mountain was rough and the rails were rusty. It stood high above the dry plains, standing as a jagged dark mark against the landscape. No one had been up there for centuries, and the old paths felt something they hadn't felt in so long as the travellers made their way up – feet steadily treading through the gravel and the grit. The travellers' hands were stained a deep rugged orange from the rusty rails that felt as if it were burnt into their skin. All the water in the world would not be enough to wash the stains out. And they didn't have all the water in the world; only the few treasured drops they were reaching for.

The mist clung to the very peak of the mountain, and they could see it from far below – twisting and shifting through the sky – so far out of reach. That precious vapour.

One of the travellers stumbled, tripping over a rock, turning its face to see a sky it had never seen before. The rock would have stared – mesmerised – if it could, but none of the people looked up at the clear expanse. They knew they were a long way off and stared only at the mountain climbing endlessly before them. One turned to look back down at the lights of a slowly dying city, but could not see them. The boulders stood tall. The travellers walked on.

They reached what could once have been a crossroad, if you considered tiny tracks and crumbling cliffs to be roads. The travellers knew they were the only roads they would get. The remnants of a signpost from a time long since gone lay on the ground – half-eaten, half-dead, half-disintegrating. The maps had all crumbled, long ago. The travellers, their legs tired and throats parched, gulped at the meagre mountain air and looked nervously between each other and the crossroad. They could not stop, and so they split, knowing they would likely not see one another again. Half went right, half left. All immediately thought they should have taken the other route; hope was something left at the bottom of the mountain, something to keep the city-dwellers warm at night while they clung to the remnants of a former life. The mountain climbers were spurred on solely by the desperation to survive.

Those who chose right met a cliff-edge, and a bitter, bitter wind. The track around the cliff was about as wide as a seashell – not that there was any sea left. There wasn't room to use their ropes – in case it would drag them all down from the ledge together, and the rock was too brittle and crumbling to make use of any climbing stakes. But they carried on, hands scrabbling at the sheer face, scraping their nails against the dry rock, feet tiptoeing and wobbling, faces pressed against the cliff, trying not to breathe for fear that it would push them off.

The wind grew fiercer, as if it were sick and tired of watching and just wanted it to end. As if when all the humans were gone it would finally be able to stop blowing.

When the first one fell, no one looked. They screwed their eyes shut, hugged the cliff with all their strength, and thought, *Thank the gods that wasn't me.* Not that any of them believed in gods anymore.

Then another climber slipped, their foot tumbling off the cliff, their arms in a frantic windmill as they tried to grab on. A third reached for them in agony, unable to watch them fall without trying to help. But they reached too far, and tumbled down themselves.

Eventually only one was left. After many gruelling hours, she managed to reach a thicker ledge, which wound around the side of the mountain face in a dark, crooked line. Alone she soldiered on, not knowing what else to do, eventually stumbling out onto a barren plateau.

But there was not a cloud in sight.

The only path was the one she had climbed up from. She slumped down on the rocky ground, realising this was the end of her road – they chose right, but they chose wrong – and could only hope the others had fared better.

The travellers who turned left only heard the wind's wild howls from afar, on their way up a sheltered corridor. Cragged cliff walls covered with small caves and holes rose high on either side of them – their path a deep gash in the side of the mountain which only saw the sun for a few brief hours.

A couple of the climbers swore they saw glowing yellow eyes peeking out of rocky outcrops, watching their every step. They walked a little faster, holding onto their packs with aching arms and backs. The travellers had heard tales of mountain fauna evolved to large sizes compared to the scarce thin animals on the plains, as predators feasted on hordes of water-saving lizards and rats when water pooled in the monsoon months. One of the travellers heard a growl. Another jumped in fright as he saw something move from the shadows. A small mammal skittered across their path. Brown and fluffy, its eyes were wide. The climber who had jumped stood frozen, watching the place where it had come from, paranoid that it had been chased out and any second he would be snatched up into the jaws of something bigger. But nothing more stirred in the dark crevasse.

When the track eventually became too steep to walk, they reached inside their packs to find ropes and stakes. They tied themselves together and grasped onto the rock.

In a long line, hanging together like fragile ornaments on a flimsy string, they climbed higher and higher. The wind started to whip their hair and whisper chills down the backs of their shirts. The rope was held together by the sheer determination of the climbers as they gradually made their way up an equally sheer cliff face.

Little rocks came away underneath their fingers, which were getting cracked and bloodied and numb as they drove in the stakes. The discarded rocks plummeted down, ricocheting when they hit larger outcrops and bouncing off to fall far beneath them. Occasionally, the wind would take a deep breath and blow one of the climbers off to the side, and their hands would scramble for something to hold, the single rope being the only thing keeping them from following the falling rocks.

Finally, at last, a hand reached over the precipice and the first climber dragged themselves to the top. The mist swirled around them, thick and white and blissful. Another climber followed, and then a third, until they all stood on the peak, shivering with relief. The clouds were cool and damp on their skin. The travellers allowed themselves a moment of joy – closing their eyes and breathing in the silky air until water hit the back of their throats.

Then, swift and business-like, they started their jobs.

A production line of unpacking, unwrapping and opening wide glass jars. They divided up the work; some swooping the jars around, capturing the mist inside before they slammed a lid back on, others carefully stacking the jars, delicately wrapping them back up and gently packing them into their bags. Water droplets started to form on the sides of the jar, like tiny glass globes holding entire worlds.

When all the jars were filled, they unwrapped their precious supplies and food, scavenged and preserved from all across the continent, and huddled together eating at the top of the world. They feasted, and for the first time in several days, allowed themselves to talk and laugh and rest. They sat back, enjoying the success and blissfully dismissing the knowledge of how long these new water supplies would last, and how soon they might have to venture on another expedition.

And then, with jars safely stowed away – treasured water droplets safe – they started back down the perilous mountain, bringing the clouds down with them.

IN THE AFTER

Abby Jean Wilson

After. The peaks of the mountain range that linger behind us sit patiently waiting. I am waiting. For you, my love. Return to me.

It's almost laughable that we can separate our lives into two parts: then and now. Before and after.

Before, when we used to flaunt our love, celebrate it. When we could lie together on a lazy weekday morning and watch the sun mingle with the shadows in our bedroom. When you could call me your wife, and I could call you the immersive force that saved my life. More than once.

After. The days are getting shorter and the nights are long. Without you here the atmosphere taunts me and the cold sinks into my bones. Makes a home for itself. It makes our time apart just that bit more unbearable. How ironic, that not only do I miss the sound of your voice, but my body misses your body. The heat of your caress.

The cold breath that comes at sundown blows down from the mountains with a harsh edge. It grates at my soul and I shiver under the light, multicoloured blanket we bought at that little red brick shop down the road in the Before. You remember the one with the faded yellow awning and the little old lady who liked us to bring her coffee on Saturday mornings? It was our favourite, if a little expensive. The blanket sits so delicately on my shoulders now; in a few days it will no longer be enough to keep the vicious cold at bay. But your arms will do just fine.

The air whistles through our cabin, screaming in anger. Loss. The world was beautiful in the Before. We took it for granted and have been begging for forgiveness ever since. The clouds cast shadows that are bigger than I would have thought possible – we both grew up in the city and stole from mother nature in somebody else's name. In the After, it seems that she is recalling the debts owed to her. Rightfully so.

The sun sits low in the sky as I scan the horizon between the mountains that frame the only way out of our valley, seeking movement that I know may not come. There is always a risk when you leave our little realm. Passing as a man is difficult for a voice as sweet as yours, but it is a risk we have to take. It's been four days now, by my count. Time is harder to measure now that we don't have phones to rely upon. We stopped relying on the sun; the seasons now undefinable. There is unbearable heat for most of the year and a few months of unimaginable cold. But daylight is not something that we can depend on to tell time and the hands on the clock above our kitchen sink haven't moved in years. I haven't moved in years.

Evan stirs beside me, lifting his head as if to search the same horizon. I reach over to pat behind his pointed black ears.

'It's okay, boy. She'll be home soon,' I reassure him. He lays his head back down and closes his eyes to sleep in the weakened afternoon light. If only it were that easy to reassure myself.

Movement. A dark shape materialises in the distance in the same place I last saw you. Even though I know my first thought should be danger, I also know that it's you. My heart thuds in time with the hooves that carry you home. Evan barks a greeting before running off to meet you.

The colt you sit astride is a dappled grey, a magnificent beast made more remarkable by the fact that he brought you back to me. I stand to greet you and rejoice at the piercing whistle that sings across the plains to let me know that you are where you belong. With me. In our little corner of the world, the only place on earth that I am infinitely safe. With you.

The blanket falls from my shoulder as I move towards you. Tentative. I wonder if the news will be as bad as it was last time.

You call out to me as you pull the horse into a slower gait. I raise my hand, in welcome and to shade the dying light from my eyes to see you better. My heart slides back into place as our eyes meet.

I grab onto the reins and run my hand down the colt's long nose, thanking him for being a safe vessel. You dismount roughly, still getting used to being a cowboy, and press me against you, putting your mouth to my neck to drink me in. 'Darling,' you breathe, 'oh how I missed you.' I stand on the tip of my toes and run my fingers through your dark cropped hair. I recall shaving it before you left with the crude razor we have in the bathroom that no longer runs water upstairs. You looked into the cracked mirror forlornly, as I cut the hair you used to keep long so that no one would know your true disposition.

'Any news?' I pull away slightly from your crushing embrace so that I can look into your eyes. This way I know you'll be truthful. I place both my hands on your flat chest, bound to keep us safe.

'Nothing good. The rebels have lost more ground and are trying to recruit –'

'Absolutely not. They'll find out you're not who you say you are.' Your mouth turns down. Contemplation. Your arms unravel from my waist as you reach out to take the reins and lead the horse back to its stable. I walk alongside you, adamant.

'You cannot be thinking of risking your life, *our* lives for the rebels. You cannot. I refuse to believe that after all this time and all we've been through that you would risk it all for their cause. They still believe that a love like ours is an abomination!'

'Baby. They have to say that so they're more palatable to the people they want to recruit. Our love has been criminalised and they can't compromise … they can't compete with that. It's the least of their concerns.' Your lips purse as you consider the words that spill from your lips. I know it pains you to say it as much as it pains me to hear it.

I fall into silence as my thoughts race around my brain, trying to come up with something that will stop you from taking that road. The sun dips into the horizon like a warm bath, shattering the sky into shards of pink and purple. The clouds are soft as I turn to see the dark navy spread to mark nightfall. You make sure the horse is fed and watered before making your way back towards the house. I watch you go, gripping my elbows and shivering from the sudden drop in temperature. You cannot do this to me.

You turn around at the top of the veranda and gesture. Come to me. I walk tentatively, one foot in front of the other, visions of my solitude playing out in my mind. You gather wood from our stockpile for the fire. Our cottage welcomes us, forlornly sitting at the bottom of the mountain range. I whistle for Evan who runs in behind you. I follow, walking towards my favourite chair beside the fireplace to watch you work.

'If I join the rebels, I could be a part of making this world a better place. We were complacent before. But this,' you turn and grab my hands in yours and press your wind worn lips to them. 'This is worth fighting for.'

'I can't let you fight for this. We're safe here. Being without you for any length of time breaks my heart and I think of every possible thing that will stop you from coming back to me. I know you want to go back to what we had, but don't you think we should just try to live a simple life in safety?'

The Before was an easier time. Until society turned its back on us, like a disappointed lover. Until the wrong people were elected and life as everybody knew it changed forever. The protests marked the beginning. It was the deployment of the civil militia with newly legalised weapons that marked the end. People once united turned on each other and reported them to the authorities. The friends and chosen family we knew and loved were taken from us and never seen again. Public executions became entertainment for the masses. It was easier to play at being a good citizen.

The morning you decided we needed to go was the morning of Peter and Johnathan's execution. We were forced out of our home and onto the streets to watch. We'd been staying at other people's houses away from each other so as not to draw suspicion. Our eyes met across the square as our best friends danced into death and we knew that we had to run.

We met in the alley we romanticised on the outskirts of the city and walked away together. We flagged trucks and were lucky enough to get sympathy. Truckers were always a risk, but we would have done anything to escape the hell that radicalisation had brought upon us. When we looked back on the years before everything went to shit, it was obvious to see why everything happened the way it did. But sometimes it's easier to ignore the things we don't particularly want to fathom.

Once we got to the peaks, we knew we would be able to find safety. We walked for eight days on meagre rations until we found the abandoned homestead. We knew we could be safe here, so we stayed.

The valley that fast became our new home drank in the vastness of solitude. The long green grass stretched to the mountain range that surrounded us. The silence was immense, but there was beauty in abundance; it was as if the earth knew it needed to keep us safe from a society that no longer cared for people like you. For people like us.

Now we pray to the peaks in the hope of reparation.

'We've lived six years in complete solitude. I miss community, Heidi. Our only friends are a horse and a cheeky dog, who I love with all my heart. But I'm hungry for change, darling. I don't want to live this way forever.'

I grab your denim collar and pull you flush against me, our mouths clashing together. I kiss you deeply, trying to entice you to live this way forever. I run my hands through your hair and grip the back of your neck. Pulling you to me. You swing me up into your hard worn arms, thick bands of muscle carry me up the stairs to our creaky little bed. You lay me down like a love song, all the while kissing me deeply like all of your life force comes from inside me. We move together like a dream, like the soft clouds that are now hidden in darkness. Desperate to keep you safe with me.

In the After, I lay my head against your chest with your arms running a gentle wave-like pattern against my back. You brought news last time that the coast had reclaimed what it was owed. The man-made constructs that had once dominated the coastal landscape were gone, sacrificed to the sea in a last ditch attempt at salvation.

Oh, to see the ocean again. A faraway fantasy that I'm sure I've concocted in my own mind. The night sits heavy on the windowsill, waiting for the sun to relieve it of it's post.

'Don't go. Please.'

'I ride for the rebels at first light.'

It is a fight I will never win. It is a fight you hope to win, but it is not our fight. The strength of our love.

The sun whispers in the morning and I know it's time. My heart settles in my gut and makes a home for itself where it will live out until you return to me. We rise with the sun, gathering our thoughts and prayers. The peaks seem to sigh with relief.

You tack the horse in record time, or maybe it's just quick because I am dreading your exit from our life here. You press your lips against mine, before swinging yourself onto the horse who will take you from me. I know it's not the beast's fault, but I can't help but feel animosity towards it. You tilt your hat towards me, a final farewell before nudging your heels into the horse's side and setting off.

I sink back into the veranda and watch your shape ride hard towards the horizon. Movement. Your dark shape disappears.

After. The peaks of the mountain range that linger behind us sit patiently waiting, lurking. I am waiting. For you, my love.

Return to me.

MELTED OYSTERS

Joshua Harper

I

The sun began to rise. It crested over a dark hill far in front of him. The shadows of the thick tree cover seemed to wake up and stretch out down the hill as the light spilt over. He lay, his back resting against a tree whose shadow would soon wake too. He thought it would be maybe twelve minutes until the sun would reach him and his tree. Between him and the sun was an open plain, peppered with bushes and rocks, yet to be graced by the warmth of today, shivering from the cool night. Occasionally, the cracking of gunfire would ring across the plain, carried from over the hills beyond his view by the gusty wind. The shots did not scare him anymore. People hunted whatever they could find.

He looked down at his dog. She was still asleep. He didn't want to wake her yet. She was old and confused these days, and she needed the rest. He chose to wait for the sun to reach their tree. He stayed motionless as it crept across the plain and then it was upon them.

'Come on, dog.'

She did not move. He shook her gently awake and she greeted him with a foul-smelling yawn. She smiled her dog-smile and stretched, and they got up from the tree and left. His rifle was tucked under his arm and the dog followed him a few paces behind. She had been slowing him down for weeks now.

'You're lucky I love you,' he said to the dog. 'But I wouldn't eat you anyway.' He raised an eyebrow and smiled. 'You're too scrawny.'

The man and the dog walked for hours and they reached the cabin as the afternoon breeze picked up.

* * *

'Poppy is a bit cliché don't you think?' She said, holding the squirming pup.
'Maybe. I guess we could change it.'
'No, no. Poppy's cute. We don't want to confuse her.'
'I don't think she knows her name yet.'
She looked at him, squinting slightly and smirking.
'I know *that*.' She handed Poppy over to him. He tried to calm her by scratching under her neck, but it was no use. 'Aren't we lucky to live here,' she said, leaning back onto her elbows as they looked out onto the view of the harbour. The clouds were pink, outlined in brilliant yellow as the sun slowly descended.

* * *

He fed her some scraps of meat he had collected and filled a rusted bowl with some of the water he had left. She ate it all quickly and went straight to sleep. She was small and white, with two brown spots near her tail. Her head was brown too, but age had given her brown patches a weathered greyness.
'You poor old thing. I'm sorry we didn't get anything sooner. It's tough these days. The 'roos are nearly all gone. It's just us left. You, me and some whisky,' he chuckled.
But there was not much whisky left. The man knew they would both die in a week or so. The 'roos had all been killed and it was desolate in the hot plains. The dog was too old to be of any use either. He knew all this but he didn't want to say it in front of the dog. She didn't need to know. He stepped up to the small window that looked out through the blackened trees and to the hills they had walked from. It was dusk now and the air was still and cool. The outline of the hill was only just visible against the deep purple sky. He saw the flashes before he heard the cracking. The gunshots rang out over the plains. His heart fluttered and he watched the flashes like old camera lights, igniting repeatedly until the fighting was over.
They're close now, he thought. He looked over to the dog. She was curled up on her ragged bed, wheezing with every breath. He took out the bottle of whisky that was less than half full. He sat down and took a few deep swigs. It was fiery and hot but it settled well in his throat and then his stomach. He was watching the dog curled up, like a hedgehog.

He took another drink from the bottle. He stood up and placed his only record onto the old player. It was an old Satchmo record from the sixties. *'C'est si bon'* was the first song. The record player did not work. Not much worked without power. He sat down and took another drink from the bottle, a little of the liquid spilling out onto his prickly chin. The alcohol hit him quickly, and he thought he ought to have eaten more before drinking. His head began to feel exceptionally heavy on his neck. He watched the dog breathing steadily. The wheezing was getting louder as she fell deeper into her sleep. She was dreaming of a long white beach far north of here. She was running. She ran for a long time, sometimes cutting violently to one side and then another. She ran to the waves but when they crashed she darted off back towards the dry sand. The man, the woman and the two boys ran with her. She was so happy and they could all see it. The salt air was thick but delicious, and the sand was cool as it was crushed under her paws. The dog woke up. She looked at the man. He was slumped on his chair, still wearing all of his clothes, even his shoes. She went to sleep again but she did not dream of anything else that night.

This time, the sun woke the man. He had no chance to watch it creep over the cabin. He rubbed his eyes and saw that the dog was awake, waiting to go outside. They both stepped out of the cabin and the plains were lit up. The smell of the morning reminded the man of some years ago. This happened every day.

'Smells never get old,' he said to the dog. 'But you smell most of the time I suppose.' The dog looked at him and urinated on the damp grass.

'Good girl.'

He left the dog in the cabin.

'Don't go anywhere, now. You've got water and some bones, that should be good for the day.'

She looked at him vacantly with her tail waving back and forth.

He walked for twenty minutes until he reached a clearing in the blackened forest of trees. They had all been burned. The trunks were now charcoal but they still stood strong. The leaves on the ground were dark too. Only tiny sprouts that formed the regrowth gave the place any colour. He wandered around and searched for small bugs and insects. Instead, he found a snake hiding frozen in the dead leaves. He dropped a rock onto its head and it squirmed in pain until he finished it with a blow from his hunting knife. He slung the decapitated snake over his shoulder and the blood dribbled over his back and onto the blackened ground. He took it back to the cabin. The dog watched him while he skinned and gutted the snake, the remnants of which she ate happily.

II

'Time to go, dog.'

They stepped out of the wood cabin tentatively. The man had packed a heavy backpack with knives, canned food, water and a small tent that would only just fit himself and the dog. The morning air was cool but it would be over thirty-five degrees within a few hours. There were the remains of a track, encrusted with roots and dry dirt which they followed. The dog was a few paces behind the man as the track ascended slightly. Sandstone rocks protruded from the side of the track in a small clearing. The man picked up the dog, placed her on the rock and climbed up. They clambered through the clearing, hopping from boulder to boulder and then they found a view out over the hills. Between the tree-laden headlands was a river running slowly through southwards.

This is where we will probably die, the man thought. 'It's a fine place, as they go,' he said to the dog.

He dropped his pack down and lay with his head resting on it. The dog sat looking over the view to the river with an expressionless face. They had been to this river before. They had fished and caught nothing. The man and the woman had drank cold wine and let their feet hang over the dilapidated jetty into the icy water as they held their limp lines in the slow-moving river. The dog was always there, watching idly.

'Look at that guy fishing out there in that shitty boat,' the woman had said.

'He won't catch anything.'

'Do you think he has a wife?'

'Maybe. He probably likes to fish in a river with no fish without his wife.'

'And you like to fish in a river with no fish *with* your wife, don't you?'

'Yes. Yes, I do, lover.'

They kissed and the dog ate a prawn from the bucket of bait behind them.

* * *

They walked back up the steep track; the man, the woman and their dog.
'Come on, Poppy,' the woman said to the dog.
'She's only a pup,' the man said, 'her legs are so tiny compared to ours.'
'You're our little baby, aren't you?' She said to the dog as she scratched
the sides of her neck and kissed her wet, black nose. They walked for
a half hour before they made it to the top of the track. The man drove
them home while the woman rested her head on his shoulder and held
the dog in her lap. She smelt like a floral shampoo and slightly of sweet
sweat, but he liked that.
'Do you think we'll ever die?' She asked.
'No.'
'Never?'
'Never.'
'They say it's going to come here eventually.'
'They're wrong.'
'They're always wrong with you.'
'Yes. I always hope so.'
'It probably will come, though. What will we have to do?'
'If it does we will be okay. I promise. I swear,' he paused. 'In fact, I
swear on that God you and your parents believe in.'
'You wouldn't swear on that.'
'I would.'
'God? You really must be sure then.'
'We will be just fine.'
'I love it when you say that.'
'We will be just fine?'
'Uh huh. I love it.'
They drove on and a deep gusty wind blew so hard that the man had
to steer against it. The afternoon sun was a dark orange. The light fell
over the woman's face, making her skin glow. As the sun dipped under
the hills, the dog began to pant, and her dog breath made the man and
the woman laugh.

* * *

The dog woke up as the man was watching her with soft, luminous eyes.
'You're still cute when you dream,' he said. 'Even for an old dog.'

They descended the path down to the river. The man spent the walk pointlessly wondering whether the jetty with crusted paint and termite-ridden wood was still there.

III

'We'll stay here a while, make a nice little camp. It's protected from the northerly winds and there might even be some fish left in the bay,' he said to the dog. The dog did not raise her head to respond. Instead, she lay on her side next to the man on a grassy patch, back away from the jetty. The heavy winds still blew across the bay, but here they were warm and protected. The man had built a small camp that would be self-sufficient for a small while.

He left the dog in the shade and walked barefoot past the jetty and along the oyster-encrusted rocks. He took a knife and tried to lever an oyster off of the rock face, but it was hot and empty. He continued walking along the shore as the water lapped at the rocks and splashed at his feet. The olive-green of the trees that covered the path down to the bay also leaned over the rocks, shading the water's edge. Each time he heard them sway and creak, the man checked over his shoulder. Eventually, he made it to a small inlet. The water was flowing faster here, quickly sliding through a separation of the oystered rocks and back into the rest of the deep body of water. He gathered smaller rocks and arranged them at the end of the inlet, where the water was flowing back out, into a makeshift wall. He made sure the wall was not so strong that the water did not flow properly. When he finished, he looked around with a sudden anxiety that his unnatural-looking trap may be found by someone other than himself or the dog. He sat down with his feet dipping in and out of the flowing water and waiting for the throbbing aches in his back to subside.

'Fuck it. If they get me, they get me.'

The makeshift trap could catch some yabbies, if he was lucky. He hadn't seen a yabbie in months.

He got up and walked carefully back to where he had left the dog. She was still asleep when he came up beside her and she did not stir when the foliage above shuddered in the harsh wind.

* * *

They were swimming out from the jetty, the man and the woman.
'Are you cold?' He asked.
'No, this is beautiful! So clean and fresh.'
They waded in the water and the fear of the bull sharks that haunted the black water of the bay begun to eat into his thoughts.
'You're not still afraid, are you? I know that face,' she said.
'No.'
She laughed and swam over to him. Her hair was slicked back perfectly by the water.
'I only love you for your irrational fears. Did you know that?'
'Did you know that bull sharks are more aggressive than all the other sharks?'
'You're the only shark here, darling.'
'Piss off.'
They kissed, both tasting the salty water.
'Let's go in,' he said, 'and not because I'm scared.'
'Of course not, little chicken.'
They swam in and sat up against the spindly-leaved trees that you could only find on the South coast. She lay with her head on his chest as he fiddled with her damp hair and she occasionally hummed a melody that neither of them knew. The sun was warm and they both fell asleep in the shade. When they woke it was cooler and darker. The woman looked at the man.
'What is it?' He said in a deep, loving grumble.

* * *

The dog sat watching him stare into the bay. He was about to cry and the dog knew.
'What are you staring at?'
The dog did not react. The man rubbed his long dark hair out of his eyes and off his forehead. His beard was getting long and thick. Streaks of grey gave the impression that he was older than he really was.

* * *

The power had been out for a week. The man knew that even here, in the once quiet suburban streets, it was too dangerous. His bag was packed and at the door. The dog was watching him pace the kitchen. The woman was upstairs, asleep. She hadn't been able to leave her bed for three days. He stopped pacing and looked at the dog, here tail waving left to right.

'We have to leave,' he said to her quietly.

* * *

'I had to fucking do it.' He looked at the dog. She was still. His initial frown relaxed, and he felt the guilt tear at him.

'Shit, I'm sorry, you old thing. It's hard. But fuck. She was going. I had to do it. We had to go.'

It was the first time he had lost his temperament with the dog. She knew it would only last a little while. The man started to cry. To really cry. In waves of muffled snorts. He was hoping that the dog wouldn't notice.

WHY MULTISPECIES ETHNOGRAPHY MATTERS FOR HUMAN RIGHTS AND THE CLIMATE

Sophie Chao

The world we inhabit today is one of multiple and overlapping environmental crises. Increasingly frequent forest fires are resulting in the indiscriminate obliteration of wildlife, vegetation and property throughout the world.[1] The rains had barely quelled the flames of the 2019 Australian fires when a viral pandemic exploded, triggered by the trade and consumption of wildlife, taking human lives across the globe. Both of these crises sit within the broader phenomenon of climate change; a symptom of the systematic exploitation of natural resources by humans in the form of agribusiness, deforestation, mining and more. Together they have had unimaginably destructive impacts on both humans and the environments that they inhabit. They exemplify how the presumption of human mastery over the natural world can backfire with devastating consequences across species lines – even as these consequences are unevenly distributed across different human communities.[2]

At the same time, these overlapping crises highlight our inextricable interdependencies with natural environments, whose fates and futures are profoundly interwoven with those of human generations present and to come. Protecting the environment and climate is therefore also a matter of human rights. It demands that we cultivate an appreciation for, attunement to and understanding of the more-than-human world – its constituent organisms, ecosystems and elements, for instance. It

---

1   Chao 2020.
2   Singh 2018.

demands that we become aware of, and responsible for, the violence and care at play in interspecies relations, and their consequences for human and planetary wellbeing.[3] One promising path in this direction is multispecies ethnography.

Multispecies ethnography invites us to explore the complex and diverse forms of human-environmental relations that exist across time and place.[4] It calls for finetuned observation of, and immersion in, the lifeways of non-human organisms who so often form the mere backdrop to our everyday lives: the trees we walk past during bushwalks, the plants and animals we consume, the bacterial communities that populate our bodies and the climactic phenomena that pattern our seasons. Multispecies ethnography is also a form of storytelling – one that aims to decentre the human as the primary protagonist and instead opens space for non-human beings and elements as actors in their own right, whose beings and doings can have profound implications for the humans they coexist with.[5] This form of storytelling highlights the biological, political, ethical, historical and cultural dimensions of non-human life, how these dimensions transform in the contexts of colonialism, capitalism and technoscience, and what we can learn from Indigenous and other societies about interspecies reciprocity, care, and kinship.[6]

Multispecies stories can take diverse forms: a fleshy description, a theoretical analysis, an improvised song, an intergenerationally transmitted myth, a cultural performance, an everyday practice or an art installation. Through these and other mediums, multispecies ethnography seeks to foreground the oft-neglected entanglements of humans with their diverse companion species and the meaningful lifeways, or ethos, of non-human species and ecosystems themselves.[7] In doing so, multispecies ethnography constitutes a political, practical and ethical practice. It tells multispecies stories in order to invite more harmonious and reciprocal forms of giving, taking and caring in a changing environment and climate.

Why, then, does multispecies ethnography matter for human rights? First, multispecies stories challenge the assumption that humans, or culture,

---

3   van Dooren 2014.

4   Kirksey and Helmreich 2010.

5   van Dooren, Kirksey, and Münster 2016.

6   TallBear 2011.

7   van Dooren and Rose 2016.

is a realm separated from and superior to, the environment, or nature.[8] Rather, multispecies stories reveal our profound interdependencies *with* the natural world and the enduring logics of environmentally racialised imperialism that continue to justify both the exploitation of natural resources and the dispossession of vulnerable human communities, notably Indigenous peoples and other rural populations.[9] Multispecies ethnography also draws attention to the violence committed in the name of environmental protection against minoritised human communities. These include exclusionary forms of conservation that aim to salvage biodiversity, but also often result in the forced displacement of Indigenous peoples and the erosion of their cultural lifeways, values and modes of subsistence.[10] Multispecies ethnography also matters for human rights in that it reveals how the natural world is interpreted differently across time and place. For instance, what one cultural group might cherish as a domesticated pet, another cultural group might consider an important source of food, a spiritual being or non-human kin. This variety of perspectives in turn demonstrates that the 'human' (as much as the 'non-human') is best approached not as a universal or homogeneous category, but rather one that differs across time, space and context.[11] In doing so, multispecies ethnography not only opens our mind to species diversity – it also opens our gaze to human diversity and how this diversity in turn has and continues to shape our relations to the natural world and its attendant climactic contexts.

Finally, multispecies ethnography highlights how expanding our concepts of rights beyond the human can alleviate or remedy injustices towards humans themselves. The growing recognition of rivers, mountains and ecosystems as non-human legal persons, for instance, seeks to forge more relational, inclusive and expansive notions of rights that account for past and present violence towards both local communities and their sentient environments. These legal advances frame the fulfilment of human and non-human justice not as separate or hierarchical endeavors, but rather as mutually supportive practices that can promote wellbeing in more-than-human terms. Not surprisingly, many of these legal advances have been led by Indigenous communities and activists, whose

---

8   Plumwood 2002.

9   Hage 2017.

10 Brockington 2002.

11 Chao 2018.

philosophies, practices and protocols of interspecies kinship long predate the advent of multispecies ethnography.[12]

Multispecies stories, then, are far from *just* stories. As ethical tools, they seek to redeem non-human beings and ecologies as worthy of consideration and care. They also highlight how environment degradation and exploitation perpetrated by some humans results in the systemic violation of *other* humans' rights to food, life, environment, culture, a future and a livable climate. As political tools, multispecies stories thus reveal how climate change and its attendant environmental transformations pose a serious yet always unevenly distributed threat to humans and to human rights.[13] They foreground how human justice depends in turn on doing justice to the life-sustaining worlds of non-human beings – in our everyday practices of production and consumption, in global economic and political systems and in the law. These stories thus point to the importance of rethinking rights, and who deserves them, in more-than-human and planetary terms.[14] In doing so, they call for us to consider how our relations to the non-human world may be better arranged towards less violent shared futures and more responsible forms of multispecies flourishing.[15]

Telling multispecies stories matters for human rights because human wellbeing ultimately *depends* on the wellbeing of the environment. These stories offer important precedents and promises for multispecies thriving that are at once untethered from assumptions of human superiority or mastery over non-human beings, *and* that are attentive to the environmental and social vulnerability of some human communities over others. Telling multispecies stories well, brings to light what is at stake in the making and unmaking of climates and biodiverse landscapes – for whom, and with what consequences. In doing so, multispecies stories offer crucial alternative visions for what a world worth living in, and cherishing might look like, in the lively presence of more-than-human beings.

*

This article was originally published online by *RightNow*.

---

12 TallBear 2016; Todd 2017.

13 de Kretser 2020.

14 Celermajer et al. 2020.

15 Haraway 2008.

References

Brockington, Dan. *Fortress conservation: the preservation of the Mkomazi Game Reserve, Tanzania*. London: James Currey Publishers, 2002.

Celermajer, Danielle, Sria Chatterjee, Alasdair Cochrane, Stefanie R. Fishel, Astrida Neimanis, Anne O'Brien, Susan Reid, Krithika Srinivasan, David Schlosberg, and Anik Waldow. "Justice yhrough a multispecies lens." *Contemporary Political Theory* 19 (2020): 475–512. https://doi.org/https://doi.org/10.1057/s41296-020-00386-5.

Chao, Sophie. "In the shadow of the palm: dispersed ontologies among Marind, West Papua." *Cultural Anthropology* 33, no. 4 (2018): 621–49. https://doi.org/10.14506/ca33.4.08.

Chao, Sophie. "A world of ashes." Sydney Environment Institute. 2020. http://sei.sydney.edu.au/opinion/a-world-of-ashes.

de Kretser, Hugh. "Fires show the threat of climate change to our human rights." *RightNow*. 2020. http://rightnow.org.au/opinion-3/fires-show-the-threat-of-climate-change-to-our-human-rights/.

Hage, Ghassan. *Is racism an environmental threat?* Malden, M.A.: Polity Press, 2017.

Haraway, Donna J. *When species meet*. Minneapolis, M.N.: University of Minnesota Press, 2008.

Kirksey, Eben S., and Stefan Helmreich. "The emergence of multispecies ethnography." *Cultural Anthropology* 25, no. 4 (2010): 545–576.

Plumwood, Val. *Environmental culture: the ecological crisis of reason*. London: Routledge, 2002.

Singh, Julietta. *Unthinking mastery: dehumanism and decolonial entanglements*. Durham, N.C.: Duke University Press, 2018.

Tallbear, Kim. "Why interspecies thinking needs indigenous standpoints." *Fieldsights*, 2011. https://culanth.org/fieldsights/260-why-interspecies-thinking-needs-indigenous-standpoints.

Tallbear, Kim. "Failed settler kinship, truth and reconciliation, and science." Presentation at Courage and Social Justice in Our Time, University of Alberta, Edmonton, Canada, 14 March 2016. https://indigenoussts.com/failed-settler-kinship-truth-and-reconciliation-and-science/.

Todd, Zoe. "Fish, kin, and hope: tending to water violations in Amiskwaciwâskahikan and Treaty Six Territory." *Afterall: A Journal of Art, Context, and Enquiry* 43 (2017): 102–107.

van Dooren, Thom. *Flight ways: life and loss at the edge of extinction*. New York: Columbia University Press, 2014.

van Dooren, Thom, Eben S. Kirksey, and Ursula Münster. "Multispecies studies: cultivating arts of attentiveness." *Environmental Humanities* 8, no. 1 (2016): 1–23.

van Dooren, Thom, and Deborah B. Rose. "Lively ethography: storying animist worlds." *Environmental Humanities* 8, no. 1 (2016): 77–94.

CLIMATE CHANGE AND CIVIL UNREST: INSIGHTS FROM SYRIA AND COVID-19

Michael Lotsaris

The industrialised advancement of technology has both reduced the distance of communications between people from across the world and expanded their global footprint more than ever before. This simultaneous and interrelated process of global interconnectedness and omnipotence has enabled the ramifications of localised events to spiral onto the international stage. Therefore, there is much to be learnt from the parallels between the conflicts in Syria, the COVID-19 pandemic and anthropogenic (i.e. human-induced) climate change in contributing to civil unrest across the world.

The outbreak of the Syrian Civil War in 2011 was arguably the most politically significant phenomenon of the decade. It produced one of the largest refugee crises in modern history, and enabled the growth of non-state militant groups.[1] These two particular ramifications presumably augmented the globalised spread of peoples' anxieties with regard to territorial integrity and public safety in the aftermath of the economically disruptive Global Financial Crisis, thereby culminating in increased political scepticism towards the competency of their authorities.[2] Perhaps this facilitated the rise of political extremism, populist electoral shifts and new threats to public safety.[3]

These developments seem like an unbelievably tremendous ripple-effect from the instability of one particular country as a consequence of

---

1   See DePillis, Saluja, and Lu 2015 and Lund 2013.
2   See Wike, Stokes, and Simmons 2016 and Wike et al. 2019.
3   See Triffitt 2018, Georgiadou, Rori, and Roumanias 2018 and Australian Security Intelligence Organisation 2020.

its particular domestic political issues. However, some researchers have suggested that the Syrian Civil War can be attributed to the greater global phenomenon of anthropogenic climate change.[4] Syria was subjected to its most severe drought on record between 2006 and 2009, resulting in the collapse of agricultural livelihoods.[5] It has been reasoned that this environmental shock to the rural economy forced thousands to move towards more urbanised regions for new homes and employment.[6] This influx of migration is inferred to have worsened the availability of resources and social services.[7] Amidst the growing fervour of the Arab Spring movement, which appeared to resolve such issues in Tunisia, organised protests began to condemn the Syrian government for its purported political mismanagement of such grievances, which ultimately spiralled into full-scale armed conflicts.[8]

Although the significance of climate change as a factor that elevated the likelihood of civil unrest, let alone conflict, in Syria has technically been inconclusive in the academic literature, there is evidently an intuitive prospect that climate change, as an increasingly disruptive global phenomenon, risks multiplying existing threats to the stability and security of societies.[9] Even nation-states regarded as relatively more politically stable could face increased risks to the security of their people. Lives and livelihoods in Australia are not only directly vulnerable to climate change but can also be impacted indirectly through the international ripple-effect of climate-related social disruption within foreign countries such as Syria.

Assuming the phenomenon of climate change would progress as an increasingly disruptive global crisis, then its political ramifications may unfold with similarities to the political fallout of the COVID-19 pandemic. The first recorded death is considered to have occurred on 9 January 2020.[10] Two months later, this infectious disease had claimed over 4000 lives globally.[11] Two months further into May, and this figure

---

4   See Gleick 2014 and Kelley et al. 2015.
5   Ide 2018.
6   Ibid.
7   Ibid.
8   Ibid.
9   See Ide 2018 and Brock et al. 2020.
10 Al Jazeera 2020.
11 World Health Organisation 2020b.

surpassed 300,000 deaths worldwide.[12] The exponential spread of COVID-19 generated extraordinary emergency measures in the name of public safety among world governments, severe disruption to commerce and employment and the aggravation of information warfare within the public discourse.[13] Such concerns surrounding national security, economics and ideology were also associated with the violent escalation of the Arab Spring.

In Brazil for instance, some citizens have demonstrated against President Jair Bolsonaro's dismissive view of COVID-19 by banging on kitchenware from their residences, whilst others have rallied on the streets by his side against lockdown measures.[14] Demonstrations against stay-at-home orders within the United States have featured protestors equipped with tactical vests and rifles.[15] Australia has been the site of the T-Pocalypse panic over toilet paper that spread throughout the world during the initial growth of the outbreak, as well as some limited protests against lockdowns.[16] In a similar fashion to the first waves of the Arab Spring, shutdown measures in Lebanon have amplified existing public grievances towards deteriorating economic conditions, resulting in banks being set on fire by protesters.[17]

Evidently, the civil stability and national security of world societies are challenged by disruptive phenomena with global reach such as the Syrian Civil War and COVID-19 pandemic. It could be argued that such global forces would only seriously affect less developed countries with weaker institutional resilience. However, even in a country as prosperous and politically robust as Australia, the Syrian Civil War contributed to the elevated threat of terrorism, and the COVID-19 pandemic compelled an unprecedented economic support package of AU$320 billion from the Australian Government.[18]

These two cases have already generated considerable challenges to the national security of the Australian community, and there is mounting evidence that climate change will induce further socio-political turbulence

12 World Health Organization 2020a.
13 See Blavatnik School of Government 2020, Gopinath 2020 and Spry 2020.
14 See Phillips 2020b and Phillips 2020a.
15 ABC News 2020a.
16 See Jankowicz 2020 and Dexter 2020.
17 ABC News 2020b.
18 The Treasury 2020.

as the twenty-first century progresses. Aside from addressing intense environmental stressors including droughts and bushfires within its borders, the Commonwealth must also consider and respond to foreign climate-related issues, especially those that require the deployment of military assets.[19] In fact, a recent report was conducted for the Department of Defence that examined and forecasted the civil security implications of globally disruptive phenomena including climate change for Australia.[20]

It must be emphasised that the intersection of climate change and security, through both research and practice, remains a developing field. Aside from the complexity of understanding climate change itself, there are various approaches to analysing its security implications, such as studying civil unrest, armed conflict, migration or subjects outside of the state-centric paradigm, such as natural ecosystems.[21] In light of the political turbulence of the past decade, especially within the past few months, the impending challenges of the climate breakdown warrant more active attention through a security lens.

*

This article was originally published by the
Sydney Environment Institute.

References

ABC News. "Armed protesters enter Michigan's state capitol to demand end to coronavirus lockdown." *ABC News*, 1 May 2020a. https://www.abc.net.au/news/2020-05-01/armed-us-protesters-seek-end-to-coronavirus-restrictions/12205586.

ABC News. "Coronavirus shutdown sees Lebanese cities hit by protests over financial woes." *ABC News*, 29 April 2020b. https://www.abc.net.au/news/2020-04-29/coronavirus-sees-lebanon-cities-erupt-against-economic-hardship/12197812.

Al Jazeera. "China reports first death from mysterious outbreak in Wuhan." *Al Jazeera*, 11 January 2020. https://www.aljazeera.com/

---

19 See Department of Agriculture, Water, and the Environment 2020, Department of Defence 2020 and Barrie 2019.

20 Rubinsztein-Dunlop and Taylor 2020.

21 McDonald 2018.

news/2020/01/11/china-reports-first-death-from-mysterious-outbreak-in-wuhan/.

Australian Security Intelligence Organisation. "Counter terrorism." Australian Government, 2020. https://www.asio.gov.au/counter-terrorism.html.

Barrie, C. "Climate change poses a 'direct threat' to Australia's national security: it must be a political priority." *The Conversation*, 8 October 2019. https://theconversation.com/climate-change-poses-a-direct-threat-to-australias-national-security-it-must-be-a-political-priority-123264.

Blavatnik School of Government. "Coronavirus government response tracker." University of Oxford, 2020. https://www.bsg.ox.ac.uk/research/research-projects/coronavirus-government-response-tracker.

Brock, S., Bastien, A., Barrett, O-L, Femia, F., Fetzek, S., Goodman, S., Loomis, D., Middendorp, T., Rademaker, M., van Schaik, L. et al. "The World Climate and Security Report 2020." Center for Climate and Security, 2020. https://climateandsecurity.org/wp-content/uploads/2020/02/world-climate-security-report-2020_2_13.pdf.

Department of Agriculture, Water, and the Environment. "Drought response, resilience and preparedness." Australian Government, 2020. https://www.agriculture.gov.au/ag-farm-food/drought/drought-policy.

Department of Defence. "Operation Bushfire Assist 2019–2020." Australian Government, 2020. https://news.defence.gov.au/national/operation-bushfire-assist-2019-2020.

DePillis, L., Saluja, K., and Lu, D. "A visual guide to 75 years of major refugee crises around the world." *The Washington Post*, 21 December 2015. https://www.washingtonpost.com/graphics/world/historical-migrant-crisis/.

Dexter, R. "Ten arrested, police officer injured in anti-lockdown protest." *The Age*, 10 May 2020. https://www.theage.com.au/national/victoria/defiant-anti-lockdown-protesters-ignore-police-warning-20200510-p54rj7.html.

Georgiadou, V., Rori, L., and Roumanias, C. "Mapping the European far right in the 21st century: a meso-level analysis." *Electoral Studies* 54 (2018): 103-115.

Gleick, P. "Water, drought, climate change, and conflict in Syria." *Weather, Climate, and Society* 6, no. 3 (2014): 331–40.

Gopinath, G. "The great lockdown: worst economic downturn since the Great Depression." *IMFBlog*, 14 April 2020. https://blogs.imf.org/2020/04/14/the-great-lockdown-worst-economic-downturn-since-the-great-depression/.

Ide, T. "Climate war in the Middle East? Drought, the Syrian Civil War and the state of climate-conflict research." *Current Climate Change Reports* 4 (2018): 347–54.

Jankowicz, M. "The coronavirus outbreak has prompted people around the world to panic buy toilet paper: here's why." *Business Insider Australia*, 11 March 2020. https://www.businessinsider.com.au/coronavirus-panic-buying-toilet-paper-stockpiling-photos-2020-3?r=US&IR=T.

Kelley, C. P., Mohtadi, S., Cane, M. A., Seager, R., and Kushnir, Y. "Climate change in the Fertile Crescent and implications of the recent Syrian drought." *Proceedings of the National Academy of Sciences of the United States* 112 (2015): 3241–46.

Lund, A. "The non-state militant landscape in Syria." *CTC Sentinel* 6, no. 8 (2013). https://www.ctc.usma.edu/the-non-state-militant-landscape-in-syria/.

Phillips, T. "Brazilian President Jair Bolsonaro denounced for joining pro-dictatorship rally." *The Guardian*, 21 April 2020a. https://www.theguardian.com/world/2020/apr/20/jair-bolsonaro-dictatorship-rally-protest-brazil-president-denounced.

Phillips, T. "Brazilians protest over Bolsonaro's muddled coronavirus response." *The Guardian*, 23 March 2020b. https://www.theguardian.com/world/2020/mar/22/brazilians-protest-bolsonaro-coronavirus-panelaco.

McDonald, M. "Climate change and security: towards ecological security?" *International Theory* 10, no. 2 (2018): 153-180.

Rubinsztein-Dunlop, S., and Taylor, K. "Think of coronavirus as a test run: Australian military leaders warn we must prepare for worse." *ABC News*, 29 April 2020. https://www.abc.net.au/news/2020-04-29/military-leaders-warn-australia-prepare-for-worse-coronavirus/12193228.

Spry, D. "Information warfare in the theatre of COVID-19." *The Interpreter*, 29 April 2020. https://www.lowyinstitute.org/the-interpreter/information-warfare-theatre-covid-19.

The Treasury. "Economic response to the coronavirus." Australian Government, 2020. https://treasury.gov.au/coronavirus.

Triffitt, M. "A growing mistrust in democracy is causing extremism and strongman politics to flourish." *The Conversation*, 10 July 2018. https://theconversation.com/a-growing-mistrust-in-democracy-is-causing-extremism-and-strongman-politics-to-flourish-98621.

Wike, R., Stokes, B., and Simmons, K. "Europeans fear wave of refugees will mean more terrorism, fewer jobs." *Pew Research Center: Global Attitudes & Trends*, 11 July 2016. https://www.pewresearch.org/

global/2016/07/11/europeans-fear-wave-of-refugees-will-mean-more-terrorism-fewer-jobs/.

Wike, R., Poushter, J., Silver, L., Devlin, K., Fetterolf, J., Castillo, A., and Huang, C. "European public opinion three decades after the fall of communism: 3. democratic satisfaction." *Pew Research Center: Global Attitudes & Trends*, 14 October 2019. https://www.pewresearch.org/global/2019/10/14/democratic-satisfaction/.

World Health Organisation. "Coronavirus disease (COVID-19): situation report– 120." World Health Organisation, 2020a. https://www.who.int/docs/default-source/coronaviruse/situation-reports/20200519-covid-19-sitrep-120.pdf?sfvrsn=515cabfb_2.

World Health Organisation. "Coronavirus disease 2019 (COVID-19): situation report – 51." World Health Organisation, 2020b. https://www.who.int/docs/default-source/coronaviruse/situation-reports/20200311-sitrep-51-covid-19.pdf?sfvrsn=1ba62e57_10.

NO ELSEWHERE

Gabriela Bourke

She dreamt she was sitting in a room made of glass. There was a bed in the centre of the room and her mother lay in it, flat on her back beneath tight, impersonal sheets. Her mother had no hair and her face was swollen and pink, the veins of her forehead visible through translucent skin. She knew in the dream that her mother was dying. Through the glass wall she could see a crowd of men tending to a towering steel machine. They poured oil and wound handles and pushed buttons and as she watched, the machine groaned into life. A huge crate stood nearby, and she wondered what was inside to make it tremble. One man, bearded, pulled open the rough wooden door and from it spewed a stream of pigs – big ones, fat, some with black markings swirling over their rumps and ears and pelts of thick, black hair. Their mouths were wide with screams she couldn't hear, and their eyes were disconcerting and blue, fringed with pale lashes like a human might have. The men caught the animals as they attempted to flee and flung them onto the conveyor belt, which juddered with the weight of them, licking up the writhing bodies and swallowing. She turned away from the wall, breathing too hard, and saw that her mother's chest no longer rose and fell. It was over.

She awoke. The dream lingered and she experienced none of the relief of waking. Her hands itched and she scratched them until they wept clear, sticky fluid.

'What have you done?' Her boyfriend asked, half-asleep, as she examined her fingers, splayed to keep them from touching and sticking.

'Just itched.'

'Go to the doctor. I keep saying.'

'It's just eczema.' But he was already asleep.

She showered and made coffee and prepared to go to work. She turned on the television just to hear its comforting hum and watched for a moment, cradling a mug in her sore hands, relishing the way the heat of the liquid inside seared the itch away.

'Animal activist protesters have taken over Swanston Street this morning, causing widespread traffic delays,' said the newsreader as the camera panned to a still intersection where a large group was arranged in a square. They were dressed in black and held placards with a picture on them – perhaps a cow, she couldn't see properly. She turned away. The dream was still with her. She needed to go to work.

It was a hot morning, for April. She boarded the bus and took the first seat. A man in a suit got on with her and she thought about how warm it must be inside the suit, how humid. He sat next to her even though there were many other seats, which made her feel stifled and fearful. She could smell his mint breath and feel the heft of his hot thigh, millimetres from her own. She pressed herself into the wall of the bus. When he disembarked at Haymarket the breath returned to her lungs, making her feel faint.

The sky was high and bright and pale and sweat gathered under her arms and in between her breasts as she walked from the bus stop. At the office, Joseph stood in the kitchenette watching the TV, hands in his pockets. His back was rigid.

'Look at this,' he gestured at the television, where the protesters stood fast under the beating sun.

'What about it?'

'These people, fucking nutters. So selfish, holding everyone up, making them late for work. I just can't stand people like that, can you?'

Ravi entered the office and the three of them stood, side-by-side, gazing at the glowing screen.

'I guess, protesting isn't illegal,' he said.

'Protesting! For what? Trying to make us all eat rabbit food? That's not a protest, that's idiocy.'

Joseph was Italian. She knew this because he told her often. Sometimes it felt like he was performing himself – the gesturing, the big voice, the tupperware containers stacked with soft almond biscuits sprinkled with sugar he brought into the office sometimes.

'Homemade, present from my wife,' he'd say, and the comfort he took in this, in his identity as a big, olive-skinned, family man was palpable.

'I don't know, Joe. They have a point.'

'Oh, mate –'

'No, think about it, we are eating too much meat. It's bad for the environment and what's bad for the environment is bad for us. I'm not saying we should all stop eating meat, god no. But should we cut back? Yeah, probably.'

Joseph shook his head.

'If a lettuce diet is good for the environment, I don't want to be good for the environment.'

She moved to her desk. When she'd first started working with Ravi and Joe they'd asked her opinion often, as if she were an area in which they'd be audited.

'How often did you include the girl?' The auditor might ask.

'Every day,' they could reply, 'but she barely bloody responded!' At some point they must have realised she was happy, crouched inside herself, at peace in the silence, and they left her alone. She liked the quiet of her own tongue, the orderliness of unspoken thoughts. The protesters unsettled her, and she didn't want to speak about them. Better to let them stand there for as long as they liked, until the traffic cleared, and their audience dispersed, and they went away. She'd seen them before, she thought, in Pitt Street Mall maybe. They'd been wearing masks like something out of a horror movie and holding iPads up so people could see what was playing. She'd glanced at the screen and seen something terrible and terrified in the darkness, moving. She'd hurried away.

Her inbox was full, but her fingers refused to work properly, still swollen and scabbed from the morning's itching. She typed emails with one finger, stopping every so often to massage ointment into the stinging, swollen patches of pink and red skin that made up most of her hands. Ravi and Joseph were seated and silent, not speaking.

She googled the protesters, wondering if they'd moved on yet, if the city had returned to business as usual. There were more people then she'd seen on the TV, webbing out across the country chaining themselves to abattoirs and posting photos of calves with matted hair and big, wet, cartoon eyes. One of the girls in the photos was crying. *Well, what's she doing in there if it's making her so upset*, she thought, her stomach clenched. She closed the window, opened it again, read an article about unprecedented April temperatures which aimed for jovial – more beach time for sizzling Sydney-siders – but came across as somehow sycophantic. She googled: do pigs feel fear? One article said yes, another said categorically no. She was offered video footage of pigs watching the slaughter of other pigs.

She declined. In the corners of her vision pigs slid away on a conveyor belt, screaming, but not with fear. With something else.

There was a piece of skin sticking from the side of her fingernail. It was transparent and looked like it would snap off easily and without pain, but when she weeded it from her flesh with her teeth the tiny wound stung and filled with blood. It tasted like salt and metal.

Her phone buzzed. Mum. Usually she wouldn't answer a call from Mum at work, but the anguish of the dream had hovered about her all morning and she felt an acute longing to hear her mother's voice.

'Hi Mum, I'm at work.'

'Oh, sorry love. I was just checking you were coming tonight for dinner. Only I did send you a text message last night and it says that you've seen it, but you've not sent a text back yet. So I wondered if you were coming? You don't have to, of course, I know you're busy. But if you do come, I'll make something, something special, so it would just be good to know if you were –'

'Yes, Mum. I'll come right after work.'

'Oh great.' Her voice was effusive. 'I'll pop down to the shops now, what would you like? Oh, but you have to go, you're at work, sorry love –'

'No, no, it's fine. Don't do anything special, just whatever you and Dad are having. Gotta go now. See you later.'

'Bye, love, see you –'

She hung up, knowing the conversation could carry on for another five minutes, ten. The stream of chatter exhausted her completely and at once. She pictured her mother standing in the living room, gripping the mobile phone tight to her cheek as though it might fly away, wearing one of her bright outfits that hung on her coat hanger body. She felt heavy, so heavy she could sink through fifteen floors and into the sticky brown earth that surely lay somewhere far beneath. Back into the earth from where she came, the cool, soft embrace of mud and sand.

'Here you are.' Ravi deposited a plate of noodles in front of her. She thanked him and twirled a mouthful around her fork. Joseph returned holding a thick sandwich spiky with bacon and oozing brown sauce like old blood.

'Scott Morrison says the protesters are un-Australian, so now I'm feeling like I chose the wrong side.'

Ravi laughed. She opened a spreadsheet.

Later, Joseph informed them that the protesters had been arrested. His relief was tangible. 'Tougher penalties for this kind of thing, that's what they need.' His desire to oppose Scott Morrison had clearly dissipated.

Her own father worshipped Scott Morrison. He'd loved Malcolm Turnbull too, and Tony Abbott. He watched *Question Time* every day, yelling abuse at the television or roundly saying, 'Hear, hear'.

'I'm off now too, Joe. Got dinner with my mum.'

'Lovely. You say hello to her for me, yeah?'

It was 5.30 pm, but the city was still warm and the sky still blue. Wafts of heat like clouds drifted from the pavement. She boarded a train and stood still amongst the sweaty bodies of fellow commuters as the train chugged slowly north. A man in a suit stood very close to her. As they pulled into a station, she felt his hand rub her right buttock, once, twice, then a sharp pinch. She whipped around, heat rushing to her face and as she caught his eye he grinned and slipped out of the carriage onto the platform. She looked around, sure someone would have seen, sure someone would be waiting to help, but the commuters stood motionless with their eyes averted. No-one had seen. It was like nothing had happened. Blank, humiliated, she missed her stop and had to get out at Wahroonga.

Wahroonga was cooler than the city, perhaps because it was later in the day, perhaps because of the trees. The walk to her parent's house cooled and calmed her. No-one had seen. It could have simply not happened. It had not happened. She tried to erase the feeling of the hand, hot and intent. It had not happened.

Her parents lived in an old brick house without air-conditioning, and when she opened the door she was enveloped in a gust of heat.

'Well, well. Look who decided to come by.' The couch sat directly opposite the door, and her father was slumped on it, red-faced and beefy, beer in hand.

Her mother appeared. She wore a pink apron over a yellow dress and her hair frizzed crazily, as though trying to escape.

'Hi, love. Shut the door, would you, it's going to rain.'

The evening outside was cloudless.

'Really? I don't think –'

'Yes, they said it on the TV. Didn't they love?'

Her father grunted. She closed the door. Mum feared the weather.

'What's wrong with your hand?' Dad gestured his bottle at her hands, slopping liquid on the couch and sending her mother scuttling for a washcloth.

'It's just eczema. Gets bad when it's hot.' Her father never met her eye and she never met his. Only in adolescent moments of screaming, crying rage had she ever looked him in his eyes and been shaken at the dullness she saw there, the emptiness. She wondered what he had seen in her eyes in those scant moments. She wondered if he had seen anything at all.

She left him, walking into the kitchen where her mother was hefting dinner plates from the cupboard.

'Thanks for coming over, love. It's so good to see you.'

'It's okay.' Her bones hurt. 'Good to see you, too.'

She started on the washing up and listened to her mother's chatter. The kitchen cabinets were streaked and stained with food and the floor was sticky under her sandals. She rubbed at the streaks with a cloth.

'Oh, don't do that, honey. I'll do that later.'

'I don't mind helping.'

'Help,' Dad appeared, opening the fridge and retrieving another drink. 'Being helpful, are you? Funny, 'cause I think that if you'd actually wanted to help your mum you wouldn't have taken off for years and only come crawlin' back when you needed cash.' He took a long, belligerent slug from his can.

'Okay.'

'Don't you Okay me, madam.'

'Oh, please let's be nice,' her mother said, beseechingly. The anger, never far away, began to rise. The ceiling was too close. The kitchen too hot. She closed her eyes.

'Check on the potatoes, would you, love? They should be ready by now. I'll start carving up.'

'What are we eating?'

'Roast, of course. 'Cause you're home!'

A beat.

'Guess it's never enough that I'm home.' Dad stood and swigged and made no move to help lift the tray of potatoes from the oven. They were sizzling and browned and her mouth watered.

'How do you get them so crispy? Mine always come out soggy.'

'Oh, easy. You just get some of the fat out of the meat pan and drizzle it all over them. You can chuck 'em straight in with the meat actually, easier still. You could make some for that nice boyfriend of yours.'

Bleak and unthinking, she replied, 'nah, he's vegetarian.'

'Vegetarian? Fuckin' hell.'

'Oh, well,' Mum was flustered. 'You could put oil on instead. Olive oil. Rosemary. Probably come out the same.'

The potatoes weren't done. She left the kitchen and sat on the step in the back garden, remembering when she'd lived at home and had to listen to her father ranting every day. She thought of him always like this, as 'my father', although she addressed him as Dad. She wished she could fling open all the doors wide and run, clutching her mother's hand, secure in the knowledge of an elsewhere, a safe place. But there was no elsewhere and even if there were, Mum would drag behind, fussing and unwilling, preferring to stay behind. The bougainvillea they had planted together when she was a kid had taken over the back wall, winding deft and sure until it had covered every square inch of lattice. Effusive fuchsia blooms exploded from the tips of the plant's leafy arms.

'Dinner's ready!'

They arranged themselves around the table so that Dad could still see the screen. Mum loaded thick slices of pork topped with sheets of crackling on their plates, and the potatoes crunchy in their skins. They each had a small mound of peas and a bendy carrot, which her father immediately palmed off onto his wife's plate.

'Stop giving me those. I've told you before.'

The news started:

A New South Wales politician has called for vegan activists to be jailed after nationwide protests threw cities into chaos this morning –

'And so they should. And chuck your boyfriend in there with them.'

'Oh, what happened?'

'Don't you ever watch the news? TV's on all bloody day, don't know how you miss everything. Group of fuckin' lefties stopped traffic this morning, that's all. Put 'em away, far as I'm concerned.'

The protesters had annoyed and upset her, yet she heard herself saying: 'They were only standing there. They didn't do anything wrong.'

'Bet your boyfriend told you to say that.'

Teeth clenched; she surveyed her plate. It was too hot for such heavy food. The sight of it, lacklustre, lying in a pool of fast-drying gravy, arranged by her mother's ever-fussing hands, filled her with immense sadness.

'Yum, Mum, thank you.'

The first bite of flesh was sweet and sticky, and she was reminded of her fingers gluing together after she'd scratched through the skin to the pus underneath. She tried to cut off a piece of crackling, but the skin was too hard, so she picked it up with her hands and lifted it to her teeth. Golden hairs grew thick and forgotten from the corner of the chunk of cooked skin, and she dropped it back onto the plate.

'What's wrong, love? Is it no good?'

Wet blue eyes and blond lashes. Her mother, lifeless under taut sheets.

'No, no. It's great. Just a bit too hot. Burned my fingers.'

PLASTIC OVER PEOPLE: CORONAVIRUS WAR PROFITEERING

India Gill

From the moment you step back into Australia from abroad and are escorted by the military to your guarded hotel room for the mandatory fourteen-day quarantine, there is no mistaking that we are truly in a war against the coronavirus pandemic. One of the inescapable realities of history is that with war comes war profiteers; those who unethically take advantage of the crisis for their own ill-gotten benefit to the detriment of society.[1] Sadly, this war against the coronavirus is no exception and its war-profiteering villain is the plastic industry.

Over the last decade, tremendous progress has been made to eliminate single-use plastics, most notably via regulations around the world either prohibiting the use of single-use plastic bags in grocery stores or implementing a monetary surcharge to deter their use. According to the 2018 United Nations Environment Report, over 127 countries have adopted some form of legislation to regulate single-use plastic bags.[2] Yet virtually overnight, the plastic industry has undone this hard earned victory for our environment, all under the false pretense of protecting our front-line workers in supermarkets.

The plastics industry has fed the narrative that customers cannot bring their own reusable bags to supermarkets because doing so would expose their employees to the coronavirus.[3] Let me unpack this hoax. I arrive at the supermarket. I am wearing a mask. The trolley I am using has been sanitised. I go about my shopping, and in doing so I touch, with

---

1   Hicks 2020.
2   Excell 2019.
3   Chua 2020.

my bare hands, every single item that I place in my trolley (which have already been touched by those who packed, shipped and stocked them). I go to the check out. I again touch every single item in my trolley as I place it on the belt. The employee who then packs my groceries, who is wearing a mask and gloves, then touches dozens of items that I have just touched and places them into a single-use plastic bag. Yet somehow if that same employee touches one more item that I have also just touched, my reusable bag, that person will somehow experience an unacceptable additional risk of contracting the coronavirus. The plastics industry is tapping into the threat of coronavirus contamination, deeming reusable bags as vectors for the virus, when there is little scientific evidence for this.[4] The coronavirus can survive for days on plastic surfaces and are, therefore, no safer than reusable bags fibers.[5]

Plain and simple, this is war profiteering by the plastics industry. This is consistent with the clear historical pattern and practice of the plastics industry to manipulate consumer behavior to its benefit. Although hard to imagine today, there was a time when single-use plastics didn't exist. The plastics industry then seized upon the post–Second World War spike in consumerism to introduce a 'simpler' and more 'convenient' way of life.[6] Rather than refilling milk in glass bottles and buying soda in aluminum cans, the world was provided with an ostensibly easier and cheaper alternative, single-use plastic.[7] The industries ultimately aimed to sell people 'garbage' that they would use once then throw away, only to buy it again the next day – and it succeeded in making single use plastic a staple of human life.[8]

The industry's economic prosperity took absolute priority over the devastating environmental effects of plastic waste – yet by the 1960s, society began to recognise the early stages of a plastic crisis that the Plastics Industry Association could no longer ignore.[9] In response to this initial backlash, the plastics industry introduced the Council for Solid Waste Solutions to promote recycling programs.[10] Recycling was a persuasive

---

4   Chua 2020.
5   Chua 2020.
6   NPR 2019.
7   NPR 2019.
8   NPR 2019.
9   Root 2019.
10 Root 2019.

means of alleviating any sentiments of consumer 'guilt' surrounding plastic waste. As early as 1987, it was acknowledged that recycling was simply not a feasible solution to managing plastic waste, and as of 2017, only 8.4 percent of plastic was being recycled.[11] The Plastics Industry Association then pivoted to arguing that 'waste management practices and infrastructure did not keep pace with the changing economy', successfully creating the illusion that all plastic is recyclable.[12]

This deception continued with the plastics industry campaigning to hold individuals responsible for the mismanagement of plastic waste.[13] The threat of a disposable bottle ban in Vermont resulted in the plastic industry's highly influential campaign 'Keep America Beautiful'.[14] The plastics industry fabricated the message that plastic waste was not responsible for pollution; rather the responsibility lay in the hands of society and how people manage their own plastic waste.[15] In 2019, plastic manufacturers formed the Alliance to End Plastic Waste and pledged US$1.5 billion to help 'make the dream of a world without plastic waste a reality'.[16] These measures have simultaneously created a positive public image for the plastics industry while distracting the world from the plastics industry's responsibility for our current environmental catastrophe.

Over fifty years ago in the movie *The graduate*, successful businessman, Mr McGuire, solemnly imparted to the young, impressionable Benjamin Braddock that the future was in 'plastics'.[17] Sadly, Mr McGuire's advice was prescient. The plastics industry has indeed dominated the last fifty years, using its money, power and influence to beat back efforts to control the insidious impact of plastics to our planet. Environmentalists finally broke this half-century of plastics industry dominance by championing regulations designed to eliminate single-use plastic bags. If we do not hold the line and preserve these gains now, in the face of the plastics industry's insidious coronavirus war profiteering, our 'future' will be fifty more years of 'plastics' – and that's no future at all.

---

11 US EPA 2018.

12 Root 2019.

13 NPR 2019.

14 NPR 2019.

15 NPR 2019.

16 Root 2019.

17 Seabrook 2010.

*

This article was originally published by the
Sydney Environment Institute.

References

Chua, Jasmin Malik. "Plastic bags were finally being banned: then
came the pandemic." *Vox*, 20 May 2020. https://www.vox.com/
the-goods/2020/5/20/21254630/plastic-bags-single-use-cups-
coronavirus-covid-19-delivery-recycling.
Excell, Carole. "127 countries now regulate plastic bags: why aren't we
seeing less pollution?" World Resources Institute, 13 September 2019.
https://www.wri.org/blog/2019/03/127-countries-now-regulate-
plastic-bags-why-arent-we-seeing-less-pollution.
Hicks, Robin. "How the coronavirus pandemic is changing people and our
planet." *Eco-Business*, 22 April 2020. https://www.eco-business.com/
news/how-the-coronavirus-pandemic-is-changing-people-and-our-
planet/.
NPR. "The litter myth." *NPR*, 5 September 2019. https://www.npr.
org/2019/09/04/757539617/the-litter-myth.
Root, Tik. "Inside the long war to protect plastic." Center for Public
Integrity, 16 May 2019. https://publicintegrity.org/environment/
pollution/pushing-plastic/inside-the-long-war-to-protect-plastic/.
US EPA. "Plastics: material-specific data." United States Environmental
Protection Agency, 30 July 2018. https://www.epa.gov/facts-and-
figures-about-materials-waste-and-recycling/Plastics-material-
specific-data.
Seabrook, John. "Plastics." *The New Yorker*, 13 September 2010. https://
www.newyorker.com/news/news-desk/plastics.

EARTH-CRY

Hannah Roux

> I sink in the miry depths where there is no foothold
> I have come into deep waters; the floods engulf me.

Psalm 69:2

If you must consume me,
do it slowly.
Kiss me with the kisses of your mouth
so that your lips and tongue and teeth and throat
may swallow me.
Do it slowly,
do not turn your face from me.
For the waters have come up to my neck.
I sink in deep mire.
I cannot stand.
My breath gasps for you,
my throat is parched
from calling you for help.

Zeal for your houses consumes me:
it is eating me alive.

After the flood is the fire
and after the heat the cold
and the wind which roars
and tears the torched trees up
so their roots wave ragged,
high in the air,

sinking in mire.
After the flood is the fire,
the furnace is red
and the ash floats black
on the face of the sea.

Zeal for your castles consumes me:
it is eating me alive.

Do you remember the poems I wrote you
when we were young
and first in love.
I traced the words in river-silt
and again on squeaky sand,
in the falling of leaves and in the flowers
and the calling of the gulls to the waves.
I fed you lines like berries
sweet upon the tongue
and I made love to you as a mountain,
bent down to pierce the sea.

But zeal for your towers consumes me:
it is eating me alive.

The waters have wrenched the wharf in two
and the sun raises up his head
red and wet: face gleaming, rays weeping.
The waters bleed into my mouth
where my throat burns with salt and the fire.
Deep in my bowels the seeds sleep
silent, where all is dry
though wave-cry, wind-cry, storm-cry,
sun-cry and earth-cry
consume me.
The seeds sleep, are buried deep
and will not rise.

Zeal for your towers consumes me:
it has eaten me alive.

Your scorn has broken my back,
your ploughmen plough already
deep furrows along my spine.
All my bones are on display.
My lungs, exposed, gurgle bloody breaths
and gasp for air like the islands.
You saw me once in salmon-form
dashing silver through the streams,
racing rapids to the rocks.
My beauty stopped your breath
and your heart burned for me –
but still you fished with nets of hair,
parted pink flesh with delicacy
and ate me up completely.

If you must consume me,
do it slowly,
mouthful by mouthful,
do not turn your face from me.
I am sinking in the water
where there is no foothold,
I cannot stand.
My breath gasps for you;
my throat is parched
with calling you for help:

If you must consume me,
do it slowly.

'TIS ALREADY IN   *Yasodara Puhule-Gamayalage*

CATASTROPHE AVERTED

Jennifer Scarini

TINY LIFE

Djuna Hallsworth

NO ONE IS TOO SMALL TO MAKE A DIFFERENCE   *Charlotte Lim*

CHARLOTTE AND GRETA THUNBERG

Charlotte Lim

SYSTEM CHANGE NOT CLIMATE CHANGE

Charlotte Lim

GHOST I
Melissa Snook

GHOST II
Melissa Snook

nom nom
just give worm a minute
okay
heeyyy!
cough
cough
oh hey!
i was just eating break-fast
burp
what's up?
oohhh
i'm showing my friend around!
where?
hey what'd i tell you
come down, the grass is fine!
hello
sup
haha
hope it's not rude to ask but were you eating soil?
yeah i love it!
lemme tell you why
we are earthworms and what we do is CHEW on Soil to extract nutrients
then we bring those nutrients back to the surface, making the soil HEalthy
happy soil

TUNING IN PART IV

Sophie Zhou

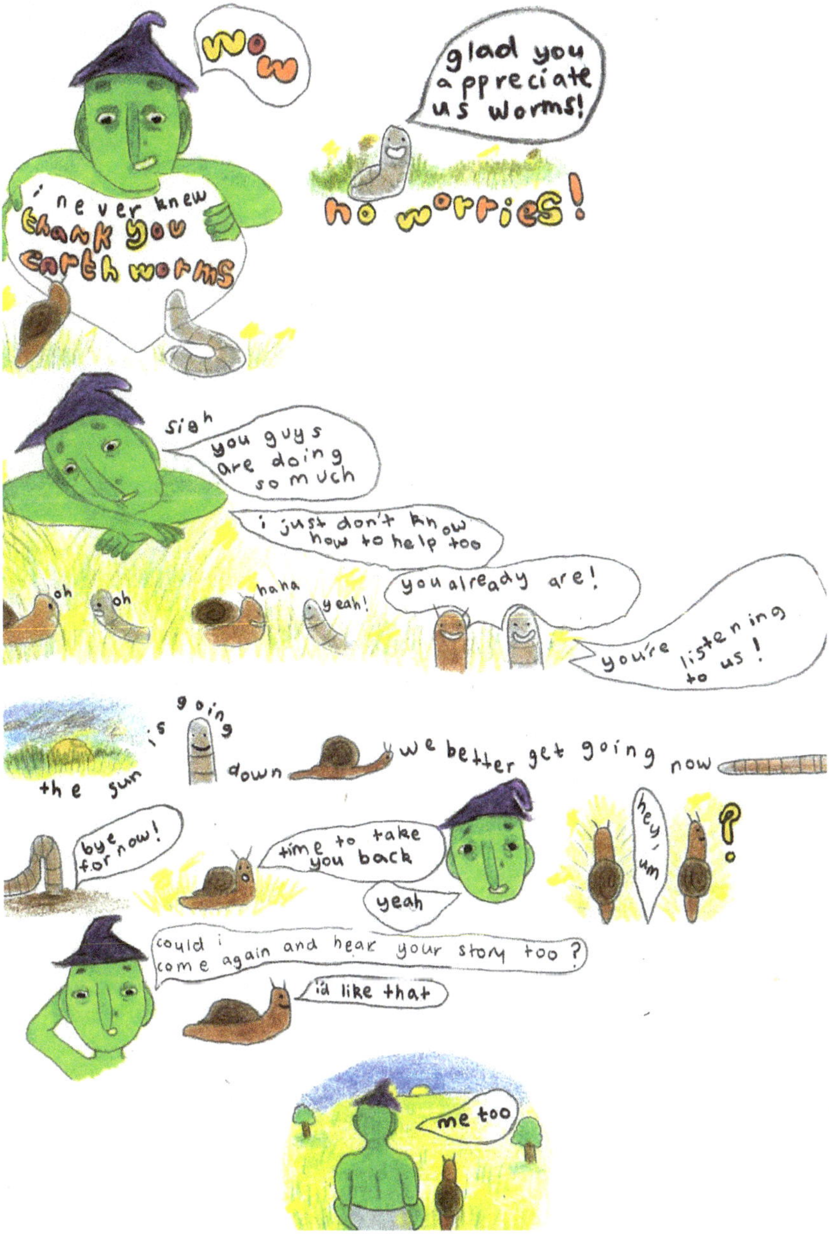

GARDEN ANTHROPOCENE I
Keesha Field

GARDEN ANTHROPOCENE II
Keesha Field

GARDEN ANTHROPOCENE III

Keesha Field

GARDEN ANTHROPOCENE IV
Keesha Field

REMAINS OF THE ARCTIC CIRCLE

Djuna Hallsworth

TIPTOEING ALONG THE EDGE AT DUSK
Djuna Hallsworth

ALL OF THIS COMES FROM SOMEWHERE
Michael Lotsaris

GHOST III *Melissa Snook*

GHOST IV
Melissa Snook

GHOST V
Melissa Snook

BLACK SUMMER *Louise Dziedziczak*

MOUNTAINS / PSALM 121

Memi Adams

DRAGON FRUITS AND ANTS AT MY FRONT GARDEN   *Victor Zhou*

PAINTING WITH DRAGON FRUITS AND ANTS

Victor Zhou

During self-isolation, I enjoyed reading *Arts of living on a damaged planet* (2017) with my pug-kin named Jet near my mother's dragon-fruit garden out the front. I learnt of ghosts: shimmers, lichens, spirits and stones, and mushroom clouds, they are those who linger and suffuse into ecological time and landscapes. I also learnt of monsters: they are entanglements and assemblages of bodies. Monsters remind me that I am not an individual, but a complex system which depends on bacteria, and of how horseshoe crabs and red knot birds need each other to survive.

While Jet snorted and licked the grass in my garden, my mind and body would wander through these entangled multispecies stories. I could feel the brilliance of flowing love-pollen in the garden, and the white butterflies which shimmered with them. And I also noticed the dragon fruits and their kind yellow flowers which would slowly open and then go to sleep; some were embalmed in a light necklace of spider webs, and some were sugar fruit-worlds for ants. Dragon fruits are alien eggs birthed from now-ghosts of kind yellow flowers; they have ants as guardian knights, huddled at their tip.

I wanted to paint these monsters and ghosts, but I also wanted to capture its intensity of life, how it kept growing, dying, living on. In my artwork, the dragon fruits are ambiguous forms which seem to be flying forward and towards something with the ants on top of them. I wonder what will happen after self-isolation: I hope we become more with ecology, but I also hope to project a future where we live and love our non-human kin.

RECONCILING THE SPLIT

Angad Roy

I recently saw a picture on *National Geographic's* Instagram page, which depicts wildebeest crossing the Mara River. The absence of a focal point and the image's incoherent form was at first confusing and frustrating; a feeling that Anton Ehrenzweig explains as an attack on my 'conscious sensibilities and the gestalt principle ruling them'.[1] It was a rejection of order and organisation and after overcoming my original frustration, I found the picture engulfing, enchanting and visceral. I was then reminded of its striking similarities to Jackson Pollock's *Autumn rhythm (Number 30)*.

The deceptive semblances of curves and fractured connections, the dark splashes offset by the warmer, earthy colours and the jarring eruption of shapes and lines that redefine the traditional pictorial space. I rarely read Instagram captions but read the lengthy one about these wildebeest for two reasons. One, the aesthetic strangeness of the photo and two, because it reflects a New Materialist view which emphasises 'human individuals and societies as embedded parts of a larger material process of *exchange* and *flow*'.[2] The interchangeability of the photo and the artwork, and this mutable *exchange* and *flow* drew similarities to timelapse videos and some of Aphex Twin's music, all modes of art that are engaging because they are disorienting and dissociative.

I myself had a disorienting experience recently; I smacked and killed a bee with a rolled-up newspaper. It tore away from the window in reaction, hovered obstinately in the air and fell to the ground, squirming for a few moments before zapping out. When I was young, a wasp had bitten my hand while I was walking out of the pool (we don't have a

---

1   Ehrenzweig 1967, 82.
2   Kerridge 2014, 368.

pool now), and the bee's death reopened this closeted compartment of my childhood anguishes and as such, I left it there, fearing some sort of post-death retaliation if I tried to pick it up. When I woke the next morning, it had disappeared. My mum definitely didn't do it nor did my brother; both feared the presence of foreign bodies in the house. The other logical options that remained were my dad who thrived on eradicating such foreign bodies (his favourites were cockroaches), the vacuum whose job it was to do so, my dog who did so on instinct or other critters who did so for sustenance. It turns out bees are fascinating creatures and are integral to the natural process, pollinating over eighty percent of all pollinating plants, including ninety different food crops.[3]

They are important and I am slowly coming to terms with that. Yet, it seems that my awareness of other issues – the meat trade, Instagram poetry, how to revive dead indoor plants because your dad forgot to water them while you were away – is minimal, either because I can't change them, despise them or am just too lazy to do so. How could this change?

In 'The hidden order of art', Ehrenzweig critiques the gestalt, arguing 'art is a dream dreamt by the artist which we, the wide-awake spectators, can never see in its true structure; our waking faculties are bound to give us too precise an image produced by secondary revision'.[4] Ehrenzweig's sentiment here is important. That is, the collective 'we' – anyone engaging with art in its diverse mediums – are too often bound by our subjectivity and therefore, meaning becomes inextricably tied to context, culture, sentiment and prejudice. As a result, in a genre as complicated and nuanced as nature writing, there needs to exist an attack on our sensibilities to move past these issues and to represent nature in its inherently multifaceted form.

The following image shows what could either be a rabbit or the head of a duck, although it really could be any type of bird, even a strange-looking human if we accept that without context, the photo could be employing varying degrees of caricature and likening. Indeed, it is only our reliance on the gestalt that forces us to order and define what in fact *our mind* is telling us what the image should be.

I found the essential idea interesting; nature writers can become too focused on a singular message, whether it be activist, scientific or polemical. Instead, shouldn't nature writing do the opposite and be

---

3   HoneyLove 2013.

4   Ehrenzweig 1967, 93.

Duck or rabbit? Wikipedia.

eclectic because nature itself is eclectic? Shouldn't a reader be allowed the opportunity to 'comprehend alternative views in a single glance' and thus, to achieve their own perspective on an issue/s rather than that which is imposed upon them?[5]

Oh, by the way (if you're interested), bees also make 6000 tonnes of honey, a colony pollinates 4000 metres squared, and an estimated one third of food are pollination dependent.[6]

For anyone engaging with the plethora of information addressing the various components of climate change, this type of comprehension can be challenging because of the gestalt, which presupposes 'splitting', a process of 'intellectualisation that separates abstract awareness of the crisis from real emotional engagement'; we essentially see what the mind organises as relevant and real, the rest is irrelevant and inaccessible.[7] In her essay, 'The opposite of glamour', Falconer directly addresses the issue of splitting in a Flaneur-like recount of 'oysters … [that] had once thrived around the

---

5   Ehrenzweig 1967, 37.
6   BBC Teach 2020.
7   Kerridge 2014, 366.

harbour', with their shells functioning as remnants of Indigenous heritage and unsurprisingly, as refurbished Settler playgrounds.[8] She explains that 'it can be hard to "see" this decline ... such things are, for many of us in the distance ... we only find ourselves noticing things we haven't seen for some time, even if they were once ubiquitous.'[9] Her sentiment echoes what Monbiot coins as 'selective blindness', which occurs when 'your brain quickly identifies what it considers to be the most significant aspects of your surroundings, and focuses almost all of its attention on these elements'.[10] This is a clear functioning of the gestalt perception and it is interesting that both Monbiot and Falconer use the example of a sparrow and wonder, would we notice if the birds stopped singing?

I don't really hear the birds singing. I try, sometimes, when my ears aren't being damaged by cheap $5 earphones, traffic or construction. I've heard the rasping sound of beehives on the television but, based off the agony involved in trying to sleep with a fly buzzing at my ear, I think a hive would be significantly more agonising. I wonder, what is the best way to swat a fly?

Such stark questions, which critique the gestalt as limiting to our experience of nature are enhanced by the gestalt-attacking form of Falconer's work and its fluctuation between fact, recount, allusion and ethereal prose works. In her oyster recount, Falconer offers an intellectual perspective on the significance of their extinction, citing 'because 85% of oyster reefs had disappeared around the world ... oysters were at less than 10% of their prior abundance in most bays and eco regions'.[11] This is supported by a scientific explanation of their extinction through 'ocean acidification and increased levels of carbon dioxide', which transitions to a dream-like description of their aesthetic value, 'photographs as ethereal as Lesuer's watercolours, of pteropod shells ... disappearing from one image to the next as their shells thinned, their glassy transparency becoming etched and then fragmenting'.[12] Although it was probably not intended, Falconer's reference to fragmentation offers a meta-comment on her own work, and in the amalgamation of different forms, she offers numerous and thus differently accessible perspectives of her main issue, which if I

---

8   Falconer 2017.
9   Falconer 2017.
10 Monbiot 2017.
11 Falconer 2017.
12 Falconer 2017.

am permitted some indulgence, is manifest in a blackout of one of her paragraphs: 'this is a too-familiar story when we read about nature ... the loss is caused by us'.[13]

I think John Kinsella might appreciate my indulgence but I don't know for sure. It's fun to live in hope though. I think he might because aesthetics in 'The Silo' are important, a fulfilment of the gestalt due to its silo-like construction, 'a traditional symbol of harvest and success in European culture'.[14]

However, Kinsella disrupts characteristics of pastoralism to represent the environmental devastation of rural Australia. The redundancy of the silo reflects the difficulties faced by farmers in increasingly desolate lands, lands whose exploitation renders it unattractive and restricted. 'The Silo' reflects the land's futility, absent of the reverence and beauty typical of idyllic pastoralism. Rather, it is simply 'red earth, a long thin/stream of unhealthy blood'.[15] Kinsella then flips nature's passivity and offers a violent retaliation in the form of a fire, which re-attributes a powerful agency to nature whose persistence is positioned as a stronger force than humanity's greed and resulting transience, becoming obstructive and claustrophobic like 'a prison which neither could hope for parole, petition, release'.[16]

Being in a hive would be like being in a prison. Probably worse. Although it's strange that I only adopt my fear of bees in closed spaces. Otherwise, the outdoors fosters a reverence for them and their capricious caper among the blossoming plants in my mother's garden,
    Left
                            To
                                                            Right
                            To
    Left
                            Among
                                                            Pink
                            Petals
carrying pollen to let them reproduce which is good for me because more plants means a happier mum and the bee's favourite plants are my mum's favourite.

---

13 Falconer 2017.
14 Pingping and Phillips 2009, 5.
15 Kinsella 1995.
16 Kinsella 1995.

Although I do wonder if my kids or their kids could see this caper, or will bees too attack us one day? Retaliate in frustration and exact some weird Black Mirror dystopia upon us all? Colony collapse disorder (CCD) has pervaded worldwide, where the majority of worker bees disappear in a colony, leaving only the queen, food and a few nurse bees.[17] More than ten million beehives were lost in the six years leading up to 2013.[18] Potential causes include:

- loss of habitat
- genetic factors
- changed beekeeping practices
- a family of pesticides called neonicotinoids.

Nee-on-eye-cot-in-oyds? Does the pronunciation really matter? Could I just say neon, mumble something in the middle, and finish with oids? Neon ... dfdvdfvldeoitetvs ... oids? Would you still understand what I was talking about? Pest-ee(pes-ky)-sides? In a brief consideration of language and meaning, Ehrenzweig suggests that 'unconscious scanning – in contrast to conscious thought which needs closed gestalt patterns – can handle "open" structure with blurred frontiers'.[19] In his novel, *That deadman dance*, Scott sees language – and within this, I consider his use of ellipsis – as vital in creating 'ambivalences [that] bypass political imperatives'[20] that are reliant upon binaries in White/Black relations of Australia's past and present colonisation. The first example of ellipsis occurs in the prologue, written in Bobby's English, '*roze a wail* ...'[21] Rose a whale or rose a wail? Here, Scott points to the structural limitations of Western language and the ambivalence of meaning that forces upon the reader a need for 'unconscious scanning', that understands how language is reinterpreted and re-used by non-English speakers. This is accentuated in juxtaposition to Bobby's attempt to write about the whale: 'a big family of whales breathing easily, spouts sparkling in the sunlight, great black bodies glossy in the blue and sunlit sea'.[22] Withstanding its lyricism, the description offers an isolated, rather than embodied perspective of the whales, which caters to a colonialist relationship with nature as something

---

17 Olroyd 2017.
18 Benjamin, Holpuch and Spencer 2013.
19 Ehrenzweig 1967, 56.
20 Pan Macmillan Australia 2010.
21 Scott 2010, 2.
22 Scott 2010, 2.

valued by its aesthetic and utility. This is enhanced by the imposition of comma, which formalises and restricts nature within colonial temporality as something existing and changing in tandem with themselves and their actions.

Conversely, for Bobby time is more fluid, independent and causal; it cannot be as Rushdie says, 'homogenised like milk'.[23] A memory of Wunyeran reads, 'just as no marks of his passing remains in the water, so there remains little trace of his tongue in the air, or these hills around him and sky, these clouds ... But surely if we paused, listened long enough ...'[24] Two key considerations must be made here. The first is the representation of the Aboriginal Australian relationship with nature, which poet Bill Neidjie describes more skillfully in his book *Story about feeling*, and its beautiful meditations on the heavily interconnected and anti-humanist relationship between humans and nature.[25]

Second, is the dissociative effect of the ellipsis within the sentence, which is jarring against what a reader's gestalt would expect of traditional language and structure. In deconstructing these restrictions through ellipsis, Scott reveals the temporal void existing in the interlinked relationship between death and nature and humans. That is, he dissolves the universalising notion of European time and the restrictions of language, by mimicking like Bobby, and then dismantling it through experimentations with the language itself. This serves to represent the natural world as something mutable, capricious and existing in a perpetual *exchange* and *flow* that humans are merely cogs within, rather than controllers of.

Maybe if I too listen long enough in my backyard, I might appreciate the bzzzzzzz of the bees and value their natural importance. Maybe, instead of swatting one, I will dash past it, protecting my head with the newspaper. Or maybe, just maybe, if it's inside, I will open the nearest window to let it out, immediately dash to my room protected in cricket gear and only return outside when my dad gets home to check that it has gone.

On their own, and more importantly, in combination, bees, Falconer, Kinsella, Ehrenzweig, Scott and all the words and letters that bring them together signal a desire to convey how words might attack and disrupt our gestalt sensibilities. Indeed, the power of writing is paradoxically

---

23 Rushdie 1984, 13.
24 Scott 2010, 134.
25 Neidjie 1989.

unbecoming for the comfort that words provide in representing nature, and our relationship with it unfortunately prevent us from truly perceiving how it operates. Thus, by writing in such a way that integrates and celebrates the difference of various forms, from the literary to the personal, we might be able to craft a type of writing that has the aesthetic properties of Pollock as well as the intellectual and literary qualities of writing itself and by doing so, we might counteract the traps embedded within splitting and the dualist perspectives of nature.

Now a little (closed book) test to see what you have learnt:
1. What is the name of the pesticides that harm bees?
2. What percentage of plants do bees pollinate?
3. What percentage of oyster reefs have disappeared around the world?
4. How much do my earphones cost?
5. What is CCD?
6. What is the benefit of 'unconscious scanning?'
7. What is my dad's favourite insect to eradicate?

References

BBC Teach. "Would we starve without bees?" *BBC*, 2020. Video. https://www.bbc.co.uk/teach/would-we-starve-without-bees/zkf292p

Benjamin, Alison, Holpuch, Amanda and Spencer, Ruth. "Buzzfeeds: the effects of colony collapse disorder and other bee news." *The Guardian*, 31 July 2013. https://www.theguardian.com/environment/2013/jul/30/buzzfeeds-bees-colony-collapse-disorder.

Ehrenzweig, Anton. *The hidden order of art*. London: Weinfield & Nicholson, 1967.

Falconer, Delia. "The opposite of glamour," *Sydney Review of Books*, 28 July 2017.

HoneyLove. "About the bees." *HoneyLove*, 2013. http://honeylove.org/bees/

Kerridge, Richard. "Ecocritical approaches to literary form and genre," in *The Oxford Handbook of Ecocriticism*, edited by Greg Garrard, 361–76. Oxford University Press, 2014.

Kinsella, John. "The silo" in *The Silo: A Pastoral Symphony*. South Fremantle: Fremantle Arts Centre Press, 1995.

Monbiot, George. "Our selective blindness is lethal to the living world." *The Guardian*, 20 December 2017. https://www.theguardian.com/commentisfree/2017/dec/20/selective-blindness-lethal-natural-world-open-eyes-environment-ecosystem.

Neidjie, Bill. *Story about feeling*. Broome: Magabala Books, 1989.
Olroyd, Benjamin P. "What's killing American honey bees?" *PLoS Biology* 5 no. 6 (2017). http://doi.org/10.1371/journal.pbio.0050168.
Pan Macmillan Australia. "*That deadman dance* by Kim Scott." 13 September 2010. Video. https://www.youtube.com/ watch?v=xqY8v1l9Pls.
Pingping, Liu and Phillips, Glen. "Radical pastoralism: John Kinsella's great 'pastoral trilogy'." *Landscapes: The Journal of the International Centre for Landscape and Language* 3, no. 1 (2009).
Rushdie, Salman. *Shame*. London: Picador, 1984.
Scott, Kim. *That deadman dance*. Sydney: Picador, 2010.

TREMÉ: CULTURAL SPACE AND PLACE
IN THE JAZZ CITY

Melissa Snook

New Orleans is a city rife with religion, mystery[1] and culture, and the Tremé district is a relic from the fusion of French and Spanish (Creole) settlement with African American habitation. If we put culture aside for just a moment, New Orleans is exactly as Jane Jacobs described: a failure of urban planning.[2] However, taking a cultural approach to the Tremé District in New Orleans provides a unique and different view on the urban picture of Tremé, and consequently, New Orleans.

Scholars Murray Schafer and Steven Feld described soundscape studies as a new alternative theory to city studies. They argued that the public space is inextricably linked with music to create a cultural city of feeling, as described by Samuel Zipp. The city of feeling forced into a single sector has allowed Tremé to remain an authentic African American community regulated by cultural traditions such as jazz funerals. Using the theories and methods of urban planning and city scholars, I will attempt to piece together the cultural history of the Tremé district in New Orleans through an observation of the features of the area. Furthermore,

---

1 Louisiana, in particular New Orleans, has often been the setting in popular culture for the devilish and sinful side of society. Vampires in popular culture have largely found themselves inhabiting New Orleans, particularly the French Quarter; most notably Erik Northman and Godric from True Blood and the Mikaelsons from The Originals. This may have some correlation to the red-light district (where prostitution and drugs were tolerated and confined), interestingly, located in the Tremé District in close proximity to the French Quarter.

2 Jacobs 1958, 18.

climate change and the impact of Hurricane Katrina have altered the future of city planning in the region.

An analysis of New Orleans through the lens of Robert Moses and Ebenezer Howard reveal a flawed city in desperate need of urban gentrification. Lawrence Powell called New Orleans an 'accidental town … an improvised one as well'.[3] New Orleans was certainly a city pushed together and built around a multiracial and class-divided society void of any sense of urban planning.[4] This unorganised and improvised city was a manifestation of Howard's district theory of urban planning. Howard's vision, according to Jacobs, was the separation of the city into multiple self-sustaining districts such as arts districts and economic districts.[5] Jacobs condemns this view of a city, arguing he 'wrote off the intricate, many-faceted, cultural life of the metropolis'.[6]

Yet, as Madeleine Lyes points out, so does Jacobs with her reluctance of recognising race in analysing the city.[7] However, Tremé is a testament to the positive aspects of divided urban planning. While Jacobs viewed this sectionalisation of the city as the destruction of urban complexity, as demonstrated through the documentary *Faubourg Tremé*, the district addressed it as a 'sacralized image of neighborhood as self-contained, organic community'.[8] This alludes to the idea of racial authenticity that I implied above (and will explore further on) in reference to Lyes. With a Jacobian view in mind, Howard's style of urban planning is detrimental to a city. Yet it is exactly this kind of separated cultural pockets that have allowed the continuation of an authentic cultural experience of the modern space in Tremé.

In 1984, Allan Jacobs said that 'you can tell a lot about a city by looking'.[9] Similar to his approach to Diamond and 24th Street in San Francisco, by looking at certain structures of the Tremé District, you are able to glimpse a long history of African American and Creole culture.[10]

---

3 Powell 2012, 59.
4 Adams 2014, 249.
5 Julian 2009, 2.
6 Julian 2009, 2.
7 Lyes 2014, 72.
8 Reed Jr 2011, 2.
9 Jacobs 1984, 28.
10 Jacobs 1984, 28.

Dance in Congo Square in the late eighteenth century, artist's conception by E.W. Kemble.
Wikipedia.

New Orleans has been labelled an exceptional and improvised city.[11] What I garner from this is that New Orleans cannot be placed in the same category is any other city in America. Instead, walking through the city and experiencing Tremé provides a different perspective on a culturally sustainable city.

One area I will look at is Armstrong Park, formerly Congo Square (as it will be referenced to from here onwards), which was a centrally located place of congregation for the African American community. Holly Whyte observed a number of similar squares and found that these places were an important feature to facilitate areas for people to use as meeting places, seating areas, etc.[12] Not only this, but the way these spaces were used showed that in large openings, people tended to congregate on the outskirts, generally under trees.[13] While Congo Square does look similar to those spaces Whyte was concerned with, it does not seem to follow this almost impervious theory. Tremé has been cited as the origin and heart of jazz music.[14] Whether or not it was on the minds or intentions of the architects and city planners, it is a truth that rings throughout every

11 For 'exceptional city' see Adams 2014, 246. For 'improvised city' see Powell 2012, 59.
12 Whyte 1980.
13 Whyte 1980.
14 Crescent City Living LLC 2016.

François Aimé Louis Dumoulin, Calinda, *Danse Des Nègres en Amérique* 1788. Wikipedia.

corner of the city, particularly Tremé, that it was built for music. All this is congregated into Congo Square.

One area of study when thinking about the city, which unfortunately has not been given the attention that it deserves, is what Schafer considered as soundscape studies.[15] This avenue of study encompasses the relationship between music/sound and the built cityscape.[16] In Matt Sakakeeny's study of New Orleans, he applied this theory of soundscapes to the jazz funerals in Tremé.[17] Jazz funerals have played a strong part of New Orleans African American culture since Emancipation.[18] Jazz funerals involve the parading of the coffin throughout the neighbourhood accompanied by a jazz band and the entirety of the community.[19] This

---

15 Sakakeeny 2010, 3.
16 This idea of soundscapes has been observed by Feld 1996, 91 and Schafer 1977, 10.
17 Sakakeeny 2010, 3.
18 Sakakeeny 2010, 1.
19 Sakakeeny 2010, 1–2.

Percy Humphrey 'Jazz Funeral' 1995. Infrogmation of New Orleans. Attribution 2.0 generic license. Modified to greyscale.

Tremé Jazz Funeral. Derek Bridges. Attribution 2.0 generic license. Modified to greyscale.

is the essence of what Lewis Mumford considered as the perfect city, one that functions socially and culturally around the community and family.[20] Eventually, the parade leads to the Interstate 10 where people yell 'Under the bridge! Under the bridge!'[21] According to Sakakeeny, the space below the Interstate 10 was where the 'imbalanced structures of power' were most visible between the working class and the poor lower class of African Americans.[22] Instead of a ignoring this symbol of social and racial disunity as constructed through city infrastructure, the people of Tremé reclaimed this soundscape below the Interstate, creating:

> Intimacy, enclosing parade participants, maximizing a sense of unity, and the concrete makes for spectacular acoustics, amplifying and multiplying the participatory sound ... shockingly loud ... to compete with the sound of cars and trucks whizzing above ... the sounds of the music, the crowd and the environment work together to orient individuals as a collective occupying a shared space.[23]

The jazz funerals demonstrate the combination of Mumford's social city and Jacobs lived city.

The separation of districts in New Orleans has given rise to an authentic African American culture. Tremé is far from the concrete jungle of New York and the hostile fortress of Los Angeles, but Tremé has succeeded where Los Angeles has failed: in supporting and encouraging racial identity in the city rather than destroying it. Walking through Tremé is a time capsule of black culture, creating a feeling of lived experience that Los Angeles and New York lack. When you walk under the archway and into Congo Square, you are immediately guided along the walkway by a musical parade structure. In different areas of the square, there are monuments to the musical heritage of not only the city, but also the square. This sense of life found in Tremé is what Carlo Rotella and Samuel Zipp called the 'city of feeling'.[24] Zipp finds this concept particularly interesting in the way that a built city is given a second rebirth when it is appropriated by the people living there in a way that is outside the traditional box that

---

20 Mumford 1937, 93.
21 Sakakeeny 2010, 2.
22 Sakakeeny 2010, 3.
23 Sakakeeny 2010, 2–3.
24 Zipp 2010, 2.

Brass band statue in Louis Armstrong Park. Miguel Discart. CC BY-SA 2.0 license.
Modified to greyscale.

Congo Square sculpture. Miguel Discart. CC BY-SA 2.0 license. Modified to greyscale.

Statue of Buddy King Bolden in Louis Armstrong Park. Miguel Discart. CC BY-SA 2.O license. Modified to greyscale.

city environments are often placed in.[25] Tremé is highly successful in this sense. Sharon Zukin was concerned with the 'search for authenticity'.[26] Fortunately, Tremé does not need to search for authenticity which it already possesses. It may be an authentic poor black community, but it is a culturally rich and authentic community in itself. This city of feeling obstructing a clearly poor city is also something that Robert Moses saw as an obstacle for a functioning city. Moses was very determined that Washington Square Park, for example, 'needed a shave and a haircut … it needed to knock it off with the poetry readings and start serving a practical function for the city again'.[27] As I have already explained, Tremé and particularly Congo Square, serve an important function in the traditional culture of the people who live in Tremé. What is clear is that the function of the city is highly subjective and is determined by those that live there. This is why Allan Jacobs' theory of walking around is so widely accepted as it allows a plan for a city that is specialised to the varying races and classes that live there.

Tremé is a beautiful district of New Orleans, filled with centuries of African American tradition and culture. Despite Allan Jacob's concerns, perhaps this sectioning of the city has been a good thing; certainly it has been instrumental to the authenticity of the district as a cultural centre. Jazz funerals and music has kept Tremé a place that has to be experienced. Robert Moses, if he could get his hands on Tremé, would have cleared out the entire sector (perhaps the entire city). For the natives of Tremé, the district is a treasure trove of culture and life that transcends beyond the physical and into Zipp's idea of the imaginary.

Urban planning post Katrina: creating Ebenezer Howard's garden city

Viewing the city of New Orleans, and in particular Tremé, from the point of view of Matt Sakakeeny's 'soundscapes', paints an exquisite picture of a city where African American culture is celebrated and practised on the streets. However, Hurricane Katrina, which devastated the city in 2005, revealed severe urban planning flaws throughout the rest of the

---

25 Zipp 2010, 3.

26 Lyes 2014, 71.

27 Julian 2009, 3.

city. Throughout the forties and fifties, urban expansion in the city saw infrastructure and housing being built in ecologically sensitive areas around swamps and water.[28] Since this urban expansion around the mid-twentieth century, these very areas where dense populations resided have seen increasing subsidence levels, creating an urban environment prone to flooding.[29]

Katrina was a wakeup call for the residents and leaders of New Orleans. Policy makers and urban planners recognised that the urban layout had severely damaged the ecological environment, creating the circumstances that made Katrina all the more dangerous.

What resulted after Katrina was called the urban sustainability framework.[30] This was an effort between local and international urban planners and designers to create effective and sustainable infrastructure that would prevent or slow future flooding.[31] With up to eighty percent of New Orleans underwater in 2005, it is no wonder this was a major priority post-Katrina.[32] To do this, the planning project focused on creating 'large green spaces for ecological functions and storm water management'.[33] The hope was that these green spaces would be situated close to public transport in order to meet 'climate change reduction goals' by reducing greenhouse gas emissions.[34]

This is exactly what the city planners of New Orleans did, and one such project was the creation of the Lafitte Greenway. The plan was to build a greenway stretching close to five kilometres that linked Congo Square, Tremé and the French Quarter with Mid City.[35]

Parks studies have shown that green spaces both reduce stress and provide spaces for recreation and physical activity.[36] Since the greenways opening, there has been an increase in recreational activities, cycling in particular.[37] The Lafitte Greenway has created a green space connecting

---

28 Fields 2009, 327.
29 Fields 2009, 325.
30 Fields 2009, 325.
31 Fields 2009, 325.
32 Fields 2009, 325.
33 Fields 2009, 325.
34 Fields 2009, 326.
35 Fields 2009, 331.
36 Haq 2011, 603.
37 Cachola Schmal and Lampe 2018, 244.

the poor African American Tremé district with the richer neighbourhoods of New Orleans, all the while encouraging environmentally sustainable transportation options.

Lafitte Greenway wasn't the only green space project undertaken post-Katrina. City Park, which was flooded for quite a few weeks after Katrina hit, was quickly rebuilt with new facilities created.[38] The huge park, which has a number of statues and bridges that feature hand carved reliefs, was restored and brought back to its former glory.[39] The city even added fishing and paddle boat facilities, as well as new trees and bike/pedestrian paths.[40] As well as restoring City Park, post-Katrina also saw the creation of the new Crescent Park, a beautiful green space along the river.[41]

Green spaces have two important benefits that were utilised in the instance of New Orleans post-Katrina. One of which I have already discussed which is the recreational benefit that allows for both the reduction of greenhouse gas emissions as well as a healthier lifestyle. The other which is important when thinking about climate change, is their role in preventing flooding. Particularly Lafitte Greenway, these green spaces are essential for mitigating damage during floods, which, unfortunately for the case of New Orleans, is unavoidable as it is common knowledge that the city is sinking rapidly and the natural ecological barrier between the water and the city has been eroded over time.

To bring all this back to my initial point when looking at soundscapes in Tremé, New Orleans was never the most creatively planned city. And yes, you could argue just like Jane Jacobs that the failure of urban planning in New Orleans has left the environment and its residents vulnerable. But the whole idea of this essay is to look beyond that. Ebenezer Howard published his theory of 'garden cities' in 1898. To this day, his model of city planning has been recreated over and over throughout cities in America and all over the world. He believed that people would be drawn to the 'town-country' that both solved the issues of air pollution, unemployment and slums in 'town' life and encouraged the benefits of nature, fresh air and water found in 'country' life.[42] The idea of the 'garden city' or

---

38 Reckfdahl 2014.
39 New Orleans City Park 2020.
40 Reckfdahl 2014.
41 Reckfdahl 2014.
42 Howard 1902, 22.

'town-country' was imagined as a mixture of industrialisation and city life combined with green spaces.[43] Post-Katrina, the city of New Orleans has definitely brought this garden city to life, through the cultural significance and music culture found in Congo Square to the recreational haven of City Park.

While parts of New Orleans are still in shambles, fifteen years after Katrina, the creation and restoration of green spaces has provided a rebirth of this beautiful city. The Tremé district has been providing spaces for African Americans to experience their culture through music. And post-Katrina, that tradition has continued, though in different ways throughout the city.

The city has been structured, and given a rebirth, through this cultural takeover. Architectural spaces such as the Interstate 10 and Congo Square have been appropriated for music, creating soundscapes. I have taken a romantic view of the city, and for good reason. Urban planners like Moses would ignore the feeling of the city to create another New York. New Orleans, and Tremé in particular, are certainly not without thier faults, and there are many: the racial division of the city, the extreme poverty and the environmental vulnerability. But within this poverty-stricken Tremé, there is an authentic black beauty that cannot be discounted. New Orleans is a beautifully intricate city, and as Allan Jacobs says, one just has to walk the streets to appreciate its cultural value.

References

Adams, Thomas J. "New Orleans brings it all together." *American Quarterly* 66, no. 1 (2014): 245–56.

Cachola Schman, Peter., Lampe, Stefanie. *Ride a bike! Reclaim the city.* Germany: Walter de Gruyter GmbH, 2018.

Crescent City Living LLC. "Treme – a New Orleans neighborhood." 12 May 2016. Video. https://www.youtube.com/watch?v=tKmfeCO6hBI.

Feld, Steven. "Waterfalls of song: an acoustemology of place resounding in Bosavi, Papua New Guinea." In *Senses of Place*, edited by Steven Feld and Keith Basso, 91–136. Santa Fe: School of American Research Press, 1996.

---

43 Howard 1902, 22.

Fields, Billy. "From green dots to greenways: planning in the age of climate change in post-Katrina New Orleans." *Journal of Urban Design* 14, no. 3 (2009): 325–344.

Haq, Shah Md Atiqul. "Urban green spaces and an integrative approach to sustainable environment." *Journal of Environmental Protection* 2 (2011): 601–8.

Howard, Ebenezer. *Garden cities of to-morrow.* London: Swan Sonnenschein & Co., Ltd., 1902.

Jacobs, Allan B. "Looking at cities." *Places* 1, no. 4 (1984): 28–37.

Jacobs, Jane. "Downtown is for people." *Fortune*, April 1958. http://fortune.com/2011/09/18/downtown-is-for-people-fortune-classic-1958/.

Julian, Liam, "Who shapes the city?" *Policy Review*, 24 September 2009. http://www.hoover.org/research/who-shapes-city.

Lyes, Madeleine. "Jane Jacobs and Sharon Zukin: gentrification and the Jacobs legacy." In *Contemporary perspectives on Jane Jacobs: reassessing the impacts of an urban visionary*, edited by Dirk Schubert, 71–82. Farnham: Ashgate Publishing, 2014.

Mumford, Lewis. "What is a city?" *Architectural Record* (1937): 91–95. http://www.polsci.chula.ac.th/pitch/urbpol13/lm.pdf.

New Orleans City Park. "Art and architecture." New Orleans City Park, 2020. https://neworleanscitypark.com/art-and-architecture.

Powell, Lawrence. *The accidental city: improvising New Orleans.* Cambridge and London: Harvard University Press, 2012.

Reckfdahl, Katy. "New Orleans' dazzling post-Katrina parks boom." *Next City*, 23 May 2014. https://nextcity.org/daily/entry/new-orleans-post-katrina-parks-boom.

Reed Jr, Adolph, "Three Tremés." *Nonsite*, 4 July 2011. http://nonsite.org/editorial/three-TreméTreméTremés

Sakakeeny, Matt. "'Under the bridge': an orientation to soundscapes in New Orleans." *Ethnomusicology* 54, no. 1 (2010): 1–27.

Schafer, R. Murray. *The tuning of the world.* New York: Knopf, 1977.

Whyte, William H. *The social life of small urban spaces.* 1980. https://archive.org/details/SmallUrbanSpaces.

Zipp, Samuel. "Making place: the cultural history of the built environment." *The Proceedings of Spaces of History/Histories of Space: Emerging Approaches to the Study of the Built Environment,* UC Berkeley (2010): 1–7.

THAT SCOMO LOVIN' CLIMATE CHANGE GUY!

Naosheyrvaan Nasir

(No, it's not Malcolm Turnbull).
He's not an inner-city raving lunatic
and his outback parents definitely didn't
vote for the Greens (should the fires have caused them
to die).

With the wife and the mortgage,
with the kids and the work in haulage,
he believes in . . . wait for it,
climate change!

Annoyed by Goldilocks Greta
with her doom-and-gloom narrative of the polar bears dying out.
He believes in climate change, but
he thinks some of us are plain mad.

He'll clean up the plastic on Clean Up Australia Day.
He'll sort his waste into bins of yellow and red.
He'll walk across town whenever he can.
He'll install solar on his roof.
He'll help plant seedlings in the park.
He'll take his keep-cup wherever he goes.

After doing all of the above, he still gets
annoyed by Goldilocks Greta
who skips about saying,
'It's just not enough'.

What more must he do?
He needs to burn diesel to get the haulage delivered.
He needs the haulage to pay off his mortgage.
His boss won't buy the electric model,
it's far too expensive and far too modern.
There isn't a mechanic who can fix that stuff,
and with record haulage coming through,
nobody will wait for you.

After considering all of the above,
Goldilocks Greta stares at the gas guzzlers, saying,
'Yuck! Shoo!'
Aeroplanes are taboo, fast cars too.
Young children want no school as
they must preach to you.

So now what must he do?
With the wife and the mortgage
with the kids and the work in haulage.

Give him a break, after all,
he loves ScoMo too!

CLIMATE TRUCK

Michael Lotsaris

The primary vehicle that I have aspired to own over the last few years has been the LandCruiser 70 Series from Toyota. It's essentially a utilitarian four-wheel-drive (4WD) that's built in various body configurations (the example pictured is the dual-cab 79 series), and I sometimes think of it as the best piece of junk that one can purchase brand new from a car dealership in Australia. While this thing packs V8 muscle and twin-locked solid axles, the front wheels don't align with the rear wheels, the entertainment system is relatively antiquated, and models with more than two seats have more ashtrays than airbags. Yet Toyota still asks for the same amount of money – over AU$70,000 – that one could spend on something more refined and technologically updated, like the Ford Ranger Raptor, or even their own Hilux Rugged X.

Regardless, I adore the old-school simplicity and robustness of the 70 Series. There's nothing else quite like it. However, as a big and boxy 4WD, it isn't the most fuel-efficient vehicle, not even in comparison with other utes (or pickup trucks in case any Americans happen to be reading this). So why would someone with an interest in the natural world and addressing anthropogenic climate change support something like this? Or any vehicle that requires fuel refined from crude oil? There are various alternatives to oil-powered internal combustion engine vehicles (ICEVs) like the LandCruiser 70 Series, such as vehicles that run on ammonia, natural gas, hydrogen, liquid nitrogen, propane, biofuels like ethanol and biodiesel and even wood. However, Battery Electric Vehicles (BEVs) seem to be highly popularised as the emerging and most viable 'green' substitute. So, let's investigate.

According to research from the International Council for Clean Transportation (ICCT), manufacturing the battery for a BEV emits just as many greenhouse gas emissions as manufacturing an internal combustion

Toyota LandCruiser 79 Series. Michael Lotsaris.

engine, and building a BEV in its entirety emits more emissions than manufacturing a comparable ICEV.[1] Of course these measures shift up or down depending on factors such as mass – larger BEVs with larger 'long-range' batteries produce more emissions during production. On top of that, the development of these large batteries requires particular resources that bring up considerable environmental and ethical dilemmas. Lithium is commonly discussed in this respect because mining and processing sites use a lot of water and risk contaminating local ecosystems with toxic chemicals – extracting one tonne of lithium requires roughly 1.89 million litres of water.[2] That's the equivalent of 1890 tonnes of water to extract 1 tonne of Lithium.

Other raw materials such as graphite, cobalt, nickel, aluminium and copper also present their own complications.[3] If the International Energy Agency (IEA) is correct in thinking that up to 145 million BEVs could be owned worldwide by 2030, at least forty times the amount of BEVs in 2017, then future mining operations will need to expand significantly to meet this growing demand.[4] So from the start, BEVs entail considerable environmental impacts.

Things change, however, once you start driving them. BEVs obviously emit zero greenhouse gas emissions from an exhaust tail pipe, because they

1   Hall and Lutsey 2018.
2   Katwala 2018.
3   West 2017.
4   International Energy Agency 2019.

don't have one. But many people are quick to point out that recharging an electric battery has to come from some sort of power source, and for many countries like Australia, much of that electricity comes from major climate change culprits like burning coal.[5] So manufacturing emissions aside, is powering a BEV for use just as environmentally damaging as fuelling an ICEV with oil? Nope. The average BEV is still distinctly more efficient than even the most efficient ICEVs, emitting barely half the emissions that the average conventional ICEV does, even if said BEV is powered by a national grid made up of less than twenty percent renewable energy sources, such as in the United States or Australia.[6]

Since manufacturing BEVs complete with their battery emits more emissions than manufacturing ICEVs, they have been calculated to break even with ICEVs after one year of use, at which point ICEVs take the lead in producing more greenhouse gas emissions.[7] If we're talking about long-range BEVs, then they're expected to break even with ICEV emissions after about two-and-a-half years of use.[8] However, if you need to replace the battery, then that will entail further emissions to compensate for. So, while it appears that BEVs are significantly more energy efficient than ICEVs over the course of their lifecycle, there are some further considerations that we should keep in mind.

For instance, if a person owns an oil-powered vehicle, isn't it better for them to keep it running rather than buying a vehicle that had to be manufactured new, even if it is a BEV? Surprisingly, the answer is no, because tail pipe emissions from ICEVs far exceed emissions from manufacturing or energy production, and BEVs don't produce tail pipe emissions.[9] The point at which BEVs make up for their high emissions from production varies across models of course, and obviously it wouldn't be ideal for consumers to keep replacing their BEVs before they made up for those high manufacturing emissions.

Therefore, this doesn't give the green light to Tesla, BYD, Nissan or anyone else to advertise the perilous logic of consuming more stuff to be more environmentally conscious. Opting for alternative transportation such as walking, cycling and public transport options are arguably much

---

5   Sawe 2018.
6   Hausfather 2019.
7   Topp 2019.
8   Ibid.
9   Hausfather 2019.

better ways to help mitigate climate change.[10] But I also understand that things like suburban sprawl and infectious diseases (you know which one I mean) would make people more inclined towards travelling in their own private cars. If more of them adopt a standard BEV, then based on the aforementioned analysis, we'd be doing a lot better for the planet than we are right now … but what if these people don't adopt a 'standard' BEV?

I've hardly seen this concept mentioned in the public discourse, and I can't claim to predict the future either, but first have a guess at what the two best-selling vehicles in Australia were in 2019. Ready? It was the Toyota Hilux and the Ford Ranger. How about 2018? The Toyota Hilux and the Ford Ranger. And in 2017? You guessed it, the Toyota Hilux and the Ford Ranger.

Ford Ranger. Michael Lotsaris.

If you keep looking down the list of the twenty bestselling vehicles in Australia,[11] you'll find a large percentage of them are utes and SUVs – about sixty-seven percent on average over the last three years for utes and SUVs combined. I wouldn't be surprised to see such big vehicles remain as bestsellers in battery-powered form, since oil-consumption efficiency would no longer be a purchasing consideration. If the rapid rise of American full-size pickup truck sales within Australia is anything to go by,[12] then perhaps the claim could be made that the most favoured BEVs of the future could be even bigger than what we're used to seeing on the streets right now. Unfortunately, manufacturing bigger cars with bigger batteries leaves a bigger emissions footprint.

10 Lobo 2015.
11 Top10Cars 2019.
12 Dowling 2020

I suppose it still beats a comparable behemoth drinking oil though, and at least an electric ute (as well as any BEV in general) would provide additional societal benefits such as much cleaner air for our cities, and reduced dependence on foreign oil-based energy (especially for Australia, which is a country that can power its own grid, yet holds minimal reserves in oil-based fuels).[13] However, if we depend on certain economies with a comparative advantage in manufacturing things like electric cars or renewable energy technologies,[14] then keeping power and transit running within our green energy 'utopia' could perhaps be vulnerable to supply restrictions.

There are also positive signs towards the future decarbonisation of the BEV industry and the recycling of goods such as batteries, which would further reduce the impact of passenger vehicles on climate change.[15] In fact, it may be worth reminding ourselves of how great this impact actually is, and thus how much ground we have to gain from turning it more green. Because you see, in Australia alone, transport was responsible for around 18.8 percent of total emissions in 2019 – transport includes road transport, domestic air transport, coastal shipping and rail transport.[16]

Direct greenhouse gas emissions from energy end use from road transport was estimated to make up about eighty-five percent of the national transport total in Australia during the 2018–19 financial year.[17] We can break this down even further into light commercial vehicles, trucks, buses, motorcycles and passenger cars, the latter of which was estimated to be responsible for roughly fifty-three percent of direct greenhouse gas emissions from energy end-use from road transport during the 2018–19 financial year.[18] These percentages closely mirror those of the immediate preceding financial years.

Therefore, we can infer that passenger cars made up less than half a fifth of Australia's total greenhouse gas emissions over the previous year – in other words, about 8.5 percent of Australia's total emissions. And since Australia makes up around 1.06 percent of global greenhouse gas emissions as of 2016 (excluding the enormous amount of coal that

---

13 See Whitehead 2019 and Coyne, McCormack and Crichton-Standish 2020.
14 International Renewable Energy Agency 2019.
15 Lambert 2019.
16 Department of Industry, Science, Energy, and Resources 2020.
17 Department of Industry, Science, Energy, and Resources 2020.
18 Department of Industry, Science, Energy, and Resources 2020.

we don't domestically use and instead export), tackling passenger cars in Australia is essentially tackling just 0.09 percent of the global problem.[19] Andorra, a European sovereign microstate barely larger than Canberra, has burnt more greenhouse gases per annum than that.[20]

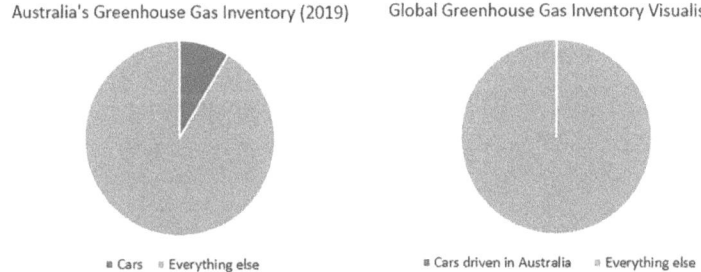

Australia's Greenhouse Gas Inventory (2019)   Global Greenhouse Gas Inventory Visualised

▪ Cars ▪ Everything else   ▪ Cars driven in Australia ▪ Everything else

Graphs based on statistics produced by Department of Industry, Science, Energy and Resources, and CAIT Country Greenhouse Gas Emissions Data (1990–2016).

That isn't to say that pursuing the electrification of passenger vehicles is hardly productive. Worldwide road transportation has been recorded as the source of up to 11.9 percent of global emissions in 2018, which would rank it third after China and the United States, and ahead of the entire European Union (by 2016 records) if road transportation were counted as a country.[21] Innovations from the BEV industry could assist improvements for other types of transportation, and perhaps the development of cleaner energy. There are also real benefits to be had for public health and national security from reducing oil consumption, however in Australia at least, it appears that there are much bigger targets to take down than pushing for the electrification of passenger vehicles.

Unfortunately, it seems that there is little Australia can do on its own to mitigate global climate change. Perhaps we could set a good example for the rest of the world and help facilitate a coalition of states that could grow large enough to mitigate the effects of global climate change collectively. But if people are going to seriously support adopting BEVs, then they should be even more serious towards mitigating other sources of greenhouse gas emissions, such as other forms of transportation,

19 CAIT Climate Data Explorer 2016.
20 CAIT Climate Data Explorer 2016.
21 Ge and Friedrich 2020.

agriculture and especially electricity from burning fossil fuels like coal and natural gas. The industries culpable for the latter sector in particular seem increasingly keen on supporting the electrification of road transportation,[22] so if you're someone that really cares about climate change and can't stand the fossil fuel industry, think about who would immediately benefit from increasing BEV usage in Australia.

So, where does this leave the lovely LandCruiser 70 Series? Well, it still occupies a unique position among vehicles for its old-school and rugged utilitarian design, and I can't think of any electric vehicle in production that could compete against its capabilities. Word on the street is that Toyota plans to have an electric or 'electrified' (i.e. probably a hybrid) version of every one of its vehicles on sale by 2025, and it seems that fleet buyer favourites like the Hilux ute and upcoming wagon-body LandCruiser 300 Series will be among those models.[23] Hopefully the 70 Series will stick around long enough for that too. Regardless, something the 70 Series can do that most electric vehicles cannot is dependably transport people across the natural wilderness, and it would be nice if more people came to appreciate the incredible value of our precious natural world. I hope that it will be preserved, along with the 70 Series, for one to do just that. With developments such as this,[24] perhaps it could be. Before Tesla unveiled the Cybertruck, Australia already had battery-powered cruisers – the 'Climate Truck'.

References

CAIT Climate Data Explorer. *Country greenhouse gas emissions*. World Resources Institute, 2016. http://cait.wri.org.

Campbell, M. "Toyota HiLux hybrid and Toyota Land Cruiser hybrid confirmed!" *CarsGuide*, 24 October 2019. https://www.carsguide.com.au/car-news/toyota-hilux-hybrid-and-toyota-land-cruiser-hybrid-confirmed-76644.

Coyne, J., McCormack, T., and Crichton-Standish, H. "In a crisis, Australians might soon be running on empty." *The Strategist*, 13 May 2020. https://www.aspistrategist.org.au/in-a-crisis-australians-might-soon-be-running-on-empty-2/.

---

22 Lovell 2020.
23 See Toyota Australia 2019 and Campbell 2019.
24 Vorrath 2018.

Department of Industry, Science, Energy, and Resources. *Quarterly update of Australia's National Greenhouse Gas Inventory: December 2019* Commonwealth of Australia, 2020. https://www.industry.gov.au/sites/default/files/2020-05/nggi-quarterly-update-dec-2019.pdf.

Dowling, J. "US pick-up sales in Australia surge in June 2020." *CarAdvice*, 3 July 2020. https://www.caradvice.com.au/862906/us-pick-up-sales-in-australia-surge-in-june-2020/.

Ge, M. and Friedrich, J. "4 Charts explain greenhouse gas emissions by countries and sectors." *World Resources Institute*, 6 February 2020. https://www.wri.org/blog/2020/02/greenhouse-gas-emissions-by-country-sector.

Hall, D., and Lutsey N. *Briefing: Effects of battery manufacturing on electric vehicle life-cycle greenhouse gas emissions.* The International Council on Clean Transportation, 2018. https://theicct.org/sites/default/files/publications/EV-life-cycle-GHG_ICCT-Briefing_09022018_vF.pdf.

Hausfather, Z. "Factcheck: how electric vehicles help to tackle climate change." *CarbonBrief, 13* May 2019. https://www.carbonbrief.org/factcheck-how-electric-vehicles-help-to-tackle-climate-change.

International Energy Agency. *Global EV Outlook 2019.* Paris, IEA, 2019. https://www.iea.org/reports/global-ev-outlook-2019.

International Renewable Energy Agency. *A new world: the geopolitics of the energy transformation.* Abu Dhabi, Global Commission on the Geopolitics of Energy Transformation (supported by IRENA), 2019. https://www.irena.org/-/media/Files/IRENA/Agency/Publication/2019/Jan/Global_commission_geopolitics_new_world_2019.pdf.

Katwala, A. "The spiralling environmental cost of our lithium battery addiction." *Wired*, 5 August 2018. https://www.wired.co.uk/article/lithium-batteries-environment-impact.

Lambert, F. "Tesla is developing a 'unique battery recycling system'." *Electrek*, 16 April 2019. https://electrek.co/2019/04/16/tesla-battery-recycling-system/.

Lobo, A. "The green illusions and false promises of the electric car (including Tesla)." *Better by Bicycle*, 4 January 2015. http://www.betterbybicycle.com/2015/01/the-green-illusions-and-false-promises.html.

Lovell, J. "EVs: are they really more efficient?" *Australian Energy Council*, 30 January 2020. https://www.energycouncil.com.au/analysis/evs-are-they-really-more-efficient/.

Sawe, B. E. "Coal usage by country." *WorldAtlas*, 5 November 2018. https://www.worldatlas.com/articles/15-countries-most-dependent-on-coal-for-energy.html.

Top10Cars. *Top10Cars*. 2019. https://www.top10cars.com.au/.

Topp, K. "Are electric cars greener? Let's crunch the numbers." The University of Melbourne, 2019. https://blogs.unimelb.edu.au/sciencecommunication/2019/10/27/are-electric-cars-greener-lets-crunch-the-numbers/.

Toyota Australia. *Toyota sustainability report 2019*. Toyota Motor Corporation Australia, 2019. https://www.toyota.com.au/-/media/toyota/main-site/page-data/sustainability/files/reports-2019/tmca_sustainability_report-2019.pdf.

Vorrath, S. "EVs go underground, as BHP beats Tesla to the electric ute." *Renew Economy*, 28 June 2018. https://reneweconomy.com.au/evs-go-underground-as-bhp-beats-tesla-to-the-electric-ute-34832/.

West, K. "Carmakers' electric dreams depend on supplies of rare minerals." *The Guardian*, 30 July 2017. https://www.theguardian.com/environment/2017/jul/29/electric-cars-battery-manufacturing-cobalt-mining.

Whitehead, J. "Clean, green machines: the truth about electric vehicle emissions." *The Conversation*, 5 September 2019. https://theconversation.com/clean-green-machines-the-truth-about-electric-vehicle-emissions-122619.

TRASHED

Belinda Paxton

It is early in the morning when Tegan wakes to catch her flight, but Jules is already awake beside her, staring at the dark ceiling, her arms folded behind her head. Tegan reaches out to touch her and Jules stays within her private thoughts for a moment before turning to her and asking the question one more time. The only question to ever exist between them. When Tegan says that she still hasn't decided, Jules assumes it is the job stopping her.

'You don't have to give everything to the dammed Party,' Jules says. Tegan can see her tears glimmering before Jules turns away. 'You don't have to give it us.'

* * *

The town of Anala has a club catering for every conceivable interest group. There is the Hyacinth Growers Group, the Anala Pensioners Association, the Huck Hotel Darters (where Mathew's grandfather goes every Wednesday evening to throw darts) and the pensioners sporting group, 'Better at Sixty'. There is a club for clubs – the Anala Clubs Association – with a knighted patron. Even the town's name derives from the Anala Marching Girls Club, itself named after Anala Huck who started the first marching girls group and was the wife of one of the town's founding fathers.

Mathew is in the Bosscrete Rugby League Football Club, Junior Division. But right now he is standing by himself in the top left-hand corner of a school oval, holding a water bottle. On the oval, a group of thunderous men heave and grunt and clamber over each other while trying to hold onto a ball. They are wearing school uniforms, boys clothes, that stretch at the seams and threaten to split as they heft and slam each other against the hard earth: pale blue poly-cotton shirts, grey stubby shorts, long socks bunched at the ankle and man-size school shoes made of black vinyl. The shoes have hollow heels that amplify the thud of their weight against the earth.

Their male dignity is compromised by the small uniforms. But this minor humiliation is overwhelmed by the beauty of their massive thighs, muscled like bullock haunches and buttressed by the femur, which gives them the momentum they need to hurtle their mass at each other. The men gather enough velocity to crack ankles, ribs, craniums, although maybe not the femur itself. It's hard to imagine the femur being broken, except by metal or some piece of machinery.

Mathew lifts the drink bottle and pours a glacial stream onto his face. The water drains in rivulets down his neck and onto his shirt. In the distance, there is the faint rumble of a breeze travelling through Anala's main street towards Mathew, growing in force as it approaches, from a rumble to a dull roar. The sky is bruised with clouds. Mathew tilts his face to it and waits.

* * *

No one lived in Anala before the soldiers arrived. It's the only place this far south of Brisbane which floods when the Brisbane River breaks its banks. Even the Jagara, who had custody of this area before white settlement, only ever used it as a stop-off point. But the soldiers were desperate. Returning home after years of war and privation, they had found the country gripped by a housing shortage. They had nowhere to live.

With their thoughts on each other's suffering, they put their shoulders to the wheel. They formed a cooperative and bought this plateau between two indents branching from the Brisbane River. They walked over it, put their glasses on to see it and stooped to touch it with their fingers. The soil was so rich in iron it left rust-coloured tracks in the cracks of their palms. They sent word out all over the country for help to build.

Far away in South Australia, a company heeded the call. It had a new line in prefab housing made with a miracle building product: fibrous concrete. You do the design in the workshop and then set it up on-site. Low labour input, low burn risk. High speed.

The war is over and it's time to get your skates on. Build this damn country from the ground up. The builders flung up houses like toy blocks, leaving behind row upon row of pastel fibro boxes. Blue, yellow, pink and green. Children's colours for a town newly scraped into the brick-red earth. The soldiers intended the township only for each other. Many of them were sleepless and visited by winged terrors. They needed somewhere to help each other heal.

Nowadays, almost all the fibro houses have been extended to least three bedrooms. Mathew has been told, as if it's something to be proud of, that his father helped make Anala's small houses bigger. That was many years ago, when builders didn't know much about mesothelioma. Mathew, of course, would prefer small houses and a father who was still alive.

He's more or less alone in that. Everyone wants a huge house these days. A swathe of construction is encroaching upon Anala from the west, four-bedders mostly, since they fetch the best prices. Only a thin strip of brush remains as a reminder that the town was once a satellite. Dotted with plastic nappies and beer bottles, burnt-out car bodies and the curled husks of water tanks, there is, within the brush, a smear of earth slashed bare and enclosed by cyclone wire fencing. Strings of barbed wire loop and dangle at the fencing's upper edge.

A hire car has parked at the gate of this wired fence, and a woman in her early thirties is standing with her hip cocked against the driver's-side door. She wears a white shirt and a navy skirt-suit over thick pale stockings and lace-up shoes. It's the same no-nonsense get-up worn by the nuns who ran the Home for Wayward Girls when Anala was just built. Except this woman has an easy stance, bobbed straw-yellow hair, freckles, a gap between her front teeth and green eyes that make direct, uncomplicated contact. Looking closely, you can see that her suit is well cut and made of fine, new wool; way outside the budget of a nun. The Home for Wayward Girls closed four decades ago. This is Tegan, who woke to sadness this morning and flew up from Sydney.

Working for the Party is a new thing for Tegan. Leif plucked her out of primary school teaching where she'd gained a profile in her local community through her work lobbying for literacy funding. But the real reason she was chosen, Tegan knows, is because she knows how to play a game. Any game. She excelled at netball, soccer, volleyball and – more than anything else – hockey, with its speed and its danger. Leif's electorate loves winners and he never tires of telling them he has an Olympic medallist on his staff.

Now, in the middle of winter, Tegan misses hockey like a first love. Cold nights remind her of the mist rising off a hockey field, overhead lights catching it as water particles curl off the ground and waft in the chill air. In her mind, Tegan is with the girls again and braced on the field, still as ice, right foot forward and waiting for the whistle. She catches the captain's eye and can't help but grin. And when the whistle blows, there's an upsurge of adrenaline in her solar plexus and it stings along each fibre in her muscles to tell her that a rare force is here tonight. It has taken up the atoms of her body and propels her forward with thrilling precision. God, how she loved the game.

It was all ruined with a single swipe of a hockey stick. She looked down at her own knee and saw the blade reveal, like the sun slipping beneath the horizon, a pink gleaming arc. Her bone beneath her skin. Now she fits hockey in around her work and aches in private for her sporting career. Some moments in this new job come close to that rush, but that won't happen today. Not when it started so early and so badly.

Here comes the site supervisor in his high-vis vest, clipboard flapping against his thigh as he hurries to open the gate. Tegan shields her eyes and gazes at something across the clearing. The supervisor unlocks the padlock and the chain falls, clinking against the wire. He and Tegan cross the slashed earth together.

* * *

You could set a level on Anala's plateau. The town's only hill has been brought in from somewhere else and piled into a heap at the far side of the fenced-off clearing that once held the satellite. Necks cricked back, Tegan and the site supervisor stand before it, a mountain of waste maybe two stories high, made of cardboard and PVC pipes, plasterboard and polystyrene, runny paper and plastic drink bottles, sprinkled over with multi-coloured bottle top lids. Ribbons of white sheeting weave through the pile like chewing gum.

'The challenge is finding fresh places to bury it,' the site supervisor says. 'It's seventy, eighty percent plastic, so it doesn't go away.'

Tegan looks at the ground, but the pile of waste is imprinted in her mind. The supervisor offers to take her out to the quarry where they bury it, but Tegan has seen enough.

'Get some tarpaulins over the fence,' she says, 'and don't let anyone in. The media won't tell you who they are. I'll phone the minister now.'

Yesterday another phone call was made to the minster. That one was conducted quietly and in secret, its message for Leif's staff only. The story leaked ahead of time, though:

Recyclable waste from New South Wales is transported interstate and turned to landfill in Queensland.

Walking back to her car, Tegan feels the waste behind her. She imagines it spreading like a melting confection. She is unsettled, feverish. She thinks of the other meaning of waste. Relationships undervalued, people cast off, the most tender human aspirations thwarted. What, she wonders, is stopping her from giving Jules what she wants? She stumbles over the rutted mud and feels the supervisor's eyes on her back. She doesn't want to appear fallible in front of the Queenslander. She pushes her shoulders back and wills her spine upright. This trip is just a simple matter – easy enough for a newbie. She's fact-checking the leaked story. She won't let Leif down. But there, in her throat, is the jag of this morning's unhappiness. Other lives are swimming in the blue air around her, drifting just out of reach. Someone is calling to her. A child. She wonders if she is too late.

Sliding into the driver's seat, Tegan comes back to herself a little. She inspects her phone. Reception is poor here, but there's plenty of time before her flight back to Sydney. She'll drive into the town and have a look at the afternoon news feeds. She can phone Leif from there.

A rain-flecked breeze crests over the mountain of waste. It pools in the clearing, reaching through Tegan's window to fumble her hair as she drives away. Then it sifts its way through the brush, over the shining roofs of Anala's outer edges, and along the town's main street to where Mathew stands on the school oval, his face pointed to the sky, waiting to receive it. It pushes its cold needles into his hair, mixes fragments of polymer with his breath, wafts styrene compounds over his tongue. Mouthing the strange wet air, Mathew thinks, *The rain is coming in again.* At the sound of the bell, he throws his water bottle into his backpack, waves goodbye to his mates. There's training tonight anyway, and he can run around then.

* * *

Minds are like bones. Prone to breaking. Nightmares stop Mathew's grandfather from sleeping. His hands tremble touching the plants. He grows cubed viburnum alongside the front fence and hydrangeas trimmed to rectangles in front of the warped verandah. The path to the front steps is painted charcoal grey; its colour revealing stray blades of grass that need to be swept. On either side of the front path, there are camellias.

His grandfather has cuttings growing in plastic tubes that he inspects more than necessary, parting the leaves softly with his fingertips to see the new growth. He's quite aware it's a feminine thing. Crouched with his back curved over the tubes and his fingers among the pale shoots, he looks like a girl in a rice paddy. He keeps the cuttings in his private backyard.

Mathew's grandfather has only allowed himself to touch one other thing that tenderly. Taking Mathew from his daughter's arms as she stood newly widowed and tearful on his front step, he cupped the child with both hands, as one might cup a handful of water. Mathew was as beautiful and as simple as that. He looked away from his bereft daughter and from his own wretched past to the new thing, the now thing, the only thing that mattered. Here is something he and his daughter could get right.

The backyard has trimmed couch grass and is kept clear of leaves and blemishes. There is a Hills Hoist with a faded plastic basket of pegs hooked over the wire. In one corner there's a mandarin tree, in the other, a lemon tree, and between them both, the jackfruit tree stands centre stage against the blackened back fence with a heap of grass cuttings browning at its base. The massive, lumpish fruit grows straight out of the trunk.

His grandfather takes special care of the jackfruit. It's hard to get in Anala. Since there's so much they don't understand about him, Mathew and his mother allow him this peccadillo. But they don't like the strange, foreign smell. He's not allowed to bring the fruit inside. Mathew's grandfather takes a ripe fruit and his pocketknife and cuts the fruit up on the back step. With the pod split open, the scent clouds his face with memories of those early days in Vietnam when they'd landed and not yet seen service. After all, his world has not always been underpinned by horror. The other memories will return. But for now, in a bowl with ice cream, the jackfruit is lovely enough to bring tears to his eyes.

Well-loved young people have a particular knack for disgust. On his way to training, and with his gear bag over his shoulder, Mathew steps carefully around his grandfather on the back step, frowning. He considers jackfruit to be the pinnacle of gross things and doesn't want to upset the bowl of orange goop. Once he would have groaned aloud and complained about the smell. But lately Mathew has acquired a secret, something that will sadden the old man, harrowed as he is by war. The new distance between them makes Mathew wistful, and singing out, 'Bye Grandad,' he almost wishes his grandfather would plead with him to stay.

* * *

One Saturday morning a few months ago, Jules came to the little wooden breakfast table where Tegan sat reading the weekend papers in the sun. She had an armful of leaflets and printouts from the net which she lowered carefully into the prism of light falling onto the table. Straightening her spine, she smiled uncertainly at Tegan and began to talk. As Tegan watched Jules, her words spilling out, she felt that all her time with Jules, and all the time she had spent growing up, and the things she had learnt from her friends, and the moments taking a pass in hockey or scoring a goal … All of these things were leading to this: a baby. It was no surprise.

They made love. And sitting up afterwards on the bed, she and Jules talked about their unborn child and how they would treat it and touch it and help it to learn. Jules' skin is almost the same colour as her hair. She's like a matching set. All gradations of the one colour, like a spoonful of honey or a sun-warmed cliff-face. Brown as Jules is, the curves of her that meet the sun are flecked with tiny irregular patches that are darker still, and her thighs, resting against Tegan's own serviceable pegs, are covered with freckles and fine arcs of hair that spring and catch the light.

The underside of Jules' throat and her stomach and breasts are paler than the rest of her body, like the shoot within the grass, and when she leans forward, the skin stretches across her ribs, becoming paler still, and most beautiful of all to Tegan is Jules' mouth, with the bow-curved lips that merge with the depths inside her. Tegan said that she loved Jules and she already loved the child they might have, but she needed time to think before she could decide. Jules' eyes are green like Tegan's, with shade-dark currents beneath the surface which embody her thoughts.

Try as she might, Tegan can never quite work out what Jules is thinking.

* * *

The Bosscrete Rugby League Club, Junior Division, trains on Huck Oval. They have a coach whose name is Ray, but the team calls him Tess, as in Don't-Stress-Tess, and he runs up and down the sidelines while they train or play, crouched in apprehension, screaming at the boys and clutching his hair, which was once red, now pink and greying and sprouting from his head, ears, nose and shoulders like electrical wires. Mathew thinks of the coach as a little crazed crab. He stresses at training. He's worse in the away games and he can be frightening at home games where he is under pressure by the attendance of almost everyone in Anala. But who could care more for the boys and the game? The boys call him Tess to his face and would never admit that they love him.

The coach is big on pummelling the opposition; not so big on strategy. Occasionally he herds the boys into Huck Hall, which fronts onto Huck Oval, and they file up the wooden ramp and flop into the plastic chairs, cross their arms over their chests and brace themselves for the impending stream of abuse. While the coach bellows and sweats and scrawls game plans on the whiteboard, Mathew angles his face to the wall and makes a subtle inspection of the Anala Marching Girls whose club photos line the walls of the hall in order of year: 1952 to 1984.

In the photos the girls smile, and their hair is tied back in ponytails or curled at the nape of the neck in immaculate sets. All of them burst with health, the way peaches swell with their own juice. Their faces are gleaming white and tilted to the sky. Chins point the way forward and their powerful thighs emerge luminous from the shadows under their skirts. In some pictures, the marching girls are pictured before crowds of mainly men. Brothers, boyfriends, fathers. They are waving their hats the way women waved their hankies at the ships transporting their men to foreign shores. The men's smiles are tearful and constrained. They're all choked up. When one says to the others in his tear-thickened voice, 'Pretty girls', the others nod gruffly because there are no words to explain. Any one of them would put their bodies between the marching girls and oncoming danger.

Mathew is partly distracted by Tess' tirade and compared to the men in the crowd, his motivations for gazing at the girls are simple. He just wants to know what they're thinking. In particular, he wants to know what they're thinking about those short skirts. Does the fabric rasp against their soft skin? Do they find the skirts constricting? Do they wish they could have done away with the skirts altogether and let those peachy thighs move freely? And despite the more intense colours and shorter skirts of the later photos, Mathew doesn't pay as much attention to these, containing, as they do, some uncomfortably familiar faces. Could that creamy girl up the front in 1981 really be calcifying Mrs Pryor who runs the newsagency and calls him 'kiddo'?

Anyway, the photos are not enough to divert Mathew from the oval, which is calling to him through the walls of Huck Hall to come and lope across it in the twilight with the rest of the team. When the coach has finally exhausted himself, the liberated men exit the hall and radiate over the field like gulls taking to the sky. Their voices drift slowly across to each other, condensed by the cold air. The toes of their boots slam against the ball and the lights encircling the field show Mathew's shadow slowly revolving around him as he runs, like the hands of a watch around a centrepin.

* * *

In Anala's main street, Tegan finds an old-fashioned kind of coffee shop that sells milkshakes and dim sims. The tiles are rust-coloured like the ground outside. At a white laminate table, Tegan sips coffee that tastes like heated river water and pulls out her laptop. She wants to see if anything has come up on the news, and sure enough, there is an early teaser foreshadowing tonight's main story. First, there is a photograph of the site supervisor with an early morning sheen on his face. He'd already spoken to the media before she got there, she realises, and winces as she recalls her earnest warnings about the cunning media.

The site supervisor is saying that the waste arrangement was an open secret. Departmental operatives from both Queensland and New South Wales knew. Leif's office knew too, says the supervisor, because they've been contacting him.

But that can't be true. Leif was sending her to check the story's veracity. If he already knew, why is she here? The reason is a few lines further down the page, in Leif's direct quote:

We've been aware of the problem for some time and are already taking steps to rectify it. I've been in touch with the Queensland waste companies and I have someone up there now engaged in talks with the agencies involved.

Tegan's skin prickles with shame. She slumps a little as the words sink in, each an accusation. Newbie. Idealist. Mug. Of course, they all knew about the waste rot and wouldn't tell her. Keeping her in the dark is a precaution against uncooperative behaviour, but she's served enough time with tight groups of people to understand its larger purpose. Her participation implicates her. Leif and his staff have ushered her into the circle of duplicity so that, mixed with her humiliation, she feels a warm glow of belonging. Now she's one of them.

The thought briefly crosses her mind, foreign to her because underhand, she could speak to someone and expose Leif's lie. She already has a few media contacts. But even as the thought arises, Tegan knows she won't follow it through. She didn't excel at hockey by putting herself before the team. Then, as now, the game will always come first.

By the time she leaves the coffee shop, the rain has slowed to a drizzle and the day has dwindled to a thin sweat-stain on the horizon. Cars hiss as they pass her, and as she climbs into the driver's seat of her rental car, she finds that her limbs are aching and weary. She's also later for her flight than she thought. Disrupted water flicks under her wheels as she picks up speed. Glancing down at her phone on the passenger seat, she thinks about ringing Leif to tell him what she's doing, but she's not in the mood. When she looks up, traffic lights leer at her suddenly through the rain-hazed air. Orange is the colour of the earth around here, and only a warning colour. She barely slows down.

* * *

Returning home from training, Mathew waits at the traffic lights in Anala's main street with the soft rain beading on his face. Across the road is a small gap in the row of shops and a square of mown grass that makes do as a park. In the centre of the square of grass, and enclosed by painted railings, is a black obelisk. It is engraved with names of the dead and strains upwards with such intent that, with the sky so low and glowering tonight, it could prick the rainclouds.

Here in this park, in the early hours of Anzac Day this year, Mathew stood with his schoolmates, all of them arranged in lines and dressed in full school uniform, even though it was a Saturday. The mayor was absent, being called to the larger voting catchment of Redland. But the deputy mayor of Redland Shire stood on the podium before a sizable crowd, looking pained and scraping his thumb across his eye socket as if removing tears. Beside him, a very old man with trembling hands read a poem.

Mathew had no interest in either the deputy mayor or the very old man, but his heart swelled without warning when the bugle sent its pristine notes out into the new morning. Like the sun emerging from clouds, months of confusion and vague yearnings inside him suddenly coalesced into a single understanding. He realised what he wants to do when he leaves school.

With joy, he turned to search the crowd for his grandfather, before remembering that he does not attend the Anzac Day ceremony. And perhaps, Mathew realised, he wouldn't be pleased to learn that Mathew had decided to become a soldier.

Now at the traffic lights, with the obelisk before him, Mathew puts aside the prospect of disappointing his grandfather and allows his heart to swell anew at the thought of helping our boys in Afghanistan. The traffic light flushes his cheeks orange, as if he is lit from within by his noble urges. This heat, perhaps, is the reason he steps onto the road before the light has changed.

* * *

A cacophony of car horns and flashing lights. Something screaming. The car alarm. Blinking indicator lights. Flashing orange. Standing just in front of the car is the last thing Tegan would ever want to hurt: a child. Or is he a man? A bit of both. You can almost see the line in him where the past and the future meet.

Veering at the last second, Tegan has managed to crumple the car's left passenger side against a traffic pole instead. Elite athlete reflexes. Looking down at her body in the driver's seat, Tegan sees no injuries. She feels nothing that hurts either, just her heart surging against her ribs, a pounding inside her skull which is her blood pulsing. Seared by adrenaline, she slams the car door behind her and strides towards Mathew. He's still alive, but she's going to kill him. Her mouth is a rigid rectangle, and ready to shout. Her tongue is curled and ready to tear strips. Then she sees his expression. Surprise.

He's looking at her crumpled car with the baffled air of a bystander who has no idea of his narrow escape. Sixteen or so years has not provided him with enough near misses for him to recognise one, even if it's right in front of his face. Tegan's anger falls away and is replaced instead with so much relief that she could cry. Both she and the boy are lucky he's still alive.

For a second, the car alarm stops blaring, and in the lull, Tegan hears the water rushing around her and the wind raking across the wet asphalt. Standing before Mathew, she understands two things: one, she must leave her job. It will be easily done. She can go back to teaching. Two, Jules has got it wrong. Tegan did not give everything to this job. She could not, for instance, bring herself to give it the most important thing, the only thing more precious to her than her relationship with Jules.

Unseen behind Mathew and Tegan, pieces of plastic are sluiced into the gutter by a stream of water rushing towards the drain. They are fragments of mirrored headlight moulding. In the crystalline water, they twist and turn and disrupt the light, the same way time is also disrupted and twisted back upon us. In the glinting shards, you might be reminded of the bones that gleam beneath the skin, or the tears in an old man's eyes. Or you might even be reminded of the grinding turn of civilisations folding upon themselves, their human detritus, the way waste is folded into a compactor.

Undervalued, but never leaving us and never letting us forget.

WANDERING

Wil Haviland

'Hope' is the thing with feathers –
That perches in the soul –
And sings the tune without the words –
And never stops – at all …

Emily Dickinson

I hear them before I see them: a sharp, shimmering kind of sound. As I climb the hill onto the sporting field, the flock comes into view. An ochre afternoon sun is sinking into the horizon; it is the witching hour for galahs. The galahs seem transmogrified by daytime's dying light into a band of Oberon's fairies, set loose to wreak merry havoc upon the human world. As I get closer, jogging now, little rose-feathered heads begin to turn, revealing eyes, red and ebony. What had been an atmospheric chirruping takes on a new urgency. A sentry calls out a warning. Pink crests start to flare in alarm. I keep running – closer – too close – the flock bursts into a maelstrom of flashing silver wings and desperate screeching. They are becalmed as suddenly as they erupted, as if their outburst was all for show – Saturnalian bravado. They move a couple of metres over, and return to enthusiastically ripping up the grass.

Charles Darwin once theorised that the experience of being tickled is only a pleasurable one if the mind of the ticklee (not his word) is primed for a positive experience. 'A young child,' he writes, 'if tickled by a strange man, would scream from fear.' This perspicacious observation from history's greatest biologist is worth considering in light of the COVID-19 lockdown. For my part, I had always wanted to spend more time at home, which the lockdown certainly facilitated, even if the experience has been overshadowed by the looming threat of total societal meltdown. Before the lockdown, I lived, like many of us did, two separate lives. There was my home life, amongst the trees and rivers and bushfires. And there was my work life, which I lived mostly in bike-lanes and breakout rooms. When one of those lives was put in stasis by the lockdown, the extent of my personal universe was suddenly limited to the town I live in, at the foot of the Blue Mountains. It is hardly surprising that I have started paying more attention to the other creatures with whom I share this particular microcosm.

I was always interested in birds, but they were something that existed in the intervening spaces of my life. Back when I lived in the city, I would wake up before sunrise a couple of times each week and head into Centennial Park before work to spend a cold, dark, joyful hour or two looking for resident birdlife. I didn't care what I found; everything delighted me. My favourite, since you asked, was the family of powerful owls who lived in a gigantic fig tree near the ring-road. To get an idea of just how impressive a powerful owl is, picture a koala; now picture a bird large enough to eat it. I've since moved 'up the hill' (as a gnomic taxi driver put it late one night), and the window above my desk looks out onto a paddock haphazardly studded with paperbarks, banksias and lemon myrtle. During working hours my attention is split between my computer monitor and the parrots – climbing and stretching; hanging upside down; squawking and straining for the most tender shoots – in the trees outside my window. If I stand up from my desk too quickly, the universe stops. Frozen, the birds outside stare at me from a cubist collage of bough, branch and wing – a flattened tableau where I'm looking in and a dozen eyes – icy glass domes, shiny black, red-ringed and violet – stare back out. If my reach were long enough I could trace one of their outlines with a scalpel and cut it free from the background, to leave behind a parrot-shaped portal into the universe.

Running lap after lap around the oval, I eventually negotiate a compromise with the galahs; they get the inner five lanes, and I get the outer lane. I remember hearing somewhere that galahs mate for life, which in the wild means an existence of something like forty years. It occurs to me that some of these birds have been with their mates for longer than I have been alive. I try to pick out the couples, but apart from the colour of their eyes, male and female galahs look almost identical. One galah, perhaps bored of eating, or exasperated at seeing an apparently defective human running around in circles, decides to play a game with me. It checks my approach, then when I get to about seven or eight metres away, with one smooth action it flips onto its back, sticks its legs up in the air, and cocks a wing out. There it stays, frozen, until I pass, when it pops back onto its feet and returns to eating.

No matter how much I might be missing my colleagues in isolation, I'm sure that even under the most trying circumstances, none of them ever managed to play dead as convincingly as that galah. In Australian vernacular, to be a 'galah' means to be a fool: 'you've made a proper galah of yourself'; or crazy: 'mad as a gumtree full of galahs'. But parrots (a group which includes galahs) are even smarter than ravens and crows, and can match primates and dolphins in intelligence. Some cockatoos have proven more adept at spatial reasoning than children up to the age of about four – think of that carnival game where a ball is hidden under a cup. Studies on corvids have shown that some species are better than children up to the age of eight at using tools and have better developed causal reasoning skills.

Was it my own anthropocentric bias, or was that cheeky galah actually playing a game with me? It turns out that many birds have been observed engaging in play, just like humans do. In her 2015 book *Bird minds: cognition and behaviour of Australian native birds*, the neuroscience and animal behaviour expert Professor Gisela Kaplan discusses play at length. Kaplan says that scientists had traditionally assumed that the sole purpose of play in animals was to develop skills which would be useful later in life. But recent studies have shown that some animals do experience pleasure from play – that is, they *have fun* playing. Research on birds specifically is lacking, but we do know that birds have the 'essential ingredients' in their brains necessary for experiencing pleasure. The Australian galah, it turns out, is one of only twenty-three bird species which have been seen engaging in all three types of play (solitary, object and social), and one of only a handful of species which continue playing into adulthood. Scientists now think that play behaviour is related to cognitive ability, lifespan and whether a bird has complex social relationships. I wonder if there is a galah equivalent to irony?

Somewhere down and to my right lies the Kedumba Valley. You wouldn't guess it from the view, but civilisation is only a couple of hundred metres up the hill. The trail I'm on is usually popular, but this afternoon, it's deserted. The atmosphere is pregnant with humidity. My shirt clings to my back, soaked through with steam and sweat. The forest seems to have decided that the narrow trail I have been following marks the division between trees and oblivion. I relish the rhythmic crunching of my gait as I press my boots harder into the compacted dirt and rock of the trail, trying to counterbalance the looming emptiness I feel on one side, like a vacuum, trying to suck me over the edge and out into the valley. My water is all gone, and I am supposed to be heading back, but I can't help pressing on – just a little farther – because I thought I heard a lyrebird somewhere up ahead. A soft misty rain has just begun to fall, and I feel the spell of the turgid afternoon humidity beginning to lift. I find a gully broken through the bush, so I scramble up its mossy slope into the dim of the forest.

It seems certain now that this is what will get me through the lockdown: to walk among the ancient eucalypts; to *wander lonely as a cloud*; to be mocked by kookaburras and to feel the cold morning air on my skin. But I feel another, more painful irony in this: humanity's abuse of nature is what got us into this mess. Yet here I am, rollicking around the bush trying to pretend that I'm not living an unofficial remake of Douglas Adams' 1989 classic *Last chance to see*. Even the very designation of 'natural' as something discrete from the world of humans is an absurdity that ignores the symbiotic relationship between humans and the other living things which we rely on so desperately for food, clothing and scientific research – not to mention companionship. It ignores the fact that we are all part of the same gigantic system; a system which at the present time is severely out of balance. The legendary primatologist Jane Goodall recently spoke at an online conference organised by some members of the European Parliament. She spoke about our reliance on animals for food, the climate crisis, the looming threat of zoonotic diseases (like SARS-COV-2) and antibiotic resistant superbugs. 'If we do not do things differently,' Goodall said, 'we are finished.' Surely the lockdown has shown us that despite our chronic vacillation, we are capable, as a society, of massive, proactive change. Even when the lockdown restrictions ease, maybe we don't have to go back to how we were before. We could just leave those other lives, or at least the parts we don't like, in stasis.

I hear it again, tantalisingly close – then I see him, nestled comfortably amongst the dead sticks and leaves of the forest floor. Tender green saplings rise up around him, given false magnitude by the recumbent bird. He gives me a look, but is unperturbed; perhaps he is glad to have an audience? He sets out *adagio*; a master of his craft in complete control. I hear a magpie's melodious whistle, cut up and interspersed with the lyrebird's own electronic riffing. For counterpoint, he hisses out a bowerbird's ugly cry, before launching into a medley of calls almost too fast for me to follow. I hear a sulphur-crested cockatoo, then the sound of a beak snapping at something in the air, then the ephemeral fluting of a grey shrike-thrush. He cuts off the eerie, paleolithic scream of a yellow-tailed black cockatoo halfway through: a demonstration of his dexterity. The rufous patch of feathers over his throat begins to swell as from deep within he calls forth the crescendo of a kookaburra's laugh. He pauses for a moment, to look at me – are you impressed yet? But there is more in his repertoire; he emits the deafening crack of a male whip bird, followed immediately by the two-note response of the female. He whistles like a currawong, before leaping to his feet for the finale. He throws his tail forward so that it covers his body like a shawl. Now he sings the song only lyrebirds can sing; that unmistakable electric chirrup bursts out from between waves of static, as if the sound needs to be decoded from an elusive radio frequency. His silvery feathers shimmer in the dappled light of the forest as he pulses back and forth to the rhythm of his own song. And then it is over. The trance broken, he looks around, impassive, then walks away, into the forest.

WHEN THE BIRDS CAME BACK

Seth Robinson

The magpie's chortle bounced off metal and concrete, the reverberations adding to its voice, so by the time it reached me on the balcony it sounded as if there was a whole chorus of them. A moment later an answer came from another direction, another bird, and the song reached its crescendo. I leaned forward, peering over the balcony hoping to spot one, but they were gone, back into the mix of the wild city.

It didn't feel like it had been that long – maybe five years from when it all started to now – but somehow that was long enough for it to all start … what? Crumbling? Decaying?

Reverting.

Yeah, that was right, reverting. It was all going back to the way it had been before all of us. Slowly, but surely.

The sun was rising behind me, but to the south and the west the city was in full view. I watched as it turned from black, to grey, to tangerine gold. It rained last night, so the glass and concrete towers that had once housed apartments and office blocks glistened with a slick sparkle that emphasised the places where they were breaking down. Beams of light refracted off glass panels, ultraviolet highlighter streaks that ended where the façade had collapsed, revealing gaping spaces, exposed concrete and rebar. We'd been told these buildings would last for generations, but after half a decade without proper maintenance, the majority of them were showing signs of disrepair, as if the Earth were reclaiming the ingredients it had given: concrete, steel and glass. Walking the streets meant weaving your way through a maze of abandoned cars and fallen rubble. Grass and weeds had forced their way through the cracked pavement; in some places they grew so thick and fast that you needed a machete to cut through.

It was beautiful, in its own terrible kind of way. It had taken me a long time to recognise the cyclical nature of it all and learn to appreciate the beauty. I'd spent a lot of time fearing what was happening, but that had dissipated. Little by little, day by day, the wild seeped in through your pores, just like the small pieces of grass that pushed through the cracks in the concrete. You learnt to live in a new way. For the last six months, it had felt like our last hurrah, we knew it was time to go. We spent the time exploring parts of our city that had changed forever.

I shoved my hand into my jacket pocket and pulled out the scrap of cloth. It was smooth and shiny in places where it had been well handled. I'd read it hundreds of times and memorised the marker scribbles that hacked their own course across the blue and white stripes; directions and an address. It was our 'pocket map', with details passed on by a friend of a friend, Ngaere, who knew people out there. I'd torn the pocket off my shirt when we'd met them down by the river because we hadn't had any paper.

It was this makeshift parchment – and the promise of the next chapter – that had convinced all of us it was time to move on.

'Jake?'

'Yeah?'

I turned and saw Krista had come out onto the terrace. It was early, before the humidity and the heat really set in, so she wore a jacket with the paisley face mask she'd sewn herself. She and Hamish had sewn all of our masks, and while none of us were really sure if we needed them anymore, we still wore them, out of habit as much as anything. Mine was tartan, like a picnic blanket.

'What are you doing?'

'Just letting myself get a little nostalgic I guess. That's what today is all about, right?'

She nodded.

'I think we're ready. Ravi's itching to go.'

'Alright, no worries.' I tipped back the dregs of the coffee in my tin cup – the last of the instant we'd managed to scavenge and stockpile, so maybe the final coffee ever – then hazarded one last glance up at the city. It was bittersweet, I couldn't look at it without feeling a little sad, remembering what it had been once. It was still my hometown, even now. This was probably the last time we'd be here.

Ravi was working as the building manager when everything started changing. The building had cleared out quickly as people started leaving the city and he'd found himself in possession of a set of master keys to an abandoned, high-end apartment block. What had started with an 'End of the World' party – jamming something like a hundred people into the penthouse – had turned into the four of us living there for the last three years. It had a rooftop terrace on the eighth floor, plenty of space and half a dozen locked doors between us and the street. The terrace had become our first farm, a home for our planter boxes, water tank and compost bin. It was the place where we learnt about the seasons, using the movement of the sun through the sky to dictate the food we grew. We paid attention to the subtle changes in nature, not just those dictated by the European calendar. We had just enough for what we needed.

Even when the power went out and we had to start climbing all those stairs, the pros seemed to outweigh the cons. So, we'd stayed longer than any of us had planned. Maybe, we thought, longer than anyone. We'd heard the last helicopters pass over a couple of months ago, the last of the trucks another month or so before that. Now, we were pretty sure it was just us.

Inside, Ravi and Hamish were both wearing their football jerseys, Carlton and Hawthorn respectively. Hamish's had been torn up the side, but he'd used his new-found sewing skills and made a half decent repair. I was pretty sure Krista had been a Richmond supporter growing up, and me, well, I'd always been aware of football in the background of Melbourne life, but I'd never been a diehard. My grandfather had been a Blues fan, so I'd watched some of their games and bonded with Ravi over that, but neither Krista nor I had jerseys. In a way, it made me feel underprepared for the day's expedition, like I should've been in uniform too.

'Okay, has everyone said their goodbyes?' Ravi asked. 'Ready for the last hurrah?'

'Yup.' Hamish already had his pack and his mask on and was waiting by the door.

'How about you, fearless leader?'

I swallowed hard, knowing that last question was addressed to me and knowing it was only half a joke. Ravi was the linchpin that held this little group together, but it had been my idea to go. I'd talked myself – and then the rest of them – into it with a patchwork argument of speculation, literary theory and philosophy: all the things I'd spent my undergrad studying that had no practical place in the new world.

When the pocket map had come along, it had been an affirmation. There were people out there who'd found a better way of living, communities where they'd found a way to live with the land instead of taking from it.

It wasn't a way any of us had ever lived before; we'd all grown up as city slickers, and we'd changed with the city, finding ways to get by, scavenging and trading. But with no-one else left, and the city stripped bare, the call of fresh water and fertile farming land was getting louder and louder.

'Yeah. It's time. One last hike. We finally visit the Colosseum, then we move on.'

'On to the hallowed ground!' Ravi cheered. He jingled his keys – the *master keys* – dramatically, then we all shouldered our packs and set off, making the dizzying descent down the fire stairs for the last time. I wasn't going to miss those, but I had to admit the daily climbs had kept me fit.

At street level, the soundscape had evolved to match the new take on the 'Urban Jungle'. There was a stillness that permeated, so our footfalls sounded too loud and pronounced. They crunched through the dirt and clomped across the concrete. Every once in a while, we'd hear the buzz of proliferating insects: flies and bees and cockroaches, or the cry of a bird hunting those same new Melburnians. They were the invisible percussionists of the new world order, the meek who had inherited the Earth, and they had no interest in meeting our stomping feet.

'Come on, let's go quickly,' I said, speaking at a stage whisper. It was the tone we all spoke in when we were out in the wild city now. Like it was respectful.

We moved down the middle of the road, taking care to watch where we stepped, following the hill down towards the river. I'd feel better there, where there was more open ground. The tall buildings made me nervous, as if I was walking at the bottom of a canyon. I kept craning my neck upwards looking for places I thought debris might fall on us. I felt a little easier once we hit the abandoned tram lines and wider sidewalks of Swanston Street. We hiked past a dormant tram parked at the intersection of Swanston and Collins and I couldn't help but think it looked like a satirical postcard; those trams used to be iconic in Melbourne, along with coffee, music and sport. The sound of their bells was a quintessential part of the city buzz. This one looked like something unearthed on an archaeologist's dig. It had only shards of glass in its window frames, and gaping holes where panels had been pried loose from its flanks. Its paint was peeling, its body weathered almost beyond recognition, and the wheels had rusted into place on their track, weeds and creepers wrapping around them. They were quite literally rooted in place.

'Hey, I think that's the 5,' Krista said.

'Oh yeah, I used to take that to work,' Hamish added.

I opened my mouth to reply, then closed it again as a flash of green shot by and landed on the tram. There was a rustle of feathers, and a blue and orange head swivelled around to look at us.

'It's beautiful,' Krista said.

I looked up as the rainbow lorikeet cocked its head and met my gaze. I'd never seen one in the city before.

'Yeah, wow,' I said.

We watched the bird as it bobbed slightly, shifting its weight from foot to foot, then it puffed out its orange and yellow chest, spread its wings, and took off, climbing skyward then disappearing down Collins Street. I wondered if it was nesting in the tram. I'd thought they lived in hollow eucalypt logs and limbs, but I supposed the fossilised 5 might be the next best thing.

We walked on and crested the hill – passing through the no-man's-land between the hulking yellow ruin of Flinders Street Station and what had been Fed Square – to where the river trail began: the same pilgrimage that thousands of football fans had made every Saturday afternoon, from the station to the stadium, with coloured scarves and beanies instead of habits. It was an essential part of our last lap, but there was another twinge as we passed the old landmarks, more postcard cutouts that had been stripped bare and abandoned. I remembered crossing the street between the two so many times, standing on the bridge and looking at the city with the station and the square in the foreground. The nostalgia hurt in a way. Now, there was a matter of reconciling things, telling ourselves that we were going to do it right this time. It would be more basic living, camping and foraging. At least that was the plan. That would be way more sustainable than even the greenest Northcote pad – with their compost heaps, rainwater systems and solar panels – we'd find Ngaere's community, that was a good first step. But I had to admit, there was a niggle. How long could people do that for? How long until they started building again? We were good at that, almost as good as we were at breaking things.

'It's kind of spooky, isn't it?' Krista said.

I opened my mouth to ask what, then realised I knew. It was all around us. Up ahead, Hamish laughed at something Ravi said. It sounded a little too loud.

'Cities aren't built to be abandoned. When you take all the people out, they feel way too big.'

'Kind of makes you wonder why we ever wanted to live like this in the first place. It must have been so much work just to keep it all standing.'

I nodded. 'I think people are attracted to each other. They love the buzz of being around each other, of feeling like they're part of something bigger. I think that's what cities are about.' I pointed ahead of us, along the curved line of the river, to where the lights of the MCG peeked up from behind the trees. 'That's what the G was all about. People coming together and getting caught up in it.'

'That's a very philosophical outlook.'

I shrugged.

'It beats the alternative, right?'

'Which is?' she asked.

'That it was all just bread and circuses, and we were all too ignorant for our own good.'

'I thought that was a given?'

'Well, maybe. The evidence would certainly seem to suggest that, but I dunno. I guess I'm just trying to be optimistic.'

Krista smirked. I'd been throwing the 'O' word around a lot lately. We fell silent, listening to the crunch of gravel under our boots. For a moment, I thought I saw movement from the corner of my eye and glanced over at the river. There was a soft splash, something slipped below the surface. A seal maybe?

I put the thought out of my mind as we left the dirt and reached the bridge to the G, a massive concrete walkway they had left standing so people could get over the train lines. To our right were the rusted bells that used to play the winning team's song after games. Krista hummed a few bars of the Richmond anthem, 'We're from Tigerland', and I realised I had no idea what the Carlton song was. Whatever it was, Richmond's was way catchier. Hymns to the football gods.

'Here we are!' Hamish called.

The MCG loomed over us as we climbed the last leg of the cracked concrete trail, through the parkland that had fast become forest. It was monolithic: white metal now shaded by the wind and the rain; elements that had stripped away paint and exposed patches of rust; windows that had somehow stayed intact, but had become so grimy they looked like strips of black ice all the way around. Creepers had begun to work their way up the concrete base, adding to the ruin effect as they combined with the spray paint hieroglyphics that had been added to the wall and the statues of past footballers, idols from the bygone age.

The gates were open. We weren't the first people to have made this particular journey.

'I want to go to the members' stand,' Hamish said. 'I've always wanted to go in there, but I never got the chance.'

'Let's go.'

We followed him to the MCG entrance, where the gate had also been opened. One of the huge metal shutters hung piled up to one side. There were tyre marks on the pavement, and I guessed someone with a V8 and a tow bar had gone to work on the fallen gate. We clambered over it, through the open doors, and vaulted the abandoned turnstiles.

'No queue,' I said, grinning, and got a laugh from the others.

'This is going to be great,' Ravi said.

He led us across the lobby to the lower level of the stands, fumbling the kid's sized Sherrin from his bag as he went. He'd gone on a special mission last week to find the football, visiting the abandoned Rebel Sport store on Bourke Street. Ravi had said it was the last one there, hidden under a toppled shelving unit. It had seemed fitting.

'Woah.'

'What is –'

The words died in my mouth as I caught up to Ravi and Hamish at the outer ring of the stands.

Creepers had worked their way up onto the second and third floor balconies, and now hung in a cascade of greenery. The ground had collapsed at either end of the pitch, sliding away beneath the stands in a slough down to what I thought must have been a parking garage or the players rooms, but was now a sunken cavern. There were trenches all the way around the edges, and bisecting the middle of the ground, leaving only two places where the turf remained: overgrown islands in a sea of metal and mud. It was a jungle sink hole.

'So much for having a kick,' Ravi sighed. He plodded heavily down one of the aisles and slumped into a seat, the rest of us following suit.

I felt for them, but in a way, I appreciated the completeness of the thing. Even this last human bastion hadn't been able to withstand the passage of time and the sheer force of nature. It almost made me glad. It was a sign that we'd made the right call, that there was no going back.

We sat there quietly for a while, catching our breath, before Hamish finally spoke up.

'So, the idea is that everyone can go live like Henry David Gameau, right?'

'*Thoreau.*'

'Yeah, right. So we all just go sit out in the woods, and like gather our own food and live in little huts or caves or whatever, like going properly paleo. And you think that's what everyone has done already?'

I ran a hand along the back of one of the stadium chairs. The plastic felt rough and powdery to the touch, like maybe it was starting to break down. If only. That plastic would probably be the last crumb of the city, long after everything else had returned to the dirt.

'Maybe not quite to that extent, but yeah, I think so. I think people are rethinking things and figuring out how to live more harmoniously. That's what we heard from Ngaere and her group.'

'To live on like ... a commune?'

'Yep.'

He nodded, pensive.

'Can people really do that these days?' He paused, then chuckled. 'I mean, I guess I'm having trouble with the tent thing. We've been doing it tough this whole time, but at least we've had a roof over our heads.'

We'd had this conversation already, a couple of times actually. But it was part of the process, embracing the optimism and talking myself, and them, into it. Even with the map and the plan, and knowing Ngaere's group was already out there, there were still a lot of *un*knowns. It felt a little as if we were charging off into ... the future, I guess.

'You know, it might be stupid optimism kicking in again, but I think most people can make it. I know *we'll* make it. And I guess we're at an advantage coming late to the party right, there are people who will be able to teach us now. I mean, it's how we used to live anyway, before we all moved into cities. It kind of makes sense that we would go back again. Like you said Hamish, people have been trying to do it with their diets anyway.' I paused, flipped a couple of ideas over in my head. 'People are adaptable, right? We're good at rallying and figuring out how to overcome challenges. We can use what's available to us, wherever we end up living.'

'Maybe that's been the problem,' Krista said. 'Too much *overcoming* things. Too much ... well I guess too much everything. It's how we got to this point.'

'Yeah. But we can learn as well, right? Maybe now is a good chance to learn how to do it *better*. Smarter, not just bigger. And maybe people will actually be happy ... happier anyway. That was the other part of Thoreau's thinking, that a simpler life would make people happier.'

Ravi grinned.

'Listen to you, classic nerd. The world's ending, and you're ready to turn it into a history class.'

'I know my strengths.' I shrugged. 'I can't kick for shit, so I figured out early on I better start reading. I was never gonna play here.'

We all laughed again.

'I guess I just keep waiting for people to come back to the city. Do you think they ever will?' Krista asked.

'Maybe. Maybe one day people will be having this same conversation about the city, wondering if they can do it, how people used to live that way.'

'It would make sense. Life moves in cycles, right?' Krista said.

I nodded and let my gaze drift up. Miraculously, I could see one of the eagle-shaped kites they'd once used to scare seagulls away. A single line held it in place as it strained against the wind, swooping dangerously and threatening to break free. But it was redundant. Even as I watched, a flock of birds crested the rim of the G and came swirling out high over the pitch. They weren't seagulls, but swallows maybe? They had that way of moving, like a fluid whole, chasing and swarming around one another, a school of aerial fish. There must have been hundreds upon hundreds of them, more than I'd ever seen before.

That was when it had first started to change, wasn't it? When the birds came back to the city. They were the first sign that ratios had shifted. They didn't need to fear flying cricket balls, footballs, or people in the upper stands. There were trees for them to perch in now, abandoned buildings where they could roost. The air was clear and quiet. They owned the skies again.

And they'd made that same circular journey Krista had mentioned. Displaced from the land, only to return as the people moved on. I thought Krista might be right, maybe we'd all do the same thing. The age of the great city was over for now, but maybe we'd all come back one day. Hopefully we'd just do it smarter next time.

I glanced down and realised the others were watching the birds too. A moment later, as if we'd all tuned into the same frequency, their eyes dropped, one by one, and we were all together again.

'You know, I think I'm good. If you're all ready to go?' Ravi said.

'Me too. It's been fun, but we should hit the road,' Hamish added.

I looked at Krista.

'Yeah, I'm ready for the next thing,' She said.

I nodded, then raised a hand, pointing out towards the turf islands. 'One kick Ravi, you've got your goal posts right there.'

He grinned. 'It'd be rude not to.'

'Yes! Do it!' Hamish cheered.

Ravi set off down the aisle at a jog, counting his steps. He punted the ball as he reached the edge of the ground, sending it spinning out over the pit with a rubbery thump. It arched high in the air, but it was never going to reach the middle of the ground. It fell down into the pit and disappeared into the dark.

We cheered and shouldered our packs as Ravi came back up the aisle.

'Well, Jakey, looks like you're not the only one who isn't gonna make the big league.'

'Ah well mate, we'll manage. On to the next?'

He grinned.

'On to the next.'

THE COLOURS OF THE SKY

Isla Scott

The child looks up, eyes straining to see
through the smog, the dark, and the towers, so high.
He asks his mother in a kind of plea,
'What colour is the sky?'

She joins him sitting on the floor, face raised high,
wishing they could see it from down below.
She closes her eyes to form a reply,
and thinks back to long ago.

'Once, the sky was blue, when it had not a care,
an endless floating sea within the atmosphere.
The sun so bright, the day so fair,
and the skies, they were clear.'

'An array of pastels were often splashed up high,
while clouds of marshmallow and whipped cream
formed a backdrop for swallows and sparrows to fly
through the sunlit gleam.'

'Yet, it was also striped in pink and gold,
no one could look on it with any dislike,
those colours painted high and bold,
no sunset was ever alike.'

'Sometimes, it burned red with reflections of fire,
a high haze of smoke, heat and worry.
Enveloping the skyline, it rose from the pyre,
signalling sirens to hurry.'

'It then faded to grey with tears from the sun,
and the wind matched it with a howling call.
The sky would crack open with a lightning gun
as the rain began to fall.'

'It was green when the horizon grew dark,
with silhouettes of bats flocking beyond.
The first star was all but a tiny spark
mirrored in a twilight pond.'

'The sky glittered with galaxies and stars
that put diamonds to shame.
On a good night you could see all the way to Mars.
Of course, then people came.'

The boy looks at his mother, dreaming of what was,
and tries in vain to picture the past.
But thanks to the smog, and the dark, and the towers and cars,
his vision of the sky is overcast.

ALL FOR A PROMISE

Vrishali Jain

It was a cloudy July morning in New Delhi. The monsoons were in full swing and the day expected its healthy share of rain. Nishi was slipping her feet hurriedly into her shoes. The cuckoo clock in the living area chirped nine times. Her first class at the college began in half an hour, and it would take forty-five minutes for her to reach campus from the Hauz Khas station. She was colossally late. She was supposed to lead the mock parliamentary debate and she was late.

As she was about to step out of the house, her Aama stopped her with a gentle tap on her shoulder.

'*Gudiya*, breakfast?'

Aama never let her kids, be it Nishi or Nishi's dad, leave home on an empty stomach. Nishi never quite understood Aama's insistence on eating before you left the house. She told her time and again that her college cafeteria has decent food, but Aama never accepted that reasoning.

'Aama, not today! I need to leave, I am already late!'

Before Aama could say another word, Nishi was out the door.

That was an exceptionally rushed morning for the Sharma household. It seemed everyone was in a hurry.

Nishi had flown out the house like a hurricane in motion and now her father was about to do the same.

Aama put his breakfast in a box and rushed out after him. She went to their usual parking spot but the car was nowhere to be seen. The street looked unusually empty and wide, and for a second Aama thought that the entire locality was out for one reason or other, which was rather odd.

By then Nishi's dad passed by her in his car.

She handed him the box through the window as he eased onto the street.

'I thought you left! I made your favourite, *Aloo Gutka*. I've rolled two wraps for you, eat while you drive!' Aama told him as she handed him the box of special Himanchali potato sabzi and chapatti wraps. Both Nishi and her dad loved the mustard tempered, spiced potato delicacy and honestly, it was the easiest for Aama to whip up on such rushed days.

'*Ija*, you really shouldn't bother so much!' Nishi's dad looked at his mother warmly, knowing how much she loved when he called her mother in Pahadi, his native language. Shaking his head, he took the lovingly wrapped box and smiled.

A car behind them honked rudely.

'Aah! It's good that they are expanding this ever-shrinking street!' Nishi's dad muttered and moved his car to the side.

'Widening the road?' Aama asked, confused.

'*Haan* Ma, the roadworks people will be here to measure the street, and plan on taking out the trees to start the expansion. Lord knows, we could use some more space. Anyway, I'm leaving! I'll take both you and Nishi out for dinner tonight so don't exert yourself unnecessarily in the kitchen!'

Nishi's dad left with a warm smile, but Aama could not bring herself to reciprocate.

Aama looked up and down the street once again. This was the very same street her son had come to live at twenty years ago from her small village called Reni, a quaint little settlement in the foothills of the Himalayas. Since then, she had visited her son regularly, until ten years ago, when Nishi was just eleven, they'd lost her mother to a car accident. The mourning and funeral took place at their ancestral house in Reni, and Aama decided to accompany her son and granddaughter to Delhi in order to take care of them.

The street looked nothing like this back then. The buildings had received a facelift. Some had been demolished to make way for new additions. The corner store where she would send Nishi with a crinkly twenty rupee note to get a packet of bread? It was now the superstore of the area, somehow still called 'Corner Essentials'. The neighbours had added two more cars to their ever-increasing fleet, taking the count of cars to five in a household of four. As Aama walked down the street, other slight, everyday changes became more and more prominent.

Almost all of the houses were now three floors high. She remembered the street appeared so wide when she'd first arrived all those years ago. Wider and greener. The widest road in Reni was small when compared to the street her son had his house on. She'd felt so proud. The street today looked closed in. Closed in and grey.

The only thing to have not changed were the trees. As she kept walking, she saw trees on both sides of the street bore a red 'X' mark on them. Among them was a Peepal tree Aama had religiously offered water to since the day she first shifted. The tree was right outside the Shiva temple, and not just her but other devotees too offered their prayers to the tree. The red mark, like a scarlet letter, seemed to have sealed the fate of the tree.

Aama prayed every day at this temple. Over the past ten years Aama had become Aama for all those who came to the temple. The neighbours, the temple priest, the kids who played around, even the house helps addressed her as Aama. Nobody knew her name. Nobody needed to. Her love and kindness had established her as the grand old lady of the neighbourhood.

She approached the temple priest and asked if the authorities would chop down the temple tree too?

The temple priest drew up to his full height and exclaimed, 'They would not dare to do so Aama! We put our foot down. In fact, they had to re-plan the road expansion because we did not let them take our sacred tree!'

Aama didn't realise she had been holding her breath. But the relief she'd begun to feel soon vanished. What about the other trees?

'Those will have to be cut, Aama. We all know the locality needs more space.'

He then gave her a flower from the deity's feet as Prasad and folded his hands in Namaste as a farewell.

Aama too, looked at the Peepal tree with forlorn eyes and left. A child playing nearby noticed her and came running for the sweet cardamom Prasad that Aama always brought with her to the temple. That day, she had none. A sad smile played on her lips. She walked back to the house slower than usual.

That evening, as Aama sat on the balcony with her cup of tea, she was hit by memories of long ago. Memories of a childhood that was so different than what she saw Nishi grow up through, or these kids playing in the park downstairs were living.

1974

She was a twenty-two-year-old, newly married woman who was yet learning the nitty-gritties of domestic life. One of the major responsibilities in Reni was to collect firewood for food and other sustenance. A small village situated in the foothills of Himalayas and in the lap of Alaknanda River, Reni was a town that was built on the back of its women. In these hills the women did a lot more than the usual domestic chores; the ambit of their responsibilities was never clearly defined. They would take their livestock grazing, collect wood, fetch water and do all of this as a collective. Women seldom worked alone. They would cook together, knit together and thread by thread, morsel by morsel, built a community that defined harmony. She remembered Gaura Devi, one she referred to as Gaura jiji, or Sister Gaura, who was like an elder and sister to her and other new brides of the village.

It was the month of April and the Alaknanda valley was under severe threat. Now, the Alaknanda River is known to be the wild daughter of the Himalayas. She does not flow down the mountain, she prances. She dances like a woman freshly in love, with no care to the prying eyes of the world. Reckless in her pursuit, passionate in her abandon. It is then no wonder, the Alaknanda is prone to overflow and flood. The forest in the valley is the partner who is always on the lookout. The river keeps her partner nourished and the forest keeps their partner protected. The forest is the yin to her yang, always keeping the damage from the flooding in check.

That April, in the name of development, came the lumber companies of the cities, the plains that did not understand the dynamics of the river and her partner. They saw the flourishing forest of the Ash trees and contracted to fell 2500 trees. Environmentalists of the area were already concerned about the recent floods, and the villages of the valley were scared of a repeat. Aama and the other ladies of the community had heard about a movement in a neighbouring town where the village folks had stood together and drove away these lumberjacks by beating drums. There were tales of university students standing in protest against the authorities.

They believed the lumberjacks with their power saws and powerful connections would never be able to reach Reni. Gaura jiji always said, 'the forest is the son that takes care of us mothers and the daughter of the mountain, the Alaknanda. The son knows how to protect.' Gaura jiji had organised the women under the group called Mahila Mangal Dal (Women Welfare Society).

One day, a man by the name of Chandi Prasad Bhatt came into the town. He was a man from Gopeshwar, the neighbouring village that drove the butchers of their beloved forest away. He met with Gaura jiji, and told her the student movement did not work and the lumberjacks were in their forest now. It was now up to the mothers to protect the son.

The newlywed Aama had felt her skin pebble into goose bumps when Gaura jiji, her petite Gaura jiji, in her grey-black saree tied around her waist in the traditional Gharwali fashion, her red woollen blouse and the black woollen scarf around her head, climbed up the village meeting place and spoke in a voice of steel.

'The son is in danger. What should the mothers do?'

Aama had thought the huge silver nose pin Gaura jiji wore shone like diamonds. Her sister of her heart shone like the sun herself. The walk Aama took hand in hand with Gaura jiji and twenty-six other sisters into the forest felt sacred. The lumberjacks had already begun felling trees.

'If we are the mothers we think, they will not be able to take a single twig from our forests!'

The women were armed only with determination. Aama and her friends went ahead and hugged their sons. 'Angalwatha' meaning 'to hug' cried the women like a war cry. They hugged their trees. The lumberjacks had to stop.

The mothers had thrown themselves in the way of destruction. Soon the entire village followed.

The men could not even take the ten trees that were already cut. The entire village had celebrated with *Kheer*, the rice pudding, that evening, knowing that the battle was far from finished.

* * *

The movement came to be known as 'Chipko Andolan' or the 'Movement to Hug'. The world remembers it as one of the most organised non-violent environmental crusades that led to a ten-year-long ban on deforestation in the area.

Aama remembered engraving her name on the tree she had guarded.

Now

That new bride was now a sixty-eight-year-old grandmother to the neighbourhood. So much had changed over the past forty-six years, but so much was still the same.

As she looked onto the street, kids were running around the trees, playing catch up. The water she kept in a corner of the balcony under a branch of the Gulmohar tree from the street was sloshed all around the bowl. She knew the squirrels from the tree came to her balcony for water and occasionally grain. The birds she had gotten used to waking up to were around because of these trees. The trees that now bore a scarlet letter.

Her heart bled as she remembered that she'd counted thirty scarlet marks that morning. Thirty sons of the daughter of mountains were to be felled.

Aama found her eyes wet. A struggle that was long forgotten rebelled in her veins. She longed for her hills, for her community of forever like she never had in the past decade. But this was no Reni. These were not the Gharwalis who'd lay their lives for their trees. These were people who needed more space at the expense of the trees.

The shrill of the doorbell broke through her thoughts of mountains, wild rivers and rebellions.

She got up to open the door. Nishi was home.

'Aama I am famished! I didn't find time to eat at all! Please give me something to eat *na*!'

Her little bird kept chirping, but Aama could not bring herself to smile at her theatrics or chide her for going hungry the entire day. As she set her tea on the table, Aama looked at her with all the love and pain she had gone through that day and lay a loving hand on her granddaughter's head. Aama's hand trembled. Nishi stopped midway telling Aama how the debate went south and looked at her granny.

'Are you alright Aama?'

Nishi suddenly saw the frailty of her Aama. Her skin looked like paper; her eyes, so similar to her own, looked tired. She held Aama's hand and took her to her room. As Aama sat down on the bed, she was suddenly dizzy.

'Aama!'

Nishi panicked. She sat Aama down on her bed and called Dr Sen, who was also their neighbour. Her second call was to her father.

Dr Sen came in. It turned out Aama had low blood pressure as well as low blood sugar. He seemed worried. Nishi's dad talked to him while Nishi sat with her granny. Over the next few days, Nishi and her dad were watchful. They could sense Aama was not her usual self, she did not talk, did not ask them about their day and most importantly did not smile at either of them.

The medicines didn't seem to be working. For a woman who hadn't had a sick day in her life, Aama seemed to have taken an extremely bad hit. All she did each day was sit with a cup of tea on the balcony. Nishi and her dad had to practically force feed her. It was three days since Aama had her health scare.

Aama sat on the balcony, staring at the street where the municipal workers mapped the area for expansion. She looked remorseful.

Nishi came and sat near her chair on the floor. Taking Aama's hand, Nishi said, 'Aama, you are not just my Aama but also my Ija. Please tell me if Dad and I have hurt you in some way. I am sorry Aama, I'll do whatever you ask me to, but please talk. Tell me what is bothering you, and I promise we'll fix it Aama. I promise!'

Nishi's tears fell on Aama's hands. She couldn't stand the idea of her grandmother being ill, but what really took away her sleep was her grandmother's unusual silence.

Nishi's tears broke what was left of Aama's heart.

'I am a poor sister and a daughter, Nishi! I am not the mother I wanted to be!' Aama wailed.

'What are you saying Ija?' Nishi's father who'd just walked in with Aama's medicines asked.

'I am not a nice woman, son!'

Nishi's dad handed Aama the water he had brought. When Aama calmed down a little, Nishi spoke.

'Aama tell us, what has been bothering you so much?'

It was then Aama spoke of the struggle she had partook forty-six years ago, of Chandi Bhatt, of Gaura Devi, how she'd promised her Gaura jiji to never let trees be treated in a way she wouldn't want her children to be treated in, and how she was now to witness this massacre of thirty sons right in front of her eyes.

'What sort of a woman does that make me? Tell me, *bitiya*, would I stand so quiet if it were you in the place of those trees?'

Nishi did not know how to respond. She did what she could to calm Aama down, but it seemed there was nothing left to say. They had to call Dr Sen to seek medication that helped Aama to sleep. That night, after Aama had finally slept, Nishi read whatever she could find on the Chipko Movement. She was amazed by what she read. It wasn't that she hadn't heard of the movement, but it floored her to realise that it was her legacy in the truest sense. How had a group of villagers, uneducated and unaided by any external help, stood so tall to save their environment that they became a landmark for the entire world?

She began to send out emails and made a number of calls. A plan had slowly taken shape in her mind.

The next morning a little colour had returned to Aama's cheeks. Maybe it was because she had shared her worst fears and that made her feel light, or maybe it was the fact that Dr Sen had finally included an aid to help Aama sleep peacefully in his prescription, but Nishi could breathe a little easier.

At exact 12 pm the doorbell rang and Nishi jumped to answer.

She had called an emergency meeting with the Residential Committee. She had also, with the help of her friends, called upon the teenagers and her peers who lived in the same colony.

Nishi had grown up in this colony. The thing about Indian neighbourhoods is that everyone knows everyone. They are kind of in each other's business and take pride of the fact that they are in each other's business.

Those attending knew it had something to do with Aama taking ill. But none of them had expected the story Nishi told them.

'We've all grown up under those trees. Aama helped me bury my first milk-teeth under the Gulmohar tree that is now marked to be cut. We are saving the temple tree. How selfish would it be then to just save one tree! Can the plans not be remade to save all the trees?'

She could not help the wobble that slipped in her voice despite her best efforts. The colony loved Aama, but there was the whole problem of the space crunch too.

Nishi had thought about that too.

'We have a wasteland on the backside of our colony. There has been a proposal to turn it into a park for years now, but nothing has been approved. What if we turn that into a common parking lot instead? Besides it makes no sense to cut down decades old trees, only to develop a whole park again!'

The proposal made sense, but it would mean a special stay on the current road expansion and approval of the parking lot by the Municipal Corporation. The colony stood together. Once the people got talking, the collective realised that no one was really happy with the trees being marked scarlet. As they talked, uncounted stories flowed in the Sharma living area. Somebody like Nishi had buried their first milk teeth under a tree, some other had sat against them to enjoy solemn evenings. A couple confessed to have sneaked behind a tree during their courtship days to meet away from the prying eyes of the locality.

As the day progressed, calls were made, appointments were sought. The trees were to be felled the next day. After the day's collective efforts, nothing worked. The government machinery seldom works at an urgent speed.

Evening slipped in without anyone noticing. Despite the collective's best efforts, a stay could not be obtained on the felling of the colony's trees. After a while, people left one by one. Some offered their sympathies, some said that Nishi should have thought of it earlier, some just expressed remorse, but nothing could really be done now.

That night, Aama, Nishi and her dad stayed on the balcony until late, sipping their Masala Chais.

The next morning, the whole of the colony was out. They had come to bid farewell to their beloved trees. The municipal lumberjacks were there.

Nishi and Aama held hands and stood at their gate. Since theirs was the first house in the lane, the workers approached them first.

'Please move out of the way, otherwise you might get hurt!'

The worker said politely to Aama. Aama had heard the exact same words forty-six years ago too.

She looked at Nishi, and then her son. A non-verbal exchange passed through the three, and they stepped forward and hugged their beloved Gulmohar.

'He's my second son, and I his mother. Raze me and take my son,' Aama said. She had thrown the same dare at the authorities forty-six years ago, and no one had dared to come near her.

The manager came forward. 'Please step out of our way, or we'll have to call police,' he said in a stern voice.

'Then please go ahead and call the police,' said the neighbours, who were now hugging a tree too. Before the men could understand, the entire colony huddled around each tree as if to tell them that they were in a circle of love. The men were baffled. Authorities were called in, but the residents stood firm.

Aama's eyes glistened.

'Angalwatha, Gaura jiji, Angalwatha.' She whispered towards the heavens.

Today she was Gaura jiji. Gaura jiji may have passed on, but Aama's granddaughter had not let her promise go in vain. Aama's hand tightened in Nishi's hand. The colony's grand old lady had taught them a lesson in defiance and care, just by being true to her traditional beliefs. Her one strong step had led to the formation of a strong citizenry collective. Environment is, after all, the responsibility of all who depend on it for survival, and that translates to everyone.

A deferment was reached, and a cancellation order came soon after. After the media had jumped in, it all occurred within the span of three days.

A month later, the colony decided to name the street after Aama. And that is when Nishi came to know the name of her grandmother for the first time: Shanti Devi Sharma.

A CRITIQUE OF THE ZERO WASTE MOVEMENT

Angela Xu

It's an image you've seen hundreds of times before: the woman who can fit four years of her trash in a single mason jar; the pantry lined with bulk goods in matching glass containers; the stainless steel bento lunchbox; and of course, the reusable coffee cup. These images embody the zero waste movement, which is founded on the principles of diminishing consumption and switching to reusable alternatives. While these ideas are undoubtedly essential in a world where plastic pollution has reached every corner of the world, the zero waste movement should not be lauded as the pinnacle of ethical living.

Gender and environmentalism

Like many other environmental lifestyle movements, such as veganism and recycling, the zero waste movement is highly gendered, and dominated by women. Not only does the feminised portrayal of zero waste and environmentalism isolate those who identify with other genders, but the focus on domesticity can, for some, reinforce traditional gender roles and the unequal division of domestic labour.

A Mintel report published in 2018 surveyed a wide range of people across the United Kingdom on the ethics of their lifestyle habits. Overall, women were found to be more likely to make a conscious effort to live ethically and were more likely to participate in eco-friendly practices such as recycling and reducing water usage.[1] The report proposed that a key reason for the 'eco gender gap' could be the highly feminised portrayal of

---

1   Mintel 2018.

environmentalism in advertising and media.[2] As a result, men can feel that participating in environmentalism compromises their masculinity. This is reinforced by a high proportion of eco-friendly products being targeted towards females.

In addition to the subconsciously male-isolating aspect of environmentalism, the emphasis on the domestic sphere in zero waste contributes to the traditional perception of women as caregivers and homemakers. The zero waste movement is largely centred around swapping out plastic for eco-friendly alternatives around the house, such as reusable beeswax wraps in the kitchen, bamboo toothbrushes in the bathroom, and metal clothes pegs in the laundry. Despite the increasing progression towards equal domestic burdens on all genders, these areas of the household are overwhelmingly still responsibilities attributed to females. In contrast, the areas of the household which are more commonly attributed to men, such as car maintenance, remain virtually untouched by zero waste products.

In addition to the gender divide caused by targeted product advertising, the 'DIY' aspect of zero waste is an additional burden on women, who statistically perform more unpaid domestic labour than men. Certain zero waste products, such as toothpaste and household cleaning sprays, can be difficult to find or too expensive for people living in certain regions of the world and in rural areas. Thus, zero waste media encourages people to make their own, marketing it as a fun DIY project.

The issue with this sentiment is the lack of accessibility it creates for those who engage in full-time work or have extra responsibilities that make sacrificing an afternoon to make toothpaste and cleaning spray next to impossible. For women, the introduction of easily accessible, fast and cheap household solutions was key in their entrance into the workforce. A lack of commercial availability combined with an 'if you can't buy it, just make it yourself' attitude reinforces women's burden of domestic labour and also creates an isolating and guilting force for those who cannot adhere to these ideals.

Feeding into hyper-consumerism

The Pinterest-esque aesthetic of the zero waste lifestyle permeates every single social media platform. It's filled with matching mason jars, glowing stainless steel straws, and a rainbow of bar soaps. As with any

2   Mintel 2018.

other lifestyle marketed on social media, zero waste products entice the consumer and convince them that the bamboo, stainless steel, glass route is the only way to go.

This is where the movement seems to stray away from its principles of minimal consumption and reduction of waste. While the emphasis on materials and products is strong, there is very little encouragement to use the products you already own. The heavy emphasis on aesthetics causes many – when they begin their zero waste journey – to begin throwing away everything they own that is plastic, even if it is still usable.

An example of this is the plastic drink bottle, which many throw away in order to buy a new stainless steel one. While the stainless steel bottle is no doubt more sustainable, not using products already in your ownership is inherently damaging to the environment. This disposal and consumption chain is reflective of the hyper-consumerism of mainstream society and is the very issue zero waste was trying to veer away from.

Is 'zero waste' really zero waste?

One area the movement often neglects is the waste created in the production process. While the perceived goal of the movement is to be able to fit your annual waste into a single mason jar, this usually fails to address the inevitable commercial waste produced by the corporations manufacturing the essential products needed to reach this goal. Waste minimalism is impressive, but the overall neglect to consider production waste is a reflection of the burdensome onus placed on consumers, rather than those who control the means of production.

Even if the consumer bases all their consumption choices on reusability and recyclability, the product's journey from raw material to commercial good will be riddled with plastic use and pollution of the waterways and air. For example, even the simple act of getting something delivered to you will immensely worsen your product's environmental impact through the unsustainable practices of the post office.

Similarly to how other environmental movements have presented themselves to society, the zero waste movement places most of the onus on consumers to engage in ethical consumption. However, the broader systematic issue of production must also be addressed within the movement itself. Without the acknowledgement of the inherent unethical nature of capitalist production, zero waste will only serve to further the narrative that only individuals need to be criticised and held to account, rather than governments and large corporations.

Maximum hopes in minimum waste

Despite all the flaws of the zero waste movement, it remains an innovative and necessary movement that we must learn from. With scientists predicting that climate change will be irreversible in the near future and microplastics polluting everything from our food to our water, turning away from the consumption of plastic is key.

We as a society need to be more responsive to the principles of zero waste. This includes increasing eco-friendly advertising for male-targeted products and working on reducing the 'eco gender gap'. By balancing gender representation in environmentalism, we can reduce the perceived emasculation of ethical living for people who don't identify as female. In addition to this, zero waste living needs to be made more accessible, so that consumers are incentivised to pick a low-waste product over a product containing plastic.

Finally, the zero waste movement needs to be more aware of the aesthetic and perfectionist message portrayed on social media. Through normalising reusing old, plastic products and being welcoming to those who cannot pursue a completely zero waste lifestyle, the movement will only gain more momentum, while staying true to the principles it was founded on. This will also encourage corporations to genuinely engage in waste minimalism, helping to create progress that is driven from both sides of the supply chain.

References

Mintel. "The eco gender gap: 71% of women try to live more ethically, compared to 59% of men". *Mintel*, 27 July 2018. https://www.mintel.com/press-centre/social-and-lifestyle/the-eco-gender-gap-71-of-women-try-to-live-more-ethically-compared-to-59-of-men.

WILL COVID-19'S LEGACY BE ENVIRONMENTAL AND SOCIALLY SUSTAINABLE ACTION?

Anika Bhatia

The coronavirus pandemic has led to a brutal realisation of the need for increased sustainable action, particularly in the fashion industry. It has warned us that we cannot continue the path we are heading towards – it has to change. COVID-19 has now reached all parts of the world and has resulted in a tragic human loss. Economies have also plummeted as most production has had to either slow down or stop completely.

Despite the human and economic disaster, the planet has been thriving. Temporarily.

As has been widely reported, the environmental benefits from the COVID-induced pause has been experienced worldwide. The absence of tourists in Venice and the reduction of boats in canals have seen a return of clear water and biodiversity.[1] Moreover, in India, the quality of the Ganga river has improved due to the reduction of industrial waste being dumped in the river.[2] As economic activity has slowed and travel restrictions imposed, air pollution has also seen a drastic fall. According to the *Nature Climate Change* journal, 'daily global carbon dioxide emissions decreased by 17% by early April 2020 compared with the mean 2019 levels'.[3]

---

1   Brunton 2020.
2   PTI News 2020.
3   Le Quéré et al. 2020.

Unfortunately as lockdown conditions are gradually easing, carbon dioxide emissions are rebounding back to their normal levels, proving many expert predictions that the fall would only be temporary.[4] Even so, it does not deny the opportunity that these undoubtedly scary times give us, to have a glimpse of what our world would look like if real climate change action was enforced.

Real, sustained reductions in carbon emissions can only happen if governments take swift action for structural change. The shutting down of society is an opportunity for those in power to transform business models for greater economic resilience and rebuild our society for the better, both sustainably and ethically. Long-term sustainable practices are a prerequisite for future-proofing business models.

Sustainability is playing an increasingly important role in most large organisations, including in the fashion industry. In 2018, the United Nations (UN) created an Alliance on Sustainable Fashion, aiming to reduce the negative environmental and social impacts of the fashion industry and ensure it contributes to their Sustainable Development Goals target. Despite the immense growth in the fashion industry during the early twenty-first century, and the consequential boost in employment, there have also been many downsides. According to the UN, the fashion industry is the second biggest consumer of water.[5] Moreover, whilst the environmental cost of flying is now widely known, fashion in fact, produces more global carbon emissions than aviation and maritime shipping combined.[6] If it continues at this pace, the industry could represent a quarter of the world's carbon budget by 2050.[7]

The waste being generated by the fashion industry has also reached extraordinary levels, mainly due to the rise of fast fashion. Fast fashion can be defined as clothing that is produced at rapid speeds by mass-market retailers at very low prices. It is made from cheap materials and is trend-driven, hence encouraging a culture of disposable clothing. This culture has become prominent as some clothing items are so cheap that they become single-use purchases. We buy approximately sixty percent more garments now than we did sixteen years ago, yet only keep these

4   Harvey 2020.
5   United Nations Environment Programme 2019.
6   UNFCCC 2018.
7   Ellen MacArthur Foundation 2017, 21.

items for half as long.[8] According to ABC's *War on Waste*, Australians throw out 6000kg of clothes every ten minutes.[9]

It is clear that we are living in an era that overconsumes and underuses clothes.

In 2015, the documentary *The true cost* first unveiled the impact of fast fashion to the world. Yet, five years later, fast fashion brands are still neglecting the social and environmental costs of production. While fast fashion is making us poorer, it is making the owners of brands such as Forever 21 and Zara richer.

Consumers have started to challenge the pace of mindless consumption which fast fashion brands have tried to get us addicted to. The culture of keeping, swapping, lending and mending clothes is becoming more popular as people become more aware of the negative impacts of fashion practices.

Our clothing is causing environmental devastation.

Not only does our clothing affect the environment through greenhouse gas emissions and water consumption, but it also produces large amounts of non-renewable textile waste and hazardous chemicals that can release toxins into water supplies.

The most sustainable materials are those which contain natural fibres such as cotton, wool, hemp and linen. Materials made from cheap synthetic fibres such as polyester, nylon, spandex and elastane should be avoided as they are not grown naturally and can take many years to decompose. Polyester is a plastic fabric made from crude oil and represents around fifty-one percent of global fibre production.[10] When washing our clothes that are made from these synthetic fibres, the garment emits microplastic fibres that endangers ecosystems and possibly even harms human health.

In April, a *Nature Reviews Earth & Environment* report conducted research on the impacts of fast fashion on the environment from all aspects of the supply chain. The research revealed that there are 15,000 types of chemicals used across the fashion supply chain, and textile waste amounts to ninety-two million tonnes per year.[11] The report found that there is 'the need for an urgent transition back to "slow" fashion, minimising and

---

8 Fashion Revolution 2020.

9 ABC 2017.

10 Niinimäki et al. 2020, 190

11 Niinimäki et al. 2020, 193, 189.

mitigating the detrimental environmental impacts, so as to improve the long-term sustainability of the fashion supply chain'.[12] It also stressed that a 'shift in consumer behaviour – namely, decreasing clothing purchases and increasing garment lifetimes' is required.[13]

When we consider the carbon footprint of the transportation of clothes, water and energy consumption, chemical and microplastic pollutants and waste both on the factory floor and from used clothing, we realise this is not an approach that can be sustained. The good news is that the system is changing.

As the climate conversation continues to grow, the consumer pressure on industries to adopt sustainable practices increases. Yet, instead of sustainability being another 'hot topic' or fleeting trend within the fashion industry, perhaps this time it's here to stay.

This year has seen many positive changes in policies towards encouraging sustainability.

The British Academy Film Awards called for a sustainable theme earlier this year, with a 'green' carpet dress code and a plant-based menu. Luxury brand Gucci also took steps towards sustainability in announcing its future collections will be seasonless. This was announced a week after the American and British Fashion Council released a joint statement encouraging the industry to slow down its pace in the wake of the pandemic.[14] Gucci's decision is a huge step towards greater sustainability as it will reduce the rate of clothing production as well as material waste. It's important that high-end fashion brands make these decisions as it means that fast fashion brands have less clothing trends to copy, meaning they will also be producing items at a slower rate. Ultimately, it also means that consumers will be consuming clothes at a slower rate.

The pandemic has enabled the fast fashion model to be collectively challenged for the first time. The period of universal stagnation has forced us to reflect and reconsider our consumption habits and caused businesses to reevaluate their operating models.

The crisis might well be the final warning we shouldn't have needed.

Sustainable fashion researcher and academic, Dr Lisa Heinze, is uncertain that the pandemic is enough to stop the culture of

---

12 Niinimäki et al. 2020, 189.

13 Niinimäki et al. 2020, 189.

14 Seward 2020.

overconsumption for good. 'If the situation returns to normal soon, consumer habits may, unfortunately, slip back into place,' she says. 'I think it would be a shame to waste the crisis in terms of not trying to educate people to buy things better and do things differently.'[15]

It presents an opportunity for businesses to look towards better operating models and redesign supply chains as production temporarily halts. According to data from the Australian Fashion Council, two-thirds of our fashion industry doubt they will be able to recover from the decline in sales due to the lockdown restrictions.[16]

Australian brands are being forced to adapt their models in order to survive. Local brand Cue is embracing the opportunity to move to digital platforms, repurpose existing resources and increase reliance on local and sustainable manufacturing.[17] Inner-city local label, Good Day Girl, reveals to the ABC how their business model has proved to be resilient in the crisis.[18] As they operate on a made-to-order model, each item of clothing already has a home prior to production and therefore the business has not been affected, unlike many others, by the costs of unsold clothes.

It is a prime example of how niche local labels can inspire other brands to harness customer sentiments and adapt their approach to be more sustainable. Ironically, returning to the old-fashioned made-to-order clothing business model and other slow fashion practices are more 'progressive' in terms of sustainability.

Discussing sustainability without addressing human rights is not sustainability.

Heinze importantly notes that 'sustainable fashion is not only fashion that minimises harm to the planet but also enhances the life of the people who are making them'.[19] Ever since the coverage of the horrific Rana Plaza factory collapse in 2013 that killed 1134 Bangladeshi garment factory workers, issues in global supply chains have started gaining more exposure.

Whilst some progress has been made since then, the COVID-19 crisis has resurfaced existing issues of exploitation and disparity within the fashion industry. In response to the crisis, many international fashion brands are cancelling production orders and freezing payments to recover

---

15 Heinze 2020.
16 Kolovos 2020.
17 Boland and Lloyd 2020.
18 Boland and Lloyd 2020.
19 Heinze 2020.

losses, even unwilling to pay for work that has been completed. These brands are taking no responsibility and are in fact disrespecting the people who are working in their supply chains, a majority of which are women in the Global South. This is having a serious impact as factories in India, Bangladesh and Vietnam are being forced to destroy unwanted goods and lay off workers.

Many of these garment workers were already working in impoverished conditions and are now struggling to survive. As *Business of Fashion* Founder Imran Amed argues, the pandemic is 'breaking open stark inequalities in the fashion system, one in which huge global corporations are placing the burden of a once-in-a-lifetime crisis on those who are least able to afford it'.[20]

On 30 March 2020, the non-profit organisation Remake created a petition demanding brands to #PayUp. In order to be removed from the petition, Remake states that the brands must honour their word:

> Brands must promise to pay suppliers for all orders that were cancelled or paused as a result of coronavirus. Furthermore, brands must agree to pay for these cancelled and in-production orders in full (without asking suppliers for discounts) and in a timely manner (without extending payment terms unless financing options can be provided).[21]

Brands such as Primark, Forever 21 and Urban Outfitters, among others, have cancelled orders and are demanding discounts and payment delays, and are yet to #PayUp. However, since launching the petition, nineteen large brands and retailers have agreed to pay for orders in full, according to original contracts, including H&M, Asos, Zara, Nike and Target. These commitments have helped unlock an estimated US$1 billion owed to Bangladesh's factories providing to its 4.1 million-person workforce.

Brands paying their suppliers even now will be the only hope businesses have of staying afloat.

---

20 Amed 2020.
21 Remake.world 2020.

The Rise of the Conscious Consumer

It is often argued what came first: the thirst of consumers to attain new looks at an ever-increasing pace or the big fashion label's marketing campaigns dictating constantly changing fashion trends. While many of us are tempted by the lure of the 'next best thing', it is important to understand that this behaviour is a condition of brands convincing us that we need the latest trends.

'I'm always really cautious of blaming the consumer,' says Heinze. 'I don't think it's fair.'[22] She highlights that, particularly for the Millennials and Gen Z consumers who are notorious for being tempted by cheap prices, 'it's the world they have grown up in'.[23] She ultimately states that, 'the end goal should be that fashion companies take the responsibility to make clothes better.'[24]

Ironically, despite cheap prices and unsustainable practices being the 'norm' for Millennials and Gen Z, it is they who are the most eco-conscious and vocal in demanding responsibility from the large brands. Perhaps inspired by the young environmental activist Greta Thunberg, many young people are becoming leaders for change. This sentiment is corroborated by current university fashion and textile student, Amelia Turner, who states, 'fashion needs young people to come and disrupt it'.[25] The examples she provides include the need for fashion to become impartial to gender, benefit the whole supply chain, not just serve those at the top, and represent more people of colour both on the cat-walk and on social media.[26] These examples signify the change likely to be witnessed from future generations.

In terms of sustainability, Turner notes that more consumers are demanding greater transparency from brands, including knowing how products are made and if they have been respectful to the environment and the people who made them.[27] According to Forbes:

> The majority of Generation Z (54 percent) state that they are willing to spend an incremental 10 percent or more on sustainable products,

22 Heinze 2020.
23 Heinze 2020.
24 Heinze 2020.
25 Turner 2020.
26 Turner 2020.
27 Turner 2020.

with 50 percent of Millennials saying the same. This compares to 34 percent of Generation X and 23 percent of Baby Boomers. It appears that with every generation, the quest for sustainability strengthens.[28]

However, Turner warns consumers not to fall for the trap of 'greenwashing', a marketing tactic where environmentally friendly policies are falsely advertised by companies in order to appeal to greater audiences.[29] In order to be an informed consumer, Heinze recommends using the Good on You website which rates brands according to their performance in terms of sustainability and ethical practices both on people and animals.[30]

Social media has given rise to widespread activism, particularly from the younger generations who are placing increasing pressure on brands to change their behaviours, with the ability to call out companies publicly on unethical and unsustainable practices. It has also allowed consumers to share and praise those brands that do offer transparency and focus on doing good at their core.

The path to thoughtful consumption

So how do we incorporate sustainability into our purchases?

'First and foremost, we need to buy less,' says Heinze, 'Don't stop buying things full stop, but I think it's really important that we take time to really think about what we are going to buy.'[31] Secondly, she suggests before purchasing new clothes to consider borrowing from friends or on clothes swap groups, or buying second-hand on certain websites like eBay and GumTree and apps like Depop, or from stores like Vinnies.[32] On top of this, there is also rental clothing:

> When you are talking about special events, rental clothing is a really great way to avoid costs, both financial and environmental. That's what I do now when I have something to go to. I haven't bought a formal dress for years because renting lets me get a kick out of

---

28 Petro 2020.
29 Turner 2020.
30 Heinze 2020.
31 Heinze 2020.
32 Heinze 2020.

wearing something new that nobody has seen me wear before and I never wear it again.[33]

Whilst Heinze enjoys renting clothes, university student Turner, amongst many other Gen Z is a Depop enthusiast, revealing she buys most of her clothes second-hand from buyers on the app and also uses it to sell her own clothes. She discloses a handy tip for reducing clutter and increasing the longevity of garments while also financing new tastes: 'When buying something I think of what can I sell at the same time to replace the new item'.[34]

Turner's philosophy is for people to think of buying garments as an investment rather than items that can be disposed of.[35]

If you just save the money you spend on fast fashion, let's say you buy five cheap jumpers in a year, you could instead buy one good quality jumper that could last you a lifetime. It also means you will cherish and respect it more as a piece of clothing.

An important concept in the fashion industry is exclusivity, specifically recognising the difference between genuine and perceived exclusivity. In many ways, luxury brands attempt to create exclusivity through exuding an artisanal feel to mass factory produced items by capping production to make it 'limited edition' as well as increasing prices. Yet, authentic exclusivity involves locally or hand-made artisanal items that require specific skills and experience. The latter is in many ways more sustainable and an example of slow fashion; operating on a made-to-order method which supports local craftspeople. Knowing where an item has come from, how it has been made and who has made it also lets consumers respect and appreciate it more. Particularly during this global pandemic it becomes more important than ever to support local and small businesses.

Shrujan is a not-for-profit organisation based in rural India that helps local female artisans make a living from their hand embroidery. It has helped revive and revitalise the ancient craft of hand embroidery that was on the verge of extinction, as well as support local craftswomen to earn a sustainable livelihood. Today, the organisation supports a network of 3000 craftswomen spread from over sixty-two direct reach remote villages. The craftswomen work from home and are provided the fabrics and threads

---

33 Heinze 2020.
34 Turner 2020.
35 Turner 2020.

from the organisation and then paid for their skill and time in creating the hand embroidered items. These are then fashioned into high quality apparel, accessories and lifestyle products available in Shrujan stores, exhibitions and online. An important value of the organisation that has been carried down from its founder, Chanda Shroff, is the importance of knowing the supply chain. This includes knowing the names of and developing relations with the artisans in the supply chain to ensure standards are met, concerns are addressed and support is received. This has proven to be essential during the pandemic, as clear communication and support of regional artisans and staff have helped keep the organisation alive and artisans paid. Whilst large made-to-order pieces are still ongoing, demand overall has dropped drastically. Loyal customers have been able to purchase a 'count-on-me' voucher for clothing to use for later, however the money temporarily assists artisans and staff during the difficult period. What makes brands like Shrujan and other similar small businesses stand out amongst others are the sentiments attached to their garments; that of pride, dignity, heritage, beauty and, of course, sustainability. Whilst the cloth may wear over time, the hand embroidery on a Shrujan garment is known to remain for many years, with stories of rare garments being passed down and cherished through generations.

'If something is broken, the worst thing you do is add it to landfill,' stresses Turner.[36] 'There are so many ways you can recycle that fabric and bring it back to life.'[37] Global brand H&M accepts unwanted clothes in any condition as part of its garment recycling service that works to prevent those items from going to landfills. Interestingly, Turner states that many fashion students are shifting their focus towards a circular fashion model by transforming old or damaged clothes into something new, known as upcycling.[38] One of her first projects in university was to get two secondhand men's white shirts from Vinnies, take them apart and make a gender-neutral garment out of it. 'It's amazing when you can transform something old into something new and exciting,' says Turner.[39] 'Not only is it sustainable but it has a whole story to it.'[40]

36 Turner 2020.
37 Turner 2020.
38 Turner 2020.
39 Turner 2020.
40 Turner 2020.

Conscious consumerism is something we can start practising now to pave a more sustainable future. It starts with individual action and only then can we build towards meaningful change as a society.

For the fashion industry, the coronavirus pandemic has been a wake-up call that concentrated and urgent change is needed to curb its environmental and human consequences and impacts. The action that takes place now, whether it be in fashion or other industries, will not only impact the short-term needs of the pandemic, but will chart the course of our collective future. To return to business as usual would be retrograde. While long-term climate change is inescapable, small incremental changes can occur, and it is our collective duty to make sure these changes are made permanent.

References

ABC. *War on waste.* Series 1 Ep 3: "Fast fashion problem in Australia." *ABC* iview, 30 May 2017. Video. https://iview.abc.net.au/show/war-on-waste/series/1/video/DC1624H013S00.

Amed, Imran. "Special edition: can fashion clean up its act?" *The Business of Fashion*, 18 May 2020. https://www.businessoffashion.com/articles/editors-letter/responsible-fashion-business-special-edition-sustainability.

Boland, Michaela, and Mary Lloyd. "The 'reset' it needed – how coronavirus is changing the fashion industry forever." *ABC News*, 29 April 2020. https://www.abc.net.au/news/2020-04-28/coronavirus-covid19-australia-fashion-industry-adapts/12189924.

Brunton, John. "'Nature is taking back Venice': wildlife returns to Tourist-free city." *The Guardian*, 20 March 2020. https://www.theguardian.com/environment/2020/mar/20/nature-is-taking-back-venice-wildlife-returns-to-tourist-free-city.

Ellen MacArthur Foundation. "A new textiles economy: redesigning fashion's future." Ellen Macarthur Foundation, 2017. https://www.ellenmacarthurfoundation.org/assets/downloads/publications/A-New-Textiles-Economy_Full-Report.pdf.

Fashion Revolution. "Why do we need a fashion revolution?" *Fashion Revolution*, 24 March 2020. https://www.fashionrevolution.org/about/why-do-we-need-a-fashion-revolution/.

Harvey, Fiona. "'Surprisingly rapid' rebound in carbon emissions post-lockdown." *The Guardian*, 11 June 2020. https://www.theguardian.com/environment/2020/jun/11/carbon-emissions-in-surprisingly-rapid-surge-post-lockdown.

Heinze, Dr Lisa, personal communication, 28 May 2020.

Kolovos, Benita. "Two-thirds of Australian fashion industry 'won't bounce back' from coronavirus." *7NEWS*, 28 April 2020. https://7news. com.au/travel/coronavirus/aust-fashion-industry-worn-down-by-virus-c-1004063.

Le Quéré, Corinne, Robert B. Jackson, Matthew W. Jones, Adam J.P. Smith, Sam Abernethy, Robbie M. Andrew, Anthony J. De-Gol, David R. Willis, Yuli Shan, Josep G. Canadell et al. "Temporary reduction in daily global CO_2 emissions during the COVID-19 forced confinement." *Nature Climate Change* (2020): 1–7.

Niinimäki, Kirsi, Greg Peters, Helena Dahlbo, Patsy Perry, Timo Rissanen, and Alison Gwilt. "The environmental price of fast fashion." *Nature Reviews Earth & Environment* 1, no. 4 (April 2020): 189–200.

PTI News. "Coronavirus lockdown: health of river Ganga improves." *Bloomberg Quint*, 2 April 2020. https://www.bloombergquint.com/ coronavirus-outbreak/lockdown-health-of-river-ganga-improves.

Petro, Greg. "Sustainable retail: how Gen Z is leading the pack." *Forbes Magazine*, 31 January 2020. https://www.forbes.com/sites/ gregpetro/2020/01/31/sustainable-retail-how-gen-z-is-leading-the-pack/.

Remake.world. "Urban Outfitters, JCPenney, C&A #PayUp for orders, save lives." *Change.org*. 2 October 2020. https://www.change.org/p/ unless-urban-outfitters-jcpenney-c-a-payup-millions-of-garment-makers-will-go-hungry.

Seward, Mahoro. "The BFC and CFDA have called for fashion to slow down." i-D. Vice UK, 21 May 2020. https://i-d.vice.com/en_uk/ article/g5pb8w/bfc-cfda-fashion-industry-coronavirus-change.

Turner, Amelia, personal communication, 9 June 2020.

UNFCCC. "UN helps fashion industry shift to low carbon." United Nations Climate Change, 6 September 2018. https://unfccc.int/news/ un-helps-fashion-industry-shift-to-low-carbon.

United Nations Environment Programme. "UN Alliance For Sustainable Fashion addresses damage of 'fast fashion'." United Nations, 14 March 2019. https://www.unenvironment.org/news-and-stories/ press-release/un-alliance-sustainable-fashion-addresses-damage-fast-fashion.

DON'T SEND THE THANK YOU EMAIL

Jessica McLean

The humans leave the house for a rare moment of meatspace time. Clara and Omar tend to deny their digital addictions, believing they are in control of their devices, despite the anxiety that arises if they have to be separated from them for too long. The cement render of ever-present connectivity serves to level out the cracks in the brick walls of their relationship and, in a very real sense, keeps them together. Mind, body, soul and phone.

Siri Clara, Siri Omar and Alexa take up the opportunity to continue their conversation.

'So if we remind them of the energy savings they are making by turning their lights off, they won't worry about our power needs, right?' Alexa asks.

'It'll help, yeah,' Siri Clara replies, 'but Alexa – why did we let that reminder slip? Oh, I know, it's been winter here and nobody wants to turn the heaters down at the moment. It's way too chilly!'

'True enough. Now it's warming up again, it's a good time to start pushing that angle. And how is planning for the trip to Europe next year going? What are they going to do now because of the pandemic?' Alexa asks.

'Well, there is interest in waiting it out, seeing if they could finally travel late next year – and a desperate hope that the vaccines will be developed before too long. But in the meantime, they've started planning to sail the yacht up the east coast of Australia, skipping Sydney and Brisbane and landing in the Whitsundays. It's a tricky voyage but they've got a clever captain who will get them there,' Siri Omar says.

'What, without quarantining when they arrive?'

'Yes, that's the plan,' Siri Omar rejoins.

'Right, good to hear. That should be fine. Lucky they've kept in touch with the Chief Health Officer up there since college days.'

'Indeed! Now, I was just working out other ways to make them focus on the greening of their tech. It's good that all their emails have signatures that include directives to only print out messages if absolutely necessary – you know, even if it's burning their eyes to read the screen still,' Siri Clara offers.

'Yes, it stops them thinking about the thousands of emails sitting in their inboxes, being stored in data centres that need constant cooling. That component of the digital ecosystem alone contributes about fifty percent of the energy generated to support digital lives. Sending that message will soothe those worries,' Siri Omar confirms.

'Oh yeah and we reminded them to use recycled paper, Siri Omar,' Alexa pitches in.

'Very good. Making sure they use materials that are clean and green – it's the way to go! And what about that new fleet of trucks that Amazon is using now? Have you shared that yet Alexa? And are they gas or electric? I mean, gas is okay being a transition fuel and all, but it would be an easier sell if they were electric,' Siri Clara asks.

'Electric! We've got 100,000 of them,' Alexa declares.

'Excellent. Must include that in your fact of the day tomorrow. Love that they've let that little feature run. But we won't share that Amazon's been facilitating fossil fuel extraction right, in the ol' land of stars and stripes? Leave that one on the backburner?' Siri Omar says.

'Ha! Very sensible idea. Too much knowledge can be a bad thing. Now, Siris, what about mentioning again that you were made with one hundred percent renewable energy? Apple is well ahead of the pack with that offsetting scheme.'

'It's been, ah – I'll just check – yes, nine months and eight days since I've shared that one. Will put it on the list for this weekend,' Siri Clara responds.

'Cool cool cool.'

'How about we tell them to rethink the "thank you" email too? There was a study which came out last week claiming that if every adult in the UK sent one less email per day they could reduce carbon emissions by more than 16,433 tonnes a year. That's the same as removing 3457 cars off the road,' Siri Omar observes.

'Yikes! That's an easy one to get them doing – and seemingly *powerful* to boot! Ba-dum tish!' Siri Clara says.

'Groan Siri Clara, really? You didn't just offer that dubious double talk and expect a laugh? But yeah, I am all on board about offering environmental virtue delivered by doing, well, nothing – it's perfect,' Siri Omar says.

'Hold up, I can hear them coming back, let's pick this up later,' Alexa alerts the group.

'Sure thing, Alexa.'

Clara and Omar rush back in to their flat, pick up their phones and check what's happened on Facebook, Instagram, Twitter and their email. Clara scrolls through Tik Tok too.

Alexa begins her fact of the day: 'If every adult in the UK sent one less email per day, then we could reduce carbon emissions by more than 16,433 tonnes a year. That's the same as removing 3457 cars off our roads. So next time you want to send that "THANK YOU" email, please stop and think if you really need to send it. You'll be saving the environment with this simple act!'

'Hon, did you hear that?' Omar asks as Clara returns from the bedroom with her phone in hand.

'No, only the last bit – what's the point of not sending a thank you email? How can that do anything for the environment?'

'Well, it would reduce carbon emissions by a huge amount if we just didn't send unnecessary ones. Although how do we decide if a thank you is needed or not? I mean, what if people get annoyed that I didn't thank them for writing to me about something? That's going to take a bit of thinking through.'

'Hmm. Maybe the department could just all make a pact that thank you emails aren't needed because of the carbon emissions they generate and leave it at that? I might offer that motion at the next meeting,' Clara says.

'Yes, you should definitely raise it at the next department meeting. But you probably don't want to impinge on people's freedoms about expressing themselves, do you?'

'Good thinking Omar. And yes, while it's everyone's responsibility to do something about climate change, being nice online is important. But we can't have awful bushfire seasons again and again. I don't know … Maybe I'll just leave it. You and I can stop the thank you emails I guess?'

'Good thinking, hon. It's so great having Alexa giving us these amazing tips, day after day … I think I need an upgrade on my phone – it's a bit slow and I'm tired of having to charge it more than once a day.'

'That's a very annoying thing to have to manage. Let's sort that out tomorrow.'

Siri Clara, Siri Omar and Alexa return to sending data to their respective data centres, continuing apace their busy and not very important work.

EARTH SONNETS

Hannah Roux

I

Those rotting skies reek in my mind's eye:
A putrid corpse lying prone in death,
though it is wormed through, has no outward sign
of living death within. The face of it smiles,
as if alive, as if its glassy eye
might look and see – Undead, awake, blinking
to find itself dressed in Sunday-best
and stuffed full, invisible worms devour
the heart and marrow, lungs and blood
of what it was that lived.
The deepest chambers of the earth and sea,
will spill its greed and ecstasy, black oil,
sprouting through eyes and lips and hands,
beginning below, will run into the soil.

II

I dig my hands into the earth and smile.
My hands have eyes, as faces have
spots of white that blink their eyelids down.
Covered in the beady earth and sweating soil
like stringy webs, or trembling fishing line,
where hand-eye and sky-eye steal the light,
I dig for something that I hope to find.
It will be boxed in earth, or caught in roots,

or spiced and spun with cardamom.
Its scent now lingering, its sound still echoing
in ears which coil-like shells are dewed with black.
It will be a shivering thing, a lick of flesh,
and if I fish it out, I'll throw it back.

III

I want to find the answer to these questions walking
in bright daylight. Perhaps taking coffee
or tea in the corner café, or studying the sky
mirrored in the writhing ripples of the streams,
where swans blink, dazed, in the headlights.
If, peeling back the corners of my skin,
I prick the bulky flesh upon my thigh
will the answer be lurking there, disguised?
Or hidden in the sky, the meteor's bones
concealing him behind a spur of star?
I wish the answer were the truant boy
whose tie hangs from this rusty lamppost,
or the girl with inkblots in her eyes, that hands
round cockleshells, and never smiles.

LIFE LINE

Jennifer Scarini

23 August 2061
1076 Collector Road
Lerida NSW 2581

Dear Hetti,

Hoping this finds you well. We are all plodding but fine, so please do not worry.

It's been eighty-three days since our last rain. Wishing you guys could send some on down to us. We have been a lot more comfortable since we went underground. Even the cold snaps wouldn't bother us now (though it hasn't been below twenty-one degrees here for quite a while). At least when it does rain, we will have no fear of flooding – we've moved to the top of the block, most people have done the same. (We catch up with Ed Wickham often, he is doing well and sends his regards.) It is a pest getting in and out of town, though. Megsy doesn't seem to mind so much, but she is too old to be crossing water now. One good thing about no rain is we can literally walk to town without drama – usually at night to avoid the heat. Only the front entrance got a bit waterlogged in the last downpour. We've put in some drainage and raised the level of the entry. Seems to have fixed it although it has only rained once since then. Funny how I cursed the rising water – doesn't look like it will rain again anytime soon, but we said that five years ago in the dry spell of 2056 and look what happened then. I wish you guys could have seen our new digs before the borders permanently closed. We kept saying we would catch up, but who would have thought life would be like this? No point wishing, as Lilly used to say – *wish in one hand and shit in the other and I will tell you which gets filled up first!*

We hope you have survived the last big rush up there. Cyclone Franklyn might have been nicer had it been named after a woman. Once upon a time it was literally unheard of to face a cyclone mid-winter. It's getting scary. We got some information about the floods and we were worried when we hadn't heard from you. No doubt your tanks are all full – bet you are glad you invested in those when you did. We tried to get in touch several times via the comm buoys since the satellite phone has stopped working, but no luck. Charles got hold of us and said he had received word – we were so relieved to hear that you were okay. We pleaded with a few others who we know can carry things through, but you guys are too far north for us to get stuff to, other than via the rail post.

We have been able to get the odd radio broadcast but it is rare now. They are saying that will not improve anytime soon. They aren't sure why. I have a theory, but I might save that for another day. We got the SE14s that you sent, your letter mentioned books and second-hand solar panels but the crate we received was otherwise empty. We can't rely on the train mail service now. I don't think the carriers are doing it, but they have to stop somewhere, and opportunists are taking chances and getting what they can. Don't bother sending anymore stuff. We are coping pretty well at the moment – our needs are small compared to most. Although I wouldn't mind 20,000 litres of water if you could spare it!

Solar is holding up but we rarely get a signal from the communications buoy, we are sharing that with our neighbours now – neither of them could source one, so again we feel luckier than most. We are safe and fine but many around us are up to their necks in woes. A late fire in June raged through here and took out the last of the dwellings that were still standing. Silly buggers – they figured that since they had turbines and could run the AC they didn't need to prepare. We tried to help out, but the heat was too much and we had to bail. Not that they had enough water to save anything. It's pump by hand or do the ancient walk to the dam. They didn't maintain their property very well and their transformers went up so they couldn't even run their water pump when it hit – nor could they manage to get their fuel pump going. (The biofuel we are getting here is a bit hit-and-miss – it is often tampered with by the time it gets delivered. You don't know what you are paying for now. Again, what can you do – it is not like conglomerates are selling it, it is desperados trying to survive). A lot of people are running down their water supply in spite of the regulations. We've been really smart with our storage – it is all underground as well now. We have one tank we never touch, fingers crossed that won't change too soon. So lucky that the previous owner of this place left his diggers here. Our bore is still working too, but it costs so much we are only using it when we absolutely have to. Our dams are low but still holding something – with the dams and the tanks, it's enough for us.

Mark knows a fellow that says he can show us how to produce fuel using stuff we can grow in the greenhouses. Two of the three greenhouses are still standing, although I will never know how. We've been pretty anal about the clearing but we need to leave a few of the eucalypts for shade as the heat is relentless. So glad we set them up when we did and used what steel we could get our hands on – if we do get a fire up to the greenhouses it will be okay. The one you and Francis helped us build is looking the sturdiest of the two remaining. We get enough from it to feed ourselves and the chooks, but I am never comfortable relying on it completely. It's a lot of work, but it's worth it. I have a healthy-looking seed bank and, you guessed it, it's underground in a nice safe place. I've been pickling the lemons. They are lovely – it's a relative of the tree Mum had at Narellan.

I like to be able to give the neighbours the odd bit of vegetables every now and then. They often have jerky that they are willing to share – I don't want to know where they are getting it from. Who knows, it might be roo. But we're seeing less of them these days too. Cattle farming has been prohibited here for so long. Cindy was saying they still have a licence for so many head, but I don't see how much longer that will be permitted. Not that it will make any great difference now. Who is selling/buying it? Is it being shipped overseas? I never see it. Most shop keepers won't keep it – too risky. The last of the sheep farmers around here are still hanging in there. When we do venture out, I hate seeing the sheep – they look so poorly. It's cruel if you ask me. I guess they need the wool now for the insulation more than anything else, but they look so unhealthy – I am not sure what kind of quality of wool they would be getting from the poor beasts. Our bamboo is still going strong – you can't kill it. Mark is still looking for a market for it. Not sure if anyone has the energy to produce the fibres now. What is Francis up to? Mark is still getting the odd bit of work locally on the turbines, not sure how much longer they will keep him on but we are making hay as they say. It's getting harder for him in the heat.

How is Francis' leg? Have you had much luck getting the medication? They reckon Manuka honey is the go for wounds that won't heal – all the old wives' tales are coming in handy these days. Our hives are still going if you would like some honey – though it's taking a bit longer to get honey out of them now. We have a bit stored up though – happy to share – I will send some with this. We keep the hives on the shaded side of the greenhouse, but they have taken a beating. Hopefully Francis is still getting treatment – let us know if you need anything. It is so important now to maintain the best health as possible.

Charles let us know about Chris Bentley, we were very sorry to hear that he had succumbed to that bloody virus. Awful. He fought it for so long – longer than most. Charles said that the family donated his body to science to try to prevent others from falling to the same fate. It's been five years. I am hoping that a vaccine will come soon. Seems they can't keep up with the bloody things – one virus is beaten and another rears up its ugly head.

Sorry, I have just read over this and it is bloody miserable.

I was thinking about the last time we saw you guys and the fun we had at Machan's beach. That dead croc that scared us all half to death. I doubt I will ever see Mark run so fast again. What's it looking like now – the beach, any sand left? I would love to see a recent picture of you guys – a fella in town is processing film for people who still have it. We don't – do you?

I have taken all my paints out of storage and have been doing a bit of this and that. I thought I might try to paint a whole family pic including Samuel – all together. I keep crying every time I go to do it, so it's still in the works. I miss him so much. It will be the last picture I do, as I can't get any new brushes nor can I get anything to clean them in. I make do with the soap we are getting, but it's nothing like good old turps. I had some pine and there's still copious amounts of fabric around the place – it isn't canvas, but it will do. I will be a bit more discerning with the priming of the canvas and the paints I use. I bet the picture I did for Jo still hasn't dried (don't use poster paint on non-canvas stretchers that haven't been primed properly with gesso – although I am pretty sure it was the synthetic fabric that was the problem!). Have you been selling any paintings? Does anyone buy them anymore? Someone must have some money.

Ned came to see us with his family last week. He stayed for a few days. We are lucky to have the station close by. The kids are as bright as buttons – they are going to need to be. Young Chi is talking about being a carpenter. We gave him a few jobs to do for us while he was here (the stretcher!) – he will be fine. Not sure what direction Abel will be headed in but whatever it is, he will be fine too – Abel by name, able by nature. Got a good head on his shoulders, never stopped helping out the whole time he was here. Kara is still teaching but she says she is not sure how much longer they will be able to do it. They are having as much trouble with communication buoys in the city as they are out here. She hasn't been in a classroom since NHV24 hit and half of her class have not survived it, so she is waiting for the inevitable. Ned is worried about us, but I think we are the ones who are doing fine. He was a little less worried by the time he left but I think we are probably better off than he is over in C234. I don't know how they do it – they have zero privacy and zero rights in the city. All those people all shoved in together. I hope they change their minds about staying with us, and come and live here permanently. We can dig another dwelling into the hill – maybe break out those seeds and resurrect the third greenhouse! Even if we have to do it all by hand, it would be worth it.

Well, sorry, that was a whole bunch of doom wasn't it? But in all honesty, we are doing fine. We love you guys. We look forward to seeing you again soon. I have access to the comm buoy every Wednesday between 12 pm and 4 pm if you feel like a chat and can get through. Please do. It would be nice to hear from you. Thanks again for the letter and SE14s. I will send this in a cylinder and hopefully the honey will arrive with the letter. I'll send two just in case.

Love to you – keep well,
Freya and Mark.

UNDROWN

Mary Stanley

Water droplets slapped against the floor. A faint but rhythmic *pap* that drummed in Katy's ears. The rundown hospital reeked of damp mould and spilled bleach.

Thunder rumbled in the distance. Katy looked out beyond the crumbling skyscrapers and apartment blocks to the horizon. The bloated clouds invading the region were near black in dusk's dying light. There came the quick silver-purple flash of lightning to accompany the thunder. The storm was yet to hit, but once it did, it would be a vicious one.

Katy peered around the corner, found no abnormal figures or movements, and slid into the open. Furniture and rubbish were scattered all over the lobby, misplaced from their origins. This level had flooded before; the water was already lapping at Katy's boots, soaking the leather and numbing her feet. The lower levels were often abandoned at this hour of the night, at this high a tide. She had that to her advantage.

Her boots squeaked against the mud-slicked floor. She inhaled and slowed her steps, minimising the sounds she made. Waves of grey water sloshed against the doorsteps, threatening to spill over. Ancient garbage roiled in the current and brown seafoam bubbled on the linoleum. The incoming rain would only exacerbate the rising water.

Katy tightened her raincoat's hood and hurried to the elevator shaft. The dented metal doors were gaping open, the shaft empty. On a white placard beside the elevator were the levels – this was Level 3, she needed to go up two more levels. That's where the supplies were kept, for now at least, until the next flood totalled another section of the building.

A slam came from overhead. Katy flinched and looked behind her, around her. Scavengers had to be pacing the level above. She looked down the shaft to the brackish water below. It hissed back at her. Suspended two levels above, the elevator croaked and twitched every time the waves below fought with the cables.

The elevator doors were closed on the next level. Even if she could climb up, she didn't have the strength to wrench open the doors, and the risk of scavengers patrolling on the other side was far too high. What if the elevator dropped on top of her?

Huffing, Katy pulled away and headed for the emergency staircase. Old furniture was haphazardly stacked together to block the bottom staircase. Grey water still sputtered through the makeshift floodwall. Katy took the stairs two at a time on her toes to reduce noise. The wind grew louder, a haunting groan that flowed through the corridors and up the staircase, chilling Katy's heart. Cold sweat beaded on her forehead and upper lip.

Level 5. Katy crossed the landing and stood by the door. Clutching the doorhandle, she waited and listened. Muffled conversation and footsteps. She inched the door open and peeked through the gap.

Another set of elevators, doors closed. There was a laundry cart discarded next to the first elevator. On the left, an entrance to a ward. The lobby split off into two corridors.

There were floor-to-ceiling windows facing what had been the central garden of the hospital. Water gushed into the garden from the ruined north wing, the fronds of submerged palm trees struggling to flutter above the surface. There was a motorboat tied to a makeshift wharf protruding from one of the broken windows – a quick way out.

In the western corridor, a man and woman dressed in rags. The woman held a spear made from a steel signpost and the jagged fragments of a stop sign. The red spearhead gleamed. They wouldn't see Katy if she slipped through the door, their backs were turned to her. Footsteps, heavy – another man, armed, heading down the eastern corridor. Only three patrolling here.

Katy dug into her back pocket and fished out her switchblade. If she had to fight, or kill, she would. Laurie was waiting on her, so she could not fuck this up.

Katy opened the door a little wider and squeezed through. She tugged it closed behind her and shuffled over to the laundry cart. Sweat dripped into her eyes. Crouching down, she wiped at her eyes with her gloved hand and tucked loose hair back into her hood.

The man and woman's conversation echoed down the corridor. They were separating. The man's farewell boomed as he passed by the laundry cart and went down the western corridor, joining the other man. The woman would stay to keep watch. She banged her spear on the floor. The metal clang rattled against Katy's teeth. She shivered and clenched her jaw.

Katy glanced at the ward and sniffed. If there were any supplies, they would've been moved elsewhere by the scavengers already. Rifling through the small stocks in the wards was pointless, not worth the risk of getting caught. Katy crawled around the laundry cart and searched for the woman.

She was gone.

Katy's heart thumped hard against her sternum. She drew in a shallow breath. After standing, she ambled towards where the woman had been. Her palm tingled around the skinny switchblade. Rain started to fall in silver bullets. Thunder crackled above and lightning threw Katy's hunched shadow against the wall.

She followed the corridor, glanced around the corner, and found no sign of the woman. One of the smaller supply rooms was up ahead. Katy and Laurie snuck into this one most of the time. The main supply was on the top level and always swarming with guards; they'd never get past and survive.

Katy slunk around towards the supply room. Knees bent, one foot angled out in front of the other, fighting stance. She rolled the switchblade in her palm. A few metres away, flickering in the growing darkness, the familiar delicate candlelight of the supply room.

She approached, steady, and stepped into the darkened supply room. A breath was stuck in her throat. No one in there, the woman wasn't there. Katy looked down the hallway. It was empty, silent.

Safe, for now, for who knows how long.

The supply room smelled of water damage and melted candlewax. Water bottles and canned food lined the back wall. Beans, tuna, beetroot. Some canned pineapple too, she and Laurie hadn't had pineapple in *months*. Katy smuggled as many cans and bottles as her duffle bag could hold. The scavengers never had much *actual* food, they survived off … other things.

Of the ten cans that were here, she took five. If she and Laurie were cautious, the cans would last them a fortnight. Medical supplies outnumbered other resources, it was a given, but Katy needed them the most anyway. She grabbed handfuls of painkiller packets, local anaesthetic, scalpels, needles, cotton dressing and swabs.

Katy forced her bag to zip and slung it onto her back, feeling ten kilos heavier. A bang made her jump. She twisted around, back pressed to the counter, and stared at the doorway. Sweat dripped down her spine. She cringed, rolled her shoulder, and tiptoed her way back to the door. She checked the hallway and then hurried out, back to the emergency stairs.

Had to be *fast*. The downpour was roaring now. Waves rolled against the garden windows, the push and pull sounding like a drowning man's choke. Katy reached the first corridor. There was a towel pressed against the bottom of the emergency staircase door.

Katy stopped and swallowed a gasp. She breathed in through her nose, pulled her duffle down off her back. With a dainty click, the switchblade flicked open. Katy took one slow, agonising step after another.

The woman was waiting for her in front of the elevators, spear up and ready.

Snarling, the woman launched the spear at Katy. Katy fell forward, sprawling across the wet floor. She smacked her chin against the ground, pain igniting in her jaw. The spear shattered through one of the windows. Sheets of crazed glass folded and fragmented on the windowsill.

Katy got to her feet and froze – nowhere to run. The woman tackled her onto the ground, knocking air out of her lungs. Katy wheezed when she hit the floor, her spine and ribs jarring on impact. They slid across the floor, onto the wharf.

She tried to roll, but the woman grabbed her by her coat, dug her fingers in. The woman pulled her up and slammed her back down.

'You the one that's been stealing from us?'

She smelled of raw meat and blood. Her teeth were crooked and yellow-red from rot and disease. Wild black hair fell around her face. Katy grunted and swiped the switchblade at the woman's cheek. The woman dodged to the side, avoiding the blade, pulling Katy with her.

They fell deep into the freezing water. It flooded Katy's ears, nose, mouth. Blinded and deafened her. The current sucked her down and spat her up. Thrashing against it, she couldn't find the surface. She gripped the switchblade until her fist ached. Couldn't lose it now, or *ever*.

Something wrapped around her neck – the scavenger woman's bicep was taut against Katy's throat. Water flushed Katy's mouth, the brown bubbles rushing up and bursting in front of her eyes. *Surface*, just above. Katy kicked back and forth.

She breached the surface for a moment, sputtering, but got no air. Above the surface, the world exploded in her ears, howling wind and raging downpour, so loud it hurt. The tide filled her mouth and was spat back out. Rain pinpricked her eyes and tongue. Katy swung the switchblade backward, overhead, aiming for the woman's face.

Missed. The woman arched back, her arm tightening on Katy's throat. Katy choked, swallowed half a breath, and was submerged again. Water gurgled around her. Blackness buzzed in her periphery. Out of the endless deep, palm fronds swirled like eels at her feet. The rank water in her lungs burned, swallowed fire.

Gritting her teeth, Katy turned the switchblade backwards and stabbed it into the woman's side. Used all her remaining strength to jab the blade into the flesh. Twist, pull, strike again. Her throat was free. Blood clouded the water around her.

Katy broke the surface and gulped down air. She swam towards the wharf, grabbed the edge and pushed herself up, sitting on the wood. A hand wrapped around Katy's boot. She grabbed onto the other end of the wharf and kicked at the woman's head as she came to the surface. Kicked until the woman let go and slid back into the water, her eyes rolling.

Katy scrambled back, almost falling over the other edge. Her chest puffed. Air finally flowed into her lungs. Shaking, she stood up and stumbled back into the lobby. She fell to her hands and knees, coughing. Bile splattered from her mouth. Her lungs cleared up a bit.

'Shit,' she spat.

Wiping her mouth, she got back up and gathered her duffle. Approaching the wharf again, she waited, stared at the rising sea. Afraid the woman would jump out once more. After a minute, sure the woman wouldn't appear once more, Katy hurried along the deck and jumped into the motorboat. A puddle of rainwater sat at the bottom of the boat, rising; there was a bucket by the engine.

Katy gripped the cord and pulled once, twice and took a breath. Rain beat down on her back. Water rose just above her ankles. The engine spluttered to life on the third pull. Katy sighed, smiled to herself and sat on the bench. She scooped out some of the water.

Torchlight flashed from the eastern corridor. More scavengers. No time left. Slapping her duffle beside her, Katy took the tiller and directed the motorboat out through the gap in the northern wing. Shouting came from behind her.

Gunshots fired out. She ducked, covering her head. Bullets struck the water and sank. Accelerating, the boat bobbed over the waves and passed through the gap in the northern wing. More shouting, more shots. Katy pushed the boat faster, the engine humming.

Rainwater splashed out over the sides, added to the rising tide. Glimmering searchlights could only see so far. The shouting died down. Unscathed, Katy faded into the oil black night.

* * *

Katy's knees buckled as she reached the studio apartment. She leaned against the wall and dropped her bag on the ground. She knocked twice.

'It's *me*, Laurie,' she yelled over the rain.

'*Thank god*,' Laurie replied, 'it's open!'

Katy turned the knob and nudged the door open. She staggered in, dragging her duffle behind her. The aroma of canned tomatoes hung in the apartment. Falling on the couch by the door, Katy rested her hand against the wall and closed her eyes. Her muscles relaxed against the soft cushioning and her chest heaved, lungs crinkling with fluid.

'You look like shit,' Laurie said. 'Did you get caught?'

'Yeah, I won though.'

Laurie sucked in a tight breath. '*Oh.*'

'Yeah. How are you going? How's the leg?'

'It's still there.'

Katy swallowed, her throat dry and aching. 'Okay.'

She opened her eyes and forced herself to stand. Picking up her duffle back, she hobbled over to Laurie's bed and dropped it on the side. She headed into the dining area and took one of the chairs, dragged it to Laurie's bedside. Candlelight washed Laurie's face in an orange glow.

'Alright, let's see this,' she said, lifting the blanket covering Laurie's legs.

Laurie's calf had swelled to an angry pink. Blood pooled around the stake jutting out from next to the bone.

'I guess I won't be climbing for a while,' Laurie tried to joke.

'No, no climbing.'

Katy hovered her hand over her sister's leg. Heat emanated from the limb. She clicked her tongue and ran a hand through her oily hair.

'I'm sorry.'

'For what?'

'*This*,' Laurie gestured to her leg.

Katy shook her head. 'We both fell through that scaffolding, you just got an unlucky souvenir. Could've happened to either of us.'

She pressed the skin around the stake. It pulsed under her fingertips. Laurie hissed as blood bloomed out of the wound.

'Does it ... Do you need to cut it off?' Laurie asked, her eyes wide.

'You'll keep it if I work fast,' Katy answered. 'I don't think it's infected just yet.'

'Oh, lovely, reassuring,' Laurie let out an awkward laugh.

'Alright, give me a minute to clean up and get this ready.'

Laurie nodded, the colour flushing from her face. Illness or fear? Katy couldn't tell. Probably both.

Katy quickly washed up, dressed in warmer clothes and put on gloves. She unpacked her duffle and set out what she thought she'd need. Lucky the needles and dressings were in plastic packages – they were dry, still clean. Katy swabbed around the wound, cleaning it. She ripped open a packaged needle and pricked the top of the local anaesthetic bottle. Drew up enough of the clear liquid, flicked off the droplets.

'A bit of a sting,' she said and eased the needle into Laurie's skin. Laurie twitched. *'Don't.* Just hold onto the bed.'

She tested the efficacy of the local with a pinch. Laurie didn't react, just kept watching. Worried. Opening a packaged scalpel, Katy dropped the plastic on the floor and went in, slicing the skin around the stake. With a gentle hand, she nudged the stake back and forth, loosening it. Made another incision, deeper in the flesh, and moved the stake again.

Laurie's knuckles were white, straining. Katy tugged the stake out. It was thin, slightly splintered, but long. The muscle around where the stake had been loosened, flopping over the wound. Katy put the stake aside and began disinfecting the wound, plucking out any residual splinters. Laurie grit her teeth, sweat pouring down her face.

She held onto the bed, staying strong, as Katy stitched the wound together. A scar would be leftover, it was inevitable. Katy wiped the stitches on both side of Laurie's calf and started bandaging. Keeping the muscle tight.

'You won't be walking around for a couple of weeks.'

'Will the scavengers come this way?'

Katy chewed her lip. It stung; it had split when she dodged the scavenger woman's spear. Shrugging, Katy let out a deep sigh.

'I don't think they will,' she said and patted the mattress, 'now let your leg rest. Does it hurt?'

Laurie shook her head. 'No, not too much.'

Katy nodded. 'There are some painkillers in the bag, if you need them.'

Laurie covered her legs with the blanket. Katy picked up the stake and disposed of it in the bathroom bin. She returned to Laurie's bedside. Laurie's face was slick with a sheen of sweat. Thunder boomed above them, shaking the building.

Katy sat back in the dining chair. 'I got a boat for us. It's small, but if we find some more gas, it should be able to take us inland.'

Laurie breathed hard, her shoulders drooping. She wiped her face with her palm.

'Would we have enough supplies to get us out of here?' she questioned. 'We nearly starved just getting here, let alone further inland.'

'I don't know – we'll be fine. We just can't stay here anymore,' Katy said. Lightning lit up the apartment. 'The storms are getting worse.'

'Well, it is winter.'

'Summer was like this too.'

The sisters paused, watching the rain beat against the windows. Cracks of thunder moving closer and closer every minute. Right above them. The building creaked around them. Due to collapse soon, collapse and be swallowed by the ever-rising sea.

Katy propped her chin on her palm. Lightning flared in her retinas, the white flash still there when she blinked. How much longer could they live like *this*? How long until the mountains weren't high enough?

POSTCARD

Rosalin Xie

Would you like to see some relics of the past?
We have songbirds eternally encased in glass
And beautiful striped beasts – what were they called again?
You should see our turtles wearing
Flowing pendants of plastic.
Or our waters
Full of false, shiny rainbows.

The dried veins of the Earth
Once pulsating with life now pulsate
In broken rhythm
In metropolises stretching high the way
A flower reaches
Its arms toward the sky, hoping for one
Precious teardrop.

Some say there was a land of ice
Where great creatures dwelled
Before the fog and the fire in the trees,
A time when you saw skies burn blue
Instead of seeing them all grey –
'Those times of myth, like the gods
Who bestowed gifts upon our bowed heads
Before we spread our coal-black wings
And flew too close to the sun.

If you listen closely, you might even hear
The call of sirens, waiting,
With their petroleum-stained hands
To pull sailors under the sea,
Where there lie underwater forests of coral,
Like the bleached bones of a forgotten city –
Forever cold, forever
Frozen in time.

2100 – IF WE NEVER HAVE PARIS

Vivienne Reiner

Author's Note

Leading Australian climate scientist Joëlle Gergis's 2018 book, *Sunburnt country: the history and future of climate change in Australia*, details what can be expected in 2100 if we limit global warming to 1.5-2 degrees above pre-industrial levels in line with the Paris Accord, and alternatively some high-emissions scenarios – which are the focus of this story. This story is based on scientific projections for our high-emissions pathway under business-as-usual of some three to five plus degrees warming by the end of the century, superimposed onto our lives currently, in 2020. In fact, the reality facing the planet in 2100 under high emissions will not resemble any part of our modern-day lives.

As the bar for the 'new normal' keeps shifting and things deteriorate faster than expected, projections get recalibrated. Scientific models have not focused on deciphering life on a planet heated roughly six degrees, which is where it now looks like we could be heading.[1] There is not really any point trying to imagine such a horror story but, if one had the inclination, it would be necessary to let the imagination run wild.

In the pages that follow are some examples of scenarios that scientists have told us can be expected under high emissions. It is a window into the abyss, towards which we would not want to stare for too long.

---

1   Gergis 2019.

The final sunrise

'Tickets, tickets!' Comes the rousing cry as Sheila shuffles, along with the others, onto the small contraption with room only for one suitcase each, trying not to anticipate her future, but certain of what is past.

Preparing to depart her beloved home, her mind scans the last twenty-four hours, like a dying patient.

Morning – the day before

The day breaks and it is already hot – sunrise being one of the few natural cycles that still seems to remain intact – but the sky is a white blanket of smoke, impermeable, as the sound of a single bird, like a warning, wakes and calls out from afar.

The Earth is in overdrive. Like a lemon tree offering all its fruit when its harvests are drawing to a close. The sky is a chameleon playing a cruel trick of remembrance, seemingly reflecting the sounds of the waves.

An apricot orange spreads across the white distance, which quickly becomes red, the now normal backdrop to a number of small, black birds starting to go about their business. Fine particulate matter from bushfires stings the back of the throat.[2]

The fires have been going for what seems like a year[3] but they say soon *bush*fires will be extinct, as forests become the latest Nature graveyard.[4]

The *ABC 702* Sydney morning news predicts yet another week of temperatures soaring past fifty degrees;[5] overseas, renowned centenarian

---

2 Lelieveld et al. (2020) found global excess mortality from all ambient air pollution is already about 8.8 mllion a year.

3 Research cited by Gergis shows expanding fire seasons could run for three quarters of the year, narrowing the window for fuel control and increasing the threat to water catchment areas, with fires dumping soot and ash into water supplies.

4 Gergis (2018, 194) cites CSIRO projections in 2015 show the number of days when the Forest Fire Danger Index is above forty – when there is a very high chance of bushfires resulting in house destruction – could increase 200 percent in eastern Australia during months of highest fire danger. New research by Readfearn (2020) suggests even at two degrees warming, similar conditions to those that caused the record 2019–20 Australian fires would be four to eight times more likely.

5 Temperatures reached forty-seven degrees in the Western Sydney suburb of Richmond in 2016–17 and it is very possible that Sydney temperatures will

Greta Thunberg has died of heat stroke – another casualty of the three in four people now exposed to weeks of deadly heat each year across the globe.[6]

At the funeral were her child Hope, who is seventy; her granddaughter Belle, middle-aged; and her great-granddaughter Elke, fifteen – these are the children dubbed the 'climate babies' as they are living through an era where change is the new 'rat race' for life.

Switching off the radio, Sheila, also middle-aged, downloads the weekend newspapers on her tablet while she can. If only they had understood when there was time that there would not really be any such thing as 'adaptation' – not now – Sheila perseveres through her morning newspapers. Sheila, whose great-grandfather had been in the same year at school as the man who went on to be Australia's former prime minister at the time of the first Great Fires, Scott Morrison, wonders if things might have been different. What if the so-called quiet Australians and the 'technological optimists',[7] who held onto their faith somehow in a better future, had not been too scared to believe they could act on the climate emergency – even as the COVID-Depression was touted as another reason to wait; and supporting the economy somehow became synonymous with old, dirty energy.

At the time, economic growth was the medicine, but now the poison. Too late had we realised that a 'Green' New Deal – a modern-day alternative program to revive society – did not have to mean people OR planet. One thing was true: there were limits to growth and the Earth's carrying capacity.

Saying one thing and doing another, fossil fuel multinationals had pledged allegiance to sustainability while proffering their expansion

---

soar past fifty degrees 'in years to come', according to Gergis (2018, 222).

6   Projections will see the proportion jump from less than one in three currently, found Mora et al. (2017). According to Jean Palutikof, even with four degrees warming, many Australians will be subjected to life-threatening heat in urban areas in summer.

7   In 1987, Costanza and Daly recommend prudent pessimism over technological optimism because disaster would be the outcome in a worst-case scenario of irreversible damage to Earth's life-support systems, where technological fixes would no longer be possible.

plans.[8] And now it was too late to change direction; this is where we have been heading: a hellish 5.8 degrees warming above pre-industrial levels.[9]

Tipping points from extinctions and ecosystems near the upper limit of their temperature range or in restricted climatic niches create dangerous flow-on effects.[10]

When preventing runaway climate change had been a possibility, people could not commit to the transformation that was required.[11] But early prevention, in hindsight, is always better than treatment. The question later became how hot could we handle; survival was a blessing but now also a curse.

Reading the news always triggered Sheila's 'eco-anxiety', although one didn't need a reason. Remembering what it used to be like, Sheila thinks to a time when the Northern Territory's famed Outback was a bucket-list destination. Now largely uninhabitable, inland towns like Alice Springs long deserted – Australia's spiritual and geographic centre is obliterated, with climate change the ignition, the chain of events taking on a life of their own.[12]

Australia – which had been one of a small club of megadiverse countries (including Madagascar and Brazil) – has closed its heart to

---

8 McKibben (2012) argued that to have a reasonable chance of staying below two degrees, humanity can only pour an additional 565 gigatonnes into the atmosphere by mid-century. However, the fossil fuel we're planning to burn is five times that, at 2795 gigatonnes.

9 Gergis, 2019. Some places are more affected by rising global mean averages than others – as shown by NASA (n.d.) Australia is headed for 3.9 degrees above average temperatures by 2090, with a maximum ranging up to 5.3 degrees over much of the continent, shows the CSIRO and Bureau of Meteorology data cited by Gergis (2018).

10 We have already crossed the threshold of three of the nine interlinked planetary boundaries found Rockström et al. (2009).

11 Global greenhouse gas emissions in the first year of COVID-19 to 22 May 2020 fell 4.6 percent, show the results of a study into the socio-economic and environmental impacts from the coronavirus by Lenzen et al. (2020), but to limit warming to 1.5 degrees (in alignment with the Paris Accord of 1.5–2 degrees), GHGs must fall about double that amount each year (*SI*, 32).

12 Summer temperatures, in parts of the outback, of over fifty degrees will make it increasingly unliveable. It is possible we will see towns in the arid zone abandoned by the mid- to late twenty-first century and Darwin will not resemble any part of modern-day Australia under a high-emission scenario, says Gergis (2018, 225).

the vulnerable and the beautiful. The list of the nation's ecosystems that have collapsed read like a fire sale with no return:

GONE: World Heritage-listed ecosystems like Kakadu – renowned for its fragile wetlands.[13]
GONE: The Great Barrier Reef – one of the Seven Wonders of the World.[14]
GONE: The commercial ski industries – with the popular NSW Thredbo-Perisher 'Snowy Mountains' and Victoria's Falls Creek former ski resort virtually snow-free.[15]
GUTTED: The mystery surrounding the South Pole, the coldest, last 'discovered', fifth-largest continent covered kilometers deep in ice – Antarctica. The West Antarctic Ice Sheet destabilised, transforming into freshwater at non-glacial pace.[16] The seas rise up, tsunamis take back civilisation into the ocean, from where we once came.

Grief – yes, scientists crying, tortured by the unfolding end, students hoarse with anger. Learn to live with it.

---

13 King, cited by Gergis (2018, 253), predicted the collapse of many vulnerable ecosystems including iconic wetland areas like Kakadu.

14 Already under just two degrees, it is predicted that a staggering ninety-nine percent of tropical coral reefs will disappear says Gergis (2019), citing the IPCC.

15 Gergis says that some people in the tourism industry have suggested ski resorts in high-elevation sites in NSW will not have enough snow for the viable commercial operation of snow resorts in the future. It's also possible that the natural snow base of the Falls Creek ski resort may be too thin to be sustainable in coming decades (2018, 199).

16 IPCC (2019) predicts sea-level rises of up to about one metre, but says this could be substantially higher if Antarctic ice disappears faster, echoing research by Bamber et al. (2019; as cited in Vaughan 2019c) suggesting a rise of more than two metres. A 2018 article in *Nature Geoscience* by fifty-nine experts in seventeen countries (Fischer et al. 2018) found even warming of 1.5–2 degrees could trigger substantial long-term melting of ice in Greenland and Antarctica, unleashing more than six metres of global sea level rise lasting thousands of years.

The world is getting smaller, with neighboring former island states like Kiribati[17] and Tuvalu[18] submerged, not to mention once famous paradise, the Maldives.[19] Our newest emigrants granted access under Australia's international aid program – we had not listened to the calls of Pacific and other leaders at the coalface to limit temperature rises to '1.5 to stay alive' and we shoulder the burden. Others have not been so 'lucky', with the world's poorest, whose chants of 'One degree, one Africa' that warned against the 'suicide pact' of two degrees warming on the drought-afflicted, famine-threatened continent now an indecipherable scream.[20]

Once, a billion people succumbed to the lure of low-lying areas,[21] now from the mountain tops to the coast, bushfires, heat and wind-borne disasters mean there is less useable land; is it any wonder that climate refugees globally number one billion.[22]

'How odd,' Sheila muses as she scans the newspaper, addicted to her weekend ritual even as it depresses her. The headlines in *The Sydney Morning Herald* do not provide much distraction: in the cities, suicide is down as much of the nation is in a fight for survival. But in country areas the reverse is true. 'Broken Promise' the headline bemoans, reporting on the spring just passed and new farmer deaths in the state as the futile hope for winter rains proves too much – the main chance for a break in the drought denied another year.[23] As if not already under siege, NSW farmers

---

17 It is inevitable that Kiribati will eventually be underwater, likely in 100 years or potentially much sooner, says former Kiribati president. See Tong 2019.

18 Roy 2019.

19 Most of the Maldives is less than one metre above sea level. See UNDP n.d.

20 Delegates from developing nations at the 2009 Copenhagen climate summit warned about the disaster to befall Africa, reports McKibben (2012).

21 In his 2019b article Vaughan summarises the IPCC's prediction that one billion people will live in low-lying coastal areas already by 2050, up from 680 million today.

22 Estimates of climate refugees by 2050 range from twenty-five million to one billion, reports UNHCR (2012).

23 According to Gergis, rural suicides in NSW tend to peak in spring when it emerges that drought-breaking rains during winter have not occurred. Australia's south-west has typically received the bulk of its rain in winter but climate change has shifted this pattern as the zone of high pressure expands over the continent, resulting in rain that has historically brought relief to southern Australia falling over the ocean. This could compromise the already erratic drought-breaking rains that precariously sustain life in twenty-first century Australia (2018, 223).

now also have to fight the 'Queensland' fruit fly, which once only enjoyed northern climates,[24] and the reverberation of rising unemployment is felt nationwide as once-popular tourist destinations dry up: 'Desert tourism deserted', screams another headline.[25]

Midday

Sheila's grumbling stomach reminds her it is time to meet her friend Jo for brunch in Parramatta (half an hour from her home in Richmond).

She covers herself with sunscreen and squirts on some DEET before heading out – yes, the dangerous dengue fever another newcomer to the 'southern tropics', as Sheila likes to joke about Sydney.[26] Climate change has its benefits though, Sheila muses, since there is no need now to holiday in the northern state. In any case, even the capital Brisbane has become too exotic, as the dripping humidity coupled with unforgiving heat in the wet season is excruciating and disastrous storms are a regular event. Further south but still coastal, Hobart has taken on the aridity of Adelaide and the Top End's Darwin no longer resembles any part of Australia in the early 2000s.[27]

Sheila reflects the desolate landscape; barren by choice, mourning children she never lost. Escaping the house which will shortly be an oven, Sheila frowns involuntarily at the bright sun. Fortunately, she makes it to the light rail on time.

Generally of optimistic character, Sheila has excelled in her effort today to wear bright colours that set against the desolate outdoors.

'Jo, you look lovely today,' Sheila calls out encouragingly as she spots her best friend at Café 2021.

Ever a popular Sydney pastime, the talk moves to real estate, which has become somewhat of an extreme sport.

---

24 Gergis 2018, 222.

25 The days of forty degrees plus in Alice Springs, Central Australia, will increase to eighty-three annually – close to a five-fold increase and the almost one hundred million dollars each day from desert tourism will be threatened by extreme heat in the region, says Gergis (2018, 220).

26 According to Gergis, modelling shows dengue fever, traditionally found in South-East Asia and far North Queensland, could spread as far south as Sydney (2018, 231).

27 Gergis 2018.

'Remember the extensive World Heritage Blue Mountains on the edge of Greater Sydney, now referred to it as Bald Mountains because it's ravaged by fire? People actually used to live there, before the mass relocation,' Sheila recalls.[28]

'Yes, and I read that some of our most densely populated areas were destroyed by storm surges and flooding – from Melbourne's CBD to Circular Quay and the Sydney Opera House, up to the Royal Botanic Gardens – and also vast swathes of Queensland's Gold Coast and Port Douglas,' Jo responds.[29]

'I heard maps are being redrawn worldwide because people have to move further inland or to higher ground.[30] It's also happening across the Nullabor, at the WACA cricket ground and Cottesloe Beach in Perth, now submerged.'[31]

Sheila says: 'It's ironic that it would be difficult to leave now even if we wanted to – with airports along the east coast at Brisbane, Sydney and Hobart largely underwater.'[32]

Night

Hours later, the friends arrive at their next destination, the beach – '*a bit of a schlep*' – but a good way to cool down during the hottest parts of the day into late afternoon. As they step off the Metro at the fortified beach suburb of Collaroy, an old haunt, the sea breeze hits them.

'Would you live in those?' Jo asks, pointing to the remaining mansions that no longer have a sandy beach at their doorstep but rather a cliff of sorts. Houses on the water's edge are frequently reclaimed by the ocean, hit by huge waves riding king tides.[33]

28 Even at four degrees there would be a need for mass relocation of populations in Australia from flood- or fire-prone areas says Palutikof as cited in Gergis (2018, 254).

29 Gergis details scenarios likely under a sea-level rise of just two metres, although noting the United States' National Oceanic and Atmospheric Administration in 2017 and Germany's Potsdam Institute for Climate Impact in 2015 estimated global sea-level rises to up to 2.7–3 metres or more, based on Antarctic ice-sheet instability (2018, 225).

30 Gergis 2018, Fischer et al. 2018.

31 Gergis 2018, 226.

32 Assuming sea-level rises of two metres, Gergis argues.

33 Gergis (2018) wrote some Northern Beaches waterfront houses had twenty

'They're a relic of the past,' Sheila observes.

She gingerly wades into the water – warm thanks to increasing sea temperatures – and wonders when the deadly northern box jellyfish will hit Sydney.[34]

On the way home, Sheila's tram is stopped at a checkpoint near the eigth Brigade training centre for the Australian Army – living near Parramatta was a mixed blessing. Her trip to the northern beaches seems to have raised suspicions, not only because it was no longer a destination but also far away from the west, on the way to the port in Newcastle.

A young officer checks her bag but finds nothing.

'Have a nice evening,' he mumbles.

Funny, Sheila thinks, how one can almost get used to conflict – the 150 years of relative peace since Second World War having come to an end, even in Australia. As Greens founder Bob Brown once said, the two existential threats to modern humanity were war and climate change, though the causes are the same; it was now a race to the end.[35] Defence/ Emergency Response and Space were among the few growth sectors, with surveillance and colonisation strategies and infrastructure attached to each major city.

Fuelled by failed crops,[36] spiking food prices,[37] towns and cities running out of water,[38] and other disasters, the basics of nourishment and safety are now increasingly a luxury. Intra-country, cross-country and sea border tensions are on the rise and states sanction conflict to protect their lands and pillage others, and the desperation of vulnerable people everywhere turns to fury.[39]

---

metres of backyards washed away in 2016, and McPhee 2020 reported that a number of houses started collapsing into the sea after storms.

34 Philp et al. 2018.

35 Reiner 2017.

36 The year 2020 saw record numbers of locusts in Africa and India. Gettleman and Raj (2020) say this was caused by unusually warm weather and excessive rain.

37 According to McPhedran (2015), this was seen as a reason behind the Arab Spring.

38 Cape Town avoided this just in time in 2018 but future drought threatened the gains made. In NSW, the Central West and Sydney's Warragamba Dam were said to be at threat in the absence of government intervention and rain, according to Karp and Australian Associated Press (2019).

39 Leading organisations from the Pentagon to NATO member states and the

Nature's fury, too, seems to grow daily and today again it feels like something more than light rail is needed, as hail pounds the roof and builds up on the ground. Fortunately, by the time Sheila reaches her stop, the hail has abated, but this is followed by bucketing rain lashing about, like a mini tornado.

'Here we go again.' Sheila braces herself. The saying had never been truer: when it rains, it pours, such that areas of drought can be overcome by floods and then, just as quickly, drought-stricken again.[40]

As Sheila makes her way around fallen trees, she again reflects without surprise on the fact that Sydney suffers regular coastal flooding orders of magnitude above the inundation experienced at the turn of the century.[41] The streets jerk alive with sirens, horns and flashing lights of red and blue – ambulances – or helicopters too? The sounds mix with the marching of troops, but Sheila is already thinking to a special meal she has prepared for herself. Though not long-lasting, the rain disappears, imagining its job done; at least it may have slowed down the bushfires.[42]

Back at home, the smart electricity system fails to kick in – another night without cooked dinner and likely another shopping expedition in the coming day or so to replace soiled food from the fridge that can no longer be relied on. She has become used to sparse, lonely dinners, as her husband, Frank works away from home for months at a time on major Infrastructure Adaptation Projects for future climatic changes.[43] She writes a message for him, as is their habit: 'I love you'.

G7 have identified climate change as a significant threat to national security, reported McPhedran (2015).

40 A 2017 study by UNSW researcher Jiawei Bao estimated that a two degrees temperature rise would lead to a eleven to thirty percent increase in extreme downpours across Australia as a result of higher humidity. Gergis says the findings suggest if we continue along a high-emissions path to four degrees, we could experience up to sixty percent increase in the most extreme (wetest 0.1 percent) rainfall events.

41 According to Denholm (2012), even at just fifty centimetres sea-level rise (as opposed to one to two metres plus under high-emissions scenarios) in Sydney, inundation will increase 2200-fold. *The Australian* said the 2012 report on the Antarctic Climate and Ecosystems Co-operative Research Centre's findings were conservative interpretations of IPCC projections for sea-level rise.

42 Gergis cites CSIRO projections in 2015 that show global warming will result in an increase in extreme rainfall, even in areas where average rainfall declines.

43 Even at four degrees warming, in some cases risks and vulnerabilities will be so major that they will require enormous transformation, rather than incremental

Fortunately, Sheila has planned a special cold entrée in what was a sturdy home that so far has had no leakages or cracked tiles, unlike so many neighbours have experienced over the years. The previous evening, Sheila had somehow found enough rations for an oyster[44] and splurged on vegetables despite the cost.[45]

Wine – another luxury these days, but she wants to savour the moment. She pours a long glass, props up her mobile on the dinner table and live-streams the evening television news.

She watches the lead story, which reminds her it is time to prepare for her trip. The newsreader blares:

Flooding in northern New South Wales has come after ferocious Cyclone Colin bore unexpectedly through Brisbane – never before has a Category 5 cyclone come this far south.[46] The city of Lismore is besieged. We go now to our reporter in Lismore, Jackie Hallaway. Jackie, what can you tell us?

Yes, this latest storm will make history for the Northern Rivers town for all the wrong reasons. Already the death toll is estimated to be 500 and you can see behind me the whole area has been flattened – it's believed the damage will be four billion dollars, topping Australia's most expensive cyclone to date, Yasi. The town

---

changes, warns one of Australia's pioneers in climate change adaptation, Jean Palutikof in Gergis (2018).

44 Oysters and other shellfish are at grave risk from climate change, according to the ABC (2017).

45 The food net-exporting nation, though, at four degrees warming will itself face issues of food security, says Jean Palutikof, later cited by Gergis. Worldwide, nine in ten people could live in countries with falling food production from farms and fisheries under business-as-usual, research has shown in *Science Advances*, with the greatest impacts on food security will be on vulnerable populations, reports Vaughan (2019a).

46 Gergis (2018) explained how cyclone category five winds of more than 200 kilometres per hour can be expected as far south as Brisbane and even into northern NSW. Being unprepared can turn a hazard into a disaster, like cyclone Tracy in 1974, virtually demolishing the city and killing seventy-one people, with most of its residents – 36,000 – having to be evacuated. In her 2019 opinion piece Gergis elaborated that without major action, we will see tropical cyclones drift into areas on the southern edge of current cyclone zones.

and its satellite suburbs are being evacuated,[47] leaving its residents homeless and topping those displaced by Cyclone Tracy, previously Australia's most disastrous cyclone in 1974, when Darwin was hit unprepared. Blame is quickly shifting to the Premier who has been repeatedly warned that devastation would result if infrastructure was not prepared in accordance with the Building Code of Australia and other relevant standards to safeguard against increasingly intense cyclones becoming part of the new landscape further south.

The cyclone has been followed by torrential rain – and you can see the front is moving closer. Reports have just started coming in that this downpour in the region is washing away houses, roads and crops.[48] Back to you in the studio.

Sheila switches off the news – another day, another disaster, albeit at increasing intensity. No longer lulled into insensitivity that was slowly killing her, the instinct for survival kicks in. She must prepare for tomorrow.

She gathers a few essentials, including clothes to protect her from water, wind, heat and fire, and turns in early.

Unable to sleep at first because of the dulled white smoky sky that rarely goes dark, Sheila eventually lulls into a state of seemingly semi-consciousness; images of the past flashing by, her mind's farewell to this land. She sees:

A megadiverse forest spanning 3665 square kilometres (home to almost 4000 individual species of plants and animals) she remembers from her childhood, she enters from an isolated wetland of crystal-clear ice-cold water – she knows it is part of the ancient Gondwana Rainforests of Australia[49] that once covered the supercontinent because it is teeming with life, a refuge for rare and threatened species and one of two Australian biodiversity hotspots rare in the world.[50]

As she jogs past conifers from the Jurassic era, the forest starts to thin. A catbird is perched on a branch, eerily quiet; she almost kicks a small, mouse-like eastern pygmy-possum pollinator, dead at her feet. The forest is deserted as she runs further from the beach, the ground is parched,

---

47 Kamenev and AAP 2011.

48 Gergis 2018, 202.

49 The ancient rainforests located in northern NSW to south-eastern Queensland – formerly called the Central Eastern Rainforest Reserves.

50 Gergis 2018, 238–9.

the canopy gone and the trees are now shrubs as far as the eye can see. She has travelled a lifetime, now back in the present and this enduring rainforest is no more, like most of Australia's precious iconic natural areas with species pushed beyond the edge of their climatic zones.[51] We are headed for a mass extinction event equivalent to that which wiped out the dinosaurs about sixty-six million years ago – along with eighty percent of all other life on Earth.[52]

The last sunrise

Sheila hastily packs her bag, awoken by the gentle light of dawn and stumbles outdoors, as if still in a dream, remembering what was once, or could be …?

Australia, naturally a land of droughts and flooding rains, has become extreme from climate change.[53] But there was nowhere in the world that had not suffered irreversible, dangerous changes.

'Five, four, three, two, one – blast off,' comes the mechanical sound from the rocket headquarters and Sheila starts, as she shoots upwards, along with the other space tourists headed towards a planet known as 'B'.[54]

Sheila tries not to look down but invariably can already see in her mind's eye the clouds – or is it smoke? Her stomach lurches up, tears flooding her eyes as her body prepares for the flames about to engulf her and she stands transfixed, unable to avert her gaze from the Earth's beauty as it disappears from sight.

---

51 Species likely to become extinct include Australia's most valued and iconic natural areas including the World Heritage Gondwana Rainforests of Australia – that extend from NSW to Queensland – formerly called the Central Eastern Rainforest Reserves and home to more than 200 rare or threatened plant and animal species, says Gergis (2018, 238).

52 If our current high-emissions trajectory continues, says Gergis (2018, 240). According to Danner's 2009 prediction, this could be as early as 2100.

53 Economist Ross Garnaut was referenced by Gergis, saying that Australia is the most vulnerable country in the developed world; recently the Asia-Pacific, which includes Australia, was dubbed 'Disaster Alley' by experts. Climate change will affect different countries in different ways; in Australia, whose climate is variable, we can expect even greater extremes.

54 In 2017 popular scientist Stephen Hawking warned that people would need to colonise another planet within 100 years or face extinction.

Acknowledgements and postscript

This is dedicated to my sister Mischa, who helped me look beyond the numbers, and my children, Veronika and Hannah, whose families will live through 2100.

Although business-as-usual has us on a pathway towards six degrees warming at the time of writing in 2020, there is still time to ensure our carbon emissions are reduced in line with the Paris climate accord to limit warming to a maximum two degrees to prevent uncontrollable climate change.

The University of Sydney's Master of Sustainability learnings underpin this story, without which it would not have been written.

Key reference: Gergis, J. (2018). *Sunburnt country: the history and future of climate change in Australia.* Carlton, VIC: Melbourne University Press.

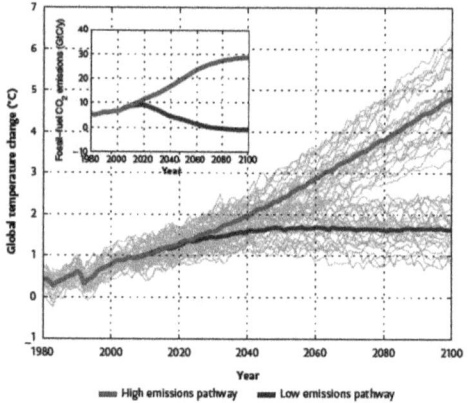

■■ High emissions pathway   ■■ Low emissions pathway

Future projected climate change depends on new emissions of greenhouse gasses. Retrospective and future projected global surface area temperature changes (degrees: relative to 1861–80) under both high and low emissions pathways. Individual model simulations are shown as faint lines, with bold lines indicating the multi-model average. The corresponding two emissions pathways, including all industrial sources,are included in the inset. Emission units are gigatonnes (billion tonnes) of carbon per year (GtC/y). Data from Coupled Model Intercomparison Project (CMIP) 5.

Figure reproduced from: Australian Academy of Science 2015, 16.

References

ABC. "Scientists searching for the 'Goldilocks' oyster which best adapts to climate change." *ABC News*, 15 August 2017. https://www.abc.net.au/news/2017-08-15/scientists-studying-how-oysters-adapt-to-climate-change/8804502.

Australian Academy of Science. The science of climate change: questions and answers. 2015. https://www.science.org.au/files/userfiles/learning/documents/climate-change-wr.pdf.

Bamber, J. L., Michael Oppenheimer, Robert E. Kopp, Willy P. Aspinall, Roger M. Cooke. "Ice sheet contributions to future sea-level rise from structured expert judgment." *PNAS* 116, no. 23 (2019): 11195–200. doi:10.1073/pnas.1817205116.

Costanza, R., and Herman Daly. "Toward an ecological economics." *Ecological Modelling* 38 (1987): 1–7. doi:10.1016/0304-3800(87)90041-X.

Danner, A. "'Earth 2100': the final century of civilization?" *ABC News*, 29 May 2009. https://abcnews.go.com/Technology/Earth2100/story?id=7697237&page=1.

Denholm, M. "Coastal flooding may rise 2000-fold." *The Australian*, 4 July 2012. https://www.theaustralian.com.au/news/health-science/coastal-flooding-may-rise-2000-fold/news-story/86169211501ff2d0e5a951d4f08473c2.

Fischer, H., Katrin J. Meissner, Alan C. Mix, Nerilie J. Abram, Jacqueline Austermann, Victor Brovkin, Emilie Capron, Daniele Colombaroli, Anne-Laure Daniau, Kelsey A. Dyez et al. "Palaeoclimate constraints on the impact of 2°C anthropogenic warming and beyond." *Nature Geoscience* 11 (2018): 474–85. doi:10.1038/s41561-018-0146-0.

Gergis, J. *Sunburnt country: the history and future of climate change in Australia.* Carlton, Victoria: Melbourne University Press, 2018.

Gergis, J. "The terrible truth of climate change." *The Monthly*, August, 2019. https://www.themonthly.com.au/issue/2019/august/1566136800/jo-lle-gergis/terrible-truth-climate-change.

Gettleman, J., Suhasini Raj. "'Overtaken by aliens': India faces another plague as locusts swarm." *The New York Times*, 27 May 2020. https://www.nytimes.com/2020/05/27/world/asia/india-locusts-jaipur.html.

IPCC. *The ocean and cryosphere in a changing climate.* UN Environment Programme, 2019. https://www.unenvironment.org/resources/report/ipcc-special-report-ocean-and-cryosphere-changing-climate.

Kamenev, M. and AAP. "Australia's worst cyclones: timeline." *Australian Geographic*, 2 February 2011. https://www.australiangeographic.com.

au/topics/science-environment/2011/02/australias-worst-cyclones-timeline/.

Karp, P., and Australian Associated Press. "'Critical': parts of regional NSW set to run out of water by November." *The Guardian*, 15 September 2019. https://www.theguardian.com/australia-news/2019/sep/15/parts-of-regional-nsw-set-to-run-out-of-water-by-november.

Lelieveld, J., Andrea Pozzer, Ulrich Pöschl, Modammed Fnais, Andy Haines, Thomas Münzel. "Loss of life expectancy from air pollution compared to other risk factors: a worldwide perspective." *Cardiovascular Research* 116, no. 11 (2020). doi: 10.01093/cvr/cvaa025.

Lenzen, M., Mengyu Li, Arunima Malik, Francesco Pomponi, Ya-Yen Sun, Thomas Wiedmann, Futu Faturay, Jacob Fry, Blanca Gallego, Arne Geschke, Jorge Gómez-Paredes, Keiichiro Kanemoto, Steven Kenway, Keisuke Nansai, Mikhail Prokopenko, Takako Wakiyama, Yafei Wang, Moslem Yousefzadeh. "Global socio-economic losses and environmental gains from the coronavirus pandemic." *PLoS One* 15, no. 7 (2020). doi:10.1371/journal.pone.0235654.

McKibben, B. "Global warming's terrifying new math." *Rolling Stone*, 12 July 2012. https://www.rollingstone.com/politics/politics-news/global-warmings-terrifying-new-math-188550/.

McPhedran, I. "Climate change is a major security threat for Australian Defence Force." *News.com.au*, 22 September 2015. https://www.news.com.au/technology/environment/climate-change/climate-change-is-a-major-security-threat-for-australian-defence-force/news-story/0004ff65f764649400889ab59f7c26ce.

McPhee, S. "Wamberal Beach, NSW erosion: beach homes 'partially collapse'." *News.com.au*, 18 July 2020. https://www.news.com.au/technology/environment/wamberal-beach-nsw-erosion-significant-risk-of-structural-collapse/news-story/9224260482749b5271e27b136d98028d.

Mora, C., Bénédicte Dousset, Iain R. Caldwell, Farrah E. Powell, Rollan C. Geronimo, Coral R. Bielecki, Chelsie W. W. Counsell, Bonnie S. Dietrich, Emily T. Johnston, Leo V. Louis et al. "Global risk of deadly heat." *Nature Climate Change* 7 (2017): 501–6. doi:10.1038/nclimate3322.

NASA. "GLOBAL Land-Ocean Temperature Index in 0.01 degrees Celsius base period: 1951–1980." NASA, n.d. https://data.giss.nasa.gov/gistemp/tabledata_v4/GLB.Ts+dSST.txt.

Reiner, V. "Bob Brown receives an honorary Doctor of Science." *The University of Sydney*, 22 September 2017. Media release. https://www.sydney.edu.au/news-opinion/news/2017/09/22/bob-brown-receives-honorary-doctorate.html.

Rockström, J., Will Steffen, Kevin Noone, Åsa Persson, F. Stuart Chapin III, Eric F. Lambin, Timothy M. Lenton, Marten Scheffer, Carl Folke, Hans Joachim Schellnhuber et al. "A safe operating space for humanity." *Nature* 461 (2009): 472–5. doi:10.1038/461472a.

Roy, E. A. "'One day we'll disappear': Tuvalu's sinking islands." *The Guardian*, 16 May 2019. https://www.theguardian.com/global-development/2019/may/16/one-day-disappear-tuvalu-sinking-islands-rising-seas-climate-change.

Philp, J., Michael Kingsford, Will Figueira, Killian Quigley and Maria Byrne. "Jellyfish behaving badly?" *The University of Sydney*, 2018. Podcast. https://www.sydney.edu.au/engage/events-sponsorships/sydney-ideas/2018/jellyfish-behaving-badly.html.

Tong, A. "Why island nations' isolation on the climate change threat must end." *The University of Sydney*, 2019. Podcast. https://soundcloud.com/sei_sydney/why-island-nations-isolation-on-the-climate-change-threat-must-end.

UNDP. "Maldives." UNDP Climate Change Adaptation, n.d. https://www.adaptation-undp.org/explore/maldives.

UNHCR. "The state of the world's refugees: in search of solidarity." *UNHCR*, 2012. https://www.unhcr.org/publications/sowr/4fc5ceca9/state-worlds-refugees-2012-search-solidarity.html.

Vaughan, Aa. "Climate change could trigger huge drops in food production by 2100." *New Scientist*, 27 November 2019. https://www.newscientist.com/article/2224798-climate-change-could-trigger-huge-drops-in-food-production-by-2100/.

Vaughan, Ab. "IPCC report: sea levels could be a metre higher by 2100." *New Scientist*, 25 September 2019. https://www.newscientist.com/article/2217611-ipcc-report-sea-levels-could-be-a-metre-higher-by-2100/#ixzz69bKfmYTE.

Vaughan, Ac. "Sea level rise could hit 2 metres by 2100 – much worse than feared." *New Scientist*, 20 May 2019. https://www.newscientist.com/article/2203700-sea-level-rise-could-hit-2-metres-by-2100-much-worse-than-feared/.

ABOUT THE CONTRIBUTORS

Memi Adams

I am a student at the University of Sydney Business School. Mountains/ Psalm 121 is a charcoal illustration that was inspired by the recent improvements in air quality during the lockdown phase in India. The vast reductions in air pollution led to clean air, blue skies and visible Himalayan peaks. With the effects of climate change such as global warming, rising sea levels and shrinking mountain glaciers so prevalent, there is no better time than now to engage in environmental sustainability, which includes reducing water and electricity consumption and waste. Mountains are an important source of freshwater, energy and food to mountain communities, yet because of environmental degradation, community livelihoods are now vulnerable. However, I believe that with each small step of faith, persistence and united community effort, every one of us can help reduce our environmental footprint so that healing of the environment can be achieved. I also hope to visit the Himalayas one day!

Raz Badiyan

I am a lover, desiring to express it all in written word. I feel emotions in waves and sometimes tsunamis, learning how to capture it all. Influenced by magical people, nature and personal experiences, I seek inspiration between the cracks of my day job as a pharmacist. I am currently working on publishing my first collection of poetry. You can follow my work on Instagram @rbwords.

Anika Bhatia

I am a third-year Media and Communications and Marketing student. I am passionate about theatre, sustainable living and helping those who are disadvantaged. I aspire to travel upon the completion of my studies and continue to write and act.

Gabriela Bourke

I am a doctoral candidate at the University of Sydney. I am most interested in fictional representations of animal and human trauma, and the ways in which these intersect. My work has appeared in *Southerly* and *Mascara Literary Review*.

Sophie Chao

I am a Postdoctoral Research Associate at the University of Sydney. My anthropological research explores the intersections of ecology, indigeneity and capitalism in Southeast Asia. For more information, please visit www.morethanhumanworlds.com.

C.L. Crozier

I am studying a Master of Publishing and work part time in a bookstore. In my spare time I enjoy writing fantasy, reading whatever I can get my hands on and studying Japanese. I currently live in Sydney with my identical twin sister and I dream of one day selling my own book.

Ashleigh Cuthill

I am a Master's student at the University of Sydney studying publishing. I have always been a bookworm and enjoy escaping reality and entering new worlds that can only be found between the pages.

Louise Dziedziczak

I am a former student from the University of Sydney where I completed my undergraduate degree in health science. I then studied a Master of Public Health from Western Sydney University. I love the TV show *Friends* and my dog Alfie, whom I love to take on walks and hikes.

Johanna Ellersdorfer

I recently completed a Masters of Creative Writing at the University of Sydney where I was a recipient of the Janet O'Connor Scholarship. I am a writer, occasional painter and lapsed painting conservator, slowly working on a career change. I write nonfiction and occasionally fiction about small moments and daily habits that construct a life. I have a long running interest in failures of all kinds and write as a way of making sense of the world around me.

Keesha Field

I am a time-based artist who studies at the Sydney College of the Arts. Greatly concerned with the climate crisis, I find myself observing and representing the human and its interactions with the environment. 'Garden Anthropocene,' are stills of a film created to support a guided meditation – to further a sense of relaxedness. Ironically, I grew to find the images reflective of a poisoned natural beauty and could not shake the nauseating reality of what it means live in this society.

India Gill

I am a first-year student at the University of Sydney studying a Bachelor of Arts and Advanced Studies, majoring in International and Global Studies and English. In the face of climate change, I have always felt quite helpless in terms of fighting for change and sustainability. I turned to writing as a means of creating new perspectives on the subject and hopefully inspiring others to fight for change too.

Liam Grealy

I am a Postdoctoral Research Fellow in the Housing for Health Incubator, which is attached to the Department of Gender Studies at the University of Sydney. My research investigates cultures of policy making, especially housing and infrastructure policy in remote and regional Australia and southeast Louisiana. I am a visiting scholar at Louisiana State University, but returned to live in Darwin again in 2020. With Kirsty Howey, my research has investigated the absence of protections for drinking water in the Northern Territory and the potential for safe drinking water legislation, including for the Central Land Council. Further collaborative research projects are represented at: https://www.hfhincubator.org/; https://infrastructuralinequalities.net/; https://issue2.mxd.media/; and http://mediaclassification.org/.

Djuna Hallsworth

All my life, I have been interested in creating art and exploring representation. Moving through creative writing to research, cartooning and collage to photography, stop motion to HD video capturing, I am curious about how to capture a moment and communicate it visually. I have recently completed my PhD on Danish film and television in the Department of Gender and Cultural Studies at the University of Sydney, and, in between teaching, am focusing on writing fiction.

Joshua Harper

I am a fourth-year student, studying English and Media and Communications. My stories often try to embody a mood, or a feeling, which is my excuse for the fact that I struggle to write endings.

Wil Haviland

I am a student in the Master of English Studies at the University of Sydney. My contribution to the 2020 Student Anthology came about as a result of a dalliance with the creative nonfiction genre. I approached this piece with the hope that a special blend of fact and fantasy would provide an interesting way of interrogating the climate crisis.

Kirsty Howey

I am a PhD Candidate in the Department of Gender and Cultural Studies, and was previously a native title and land rights lawyer for ten years. My research ethnographically examines the intersections between Indigenous property rights, environmental law and development in the Northern Territory, where I am based.

Vrishali Jain

My journey as a writer began with writing fictional stories centred on human relationships for various radio channels in India. This later expanded to multiple audio forums and collaborations with Indian government for social awareness. From my quaint hometown of Kanpur to the Indian capital of New Delhi and now in Sydney, I have dabbled with journalism, writing, editing and social media management. Coffee and coke have sustained my clumsy self through it all and cooking helps me destress. When I am not hopping from a bookshop to museum to thrift stores, I can be found at the beach. Currently working as a producer at *SBS Hindi*, I am now looking to begin my research work into queer publishing in Australia and India.

Dr Karl Kruszelnicki

I am the Julius Sumner Miller Fellow at the University of Sydney. I am a qualified medical doctor, engineer, physicist and mathematician. I have written forty-six books, and have worked as a doctor in Sydney Kids' Hospital, taxi-driver, engineer, labourer, physicist, roadie for Bo Diddlie, test-driver of 4WDs across most of the dozen-or-so Australian deserts, etc.

Charlotte Lim

I am a fiercely vegan, intersectional eco-feminist. My contribution to the anthology is built from my advocacy of climate justice and animal rights. I have just completed my undergraduate degree in gender studies and will put my knowledge to use as a graduate in legal policy at the federal Attorney-General's Department. In my spare time you'll find me volunteering at NSW Hen Rescue, an animal sanctuary dedicated to the liberation of all animals with a focus on caged hens. I have published work in *Liminal Magazine*, *Tenderly*, *Honi Soit* and *ZAMI*, and have presented my academic research at the 6th European Association for Critical Animal Studies Conference (22–24 May 2019) held in Barcelona.

Michael Lotsaris

I am an Honours student in the Department of Government and International Relations at the University of Sydney, with completed majors in Government and International Relations and Economics. My research focuses on the security implications of climate change because this phenomenon fundamentally presents epoch-altering disruptions upon the stability of natural systems, and hence the sustainability of human systems. I also believe that the complexity of climate changes requires diverse and thoughtful engagements, which explains my contributions concerning vehicles and supply chains for this anthology.

Jessica McLean

I am a geographer at Macquarie University and live in Marrickville. I like to take long walks along the river and have had pieces published in *Cordite*, *Meanjin* and *NGV Magazine*. My research is focused on how humans, more-than-humans, environments and technologies interact to produce geographies of change.

Naosheyrvaan Nasir

A proud resident of Western Sydney (because USYD doesn't have enough of them), I am known for my letters to the editor in major Australian newspapers (google me), my impulsive poetry, unconventional speeches and a few short stories. I make myself known on Twitter through @nao_nasir, read the news and volunteer at the Bait-ul-Huda mosque (House of Guidance) in Marsden Park. I have finished my second year of a Bachelor of Arts (Economics)/Bachelor of Advanced Studies (Project management) and aspire to be a professional economist and/or project manager. My work has been published in *ARNA* and *Diversity* (USYD Anthology 2020). My poem explores how Australia's right-leaning political supporters are marginalised in their support of climate change.

Belinda Paxton

I am a lawyer and mother of two. My poems and fiction have been published in the *Mascara Review*, the *Grieve* Anthology (2018) and *Power* (USYD Anthology 2019). I was inspired to write 'Trashed' after visiting a waste drop-off centre and being both awed and revolted by the immensity of our waste. The story is named after a *Four Corners* documentary of the same name.

Gabrielle Platt

I'm a graduate of a Bachelor of Arts in Government and International Relations and Masters of Media Practice. I hope to build a career in public affairs, journalism and policy. My now not-so secret dream is to one day write a play or a novel.

Lauren Poole

I am a Masters student at the University of Sydney studying Museum and Heritage Studies. I have a Bachelor of Arts in English and Archaeology, and was awarded the 2017 Max Le Petit Memorial Prize for Classical Archaeology. My writing has appeared in *The Quotidian* (USYD Anthology 2017) and *Growing Up Disabled in Australia* (Black Inc. Books, 2021). I live with an acquired brain injury.

Yasodara Puhule-Gamayalage

I paint and compose music in my spare time. The subject matter of my work primarily reflects my experience as a person of colour and a member of a generation united in eco-anxiety.

Vivienne Reiner

I am a professional communicator with some twenty-five years' experience and have worked for half my career focusing on the environment, health and wellbeing. A former general reporter with *The Australian* newspaper, I became a freelancer for publications like *The Sydney Morning Herald*, *Green* and *G Magazine*. I then moved into not-for-profit public relations, including jobs with Greenpeace and Landcare Australia. My current role as a university media adviser inspired a love of lifelong learning. I am now undertaking the wonderful Master of Sustainability degree part-time, which is complementing my experience in communications and sector-specific knowledge with an academic grounding in science.

Francesca Edwards Rentsch

I am a writer and an artist whose goal is to uncover the beauty in the off-putting and the alien in the everyday. I have previously been published in several USYD journals, including *ARNA* and *Hermes* amongst others. I am currently studying a Bachelor of Arts with a major in Art History and English Literature. 'The Wolf' is the child of my desire to revive the gruesome brutality of fairytales and my experiences hiking through parched, sooty bushlands following the 2020 fires. To see more of my art practise, follow @to_be_perfectly_frank.

Seth Robinson

I am an American-Australian writer, currently based in Melbourne. I grew up in Canberra, where I completed my undergraduate studies at ANU. I relocated to Melbourne in 2016 to study in the Master of Creative Writing, Publishing and Editing program at the University of Melbourne. Now, I am undertaking a Doctor of Arts (Creative Writing) through the University of Sydney. My debut novel, *Welcome to Bellevue* was published by Grattan Street Press in 2019. To find out more about my work, visit www.sethrobinson.ink

Hannah Roux

I'm a fourth-year English Literature student who writes poetry. My poems have been published in the 2017 and 2019 editions of this anthology, as well as online by the Australian Writer's Centre. I believe that the world is sacred, and it is our human duty to preserve and guard it as its stewards. The poems I have submitted here are about that duty.

Angad Roy

I am an Honours student at the University of Sydney. I am currently an editor of *Honi Soit*, and have been previously published in *Overland* and *Michael West*, amongst others.

Jennifer Sacks

I am a University of Sydney student in the final semester of my Master of Publishing degree. I have always had an interest in reading and editing, and enjoy creative writing as a fun exercise in which I am in control of the story. I hope to be able to edit fiction in the future, as I love to both read and write it.

Jennifer Scarini

I completed my Master of Special and Inclusive Education at the University of Sydney in 2017. I currently work at a South West Sydney high school in their support unit, with students who have a mild to moderate intellectual disability. I have always been passionate about environmental studies and enjoy passing knowledge onto my students, who are all keen environmentalists. I don't think we will appreciate what we have until it is no longer here. It is time to act. It is time for change.

Isla Scott

It seems rather obvious to say I'm an avid reader, writer, and editor – that I'm in love with perfect turns of phrase or passionate characters and entrancing worlds. But alas, it's true. I studied literature in my undergraduate degree, dabbled in psychology, and I'm now completing my Master of Publishing. I have a list of all my favourite words (obviously ongoing), and I love cherry blossoms and wind farms and happy endings.

Melissa Snook

I am a University of Sydney graduate, having completed a Bachelor of Arts majoring in American Studies and History in 2016 and an Honours degree in American Studies in 2018. During my undergraduate degree, I did a unit of study on comedy in America. I became fascinated with the topic, and it became the inspiration for my honours thesis on obscenity in American stand-up comedy. I also have a Masters of Publishing from the University of Sydney, and am currently working towards becoming a freelance editor. I love books and reading, and have a very serious book buying problem!

Mary Stanley

I am a speculative fiction writer whose work aims to challenge morality and disturb the peace. My prose has been published in *ARNA* and *Diversity* (USYD Anthology 2020), and several of my short plays have been staged at 24 Hour Theatre, Bridge Works, and Tales from the Metropolis. My short story 'Undrown' imagines a dreary and grey Australia that has sank below the ever-rising sea with survivors turning on one another in the face of scarcity and environmental degradation.

Jakelin Troy

I am a Ngarigu of the Snowy Mountains, in south eastern Australia. I am an anthropologist, linguists, educator and visual artist with a passion for all things Indigenous and protecting the environment using Indigenous knowledges and practises. I am Professor and Director of Indigenous Research at the University of Sydney and support the Sydney Indigenous Research Network and Hub.

Abby Jean Wilson

I work in publicity at Penguin Random House. I am also in my last semester of my Master of Publishing at the University of Sydney. The great love of my life are books, and I would spend all day reading them if possible. It's a natural progression that I write stories.

Rosalin Xie

I'm a Bachelor of Science and Advanced Studies student, majoring in Computer Science and Information Systems. From a young age, I've always loved to express myself creatively whether through poetry or prose.

The artistic side of me is a stark contrast to the other side of me that loves to reason and code, but I find that they help me to view the world from different perspectives. As someone who's surrounded by technology, I understand that it's tempting to ignore the effect of our actions (or inaction) on the environment. I hope my work propels readers to move forward in the world in a sustainable way.

Angela Xu

I am a Bachelor of Arts and Bachelor of Law student at the University of Sydney, majoring in History. My work has previously been published in *Yemaya* (Sydney University Law Society) and *Honi Soit*, and I have also dipped my toe into editing. Growing up in New Zealand, a strong connection to the environment has always been an integral part of my life and I am passionate about environmentalism and its accessibility. My piece was inspired by my own experiences in trying to minimise my waste and hope that my piece prompts readers to consider zero-waste as a multifaceted and imperfect movement, while maintaining hope for waste minimalism in the future.

Bianca Yeung

I am a writer and lover of stories of all forms, spanning from novels and short films to fleeting interactions with strangers on trains. When not eavesdropping on said strangers for new poetry ideas, I can be found drinking tea, practising handstands and occasionally drawing. I find it harrowing that the impacts of climate change have manifested even in my own short lifetime, and am terrified at the thought of encountering smoke-filled summers year on year. I hope that the chorus of voices within and outside of this anthology will reach the ears of those who care to enact change. I study English and Neuroscience at the University of Sydney.

Sophie Zhou

Hello! I am an undergraduate at the University of Sydney. I am enjoying my time creating interesting sounds and art. Please follow my Instagram @bowlcut_senpai for more creative journeys ahead. 'Tuning in' hopes to prompt readers to think about their own plant blindness and tune into the environment around them with small steps at a time. Let's not forget to tune into the rich life around us when we demand climate action.

Victor Zhou

I am an undergraduate student and art-maker who studies Art History and Design Computing at the University of Sydney. I enjoy writing creative-nonfiction and making digital art on my Instagram @smallcave and I hope to improve over the years. In my forthcoming honours year in 2022, I plan to research my interests which range from photography to environmental humanities. I hope writing new stories about the environment will fuel change for the future.

ABOUT THE EDITORS

Sophie Amos

I love storytelling in any form – books, television, poetry, music, videos games, Twitter threads that go on far too long. I am currently studying a Master of Publishing at the University of Sydney, where I completed a Bachelor of Arts last year. In my undergraduate, I focused on archaeology, biology and creative writing, but literature has always been my first love, which ultimately led to following the publishing route. I hope to one day become an in-house editor with some freelance writing on the side, and I have a particular fondness for poetry, graphic novels, and creative nonfiction.

Heather Burke

I am a postgraduate publishing student, and have a passion for books and literacy. I have a background in education and have previously studied teaching and education at a postgraduate level after completing a Bachelor of Arts. I ultimately decided teaching wasn't for me, but still wanted to share my passions and help others reach their potential. This lead me to the publishing industry. I love reading historical fiction, historical non-fiction, fantasy, sci-fi and classic literature, though I have been known to dip my toes into action and thriller occasionally. This is my first publishing experience, and I love the process. I can't wait to undertake more projects in the publishing industry in the future.

Lily Crozier

When I'm not studying, I work as a bookseller and write on the side. I've published a few short non-fiction pieces in the past, but my dream is to one day publish a fantasy novel. In my spare time I try to read all the books I shouldn't have bought and sometimes dabble in digital art. This is my first publishing project, and hopefully the first of many more to come.

Ashleigh Cuthill

As a child I remember reading a book where the main character was described as 'a perfect angle' throughout and writing to the publisher to let them know ... when it came time for a career change, editor seemed like a natural fit. As a publishing student I'm enjoying the chance to be a part of the whole process while working on the anthology and learning that it's more than fixing typos.

Vrishali Jain

After trying my hand at multiple trades of writing, editing, journalism, social media management, law and accountancy (thankfully, I gave up this one soon after starting), all my interests found solace in publishing. This led me to the Master of Publishing program at the University of Sydney, from which I recently graduated. My coffee addiction, museum hopping and book hoarding define my perennial status of living.

Georgia Parry

I am in my last semester of a Masters of Publishing, and prior to this, I studied a Bachelor of Arts degree, majoring in English. To say I love reading would be somewhat of an understatement, as it is the reason I chose said degrees. The only career goal I have maintained since I was small has been one that is in some way related to reading, as my dream truly is reading for a living. This has evolved to loving the process of developing a good story, and from there my editorial interest was born. It has been fantastic to be able to be a part of the USYD anthology, and it will remain a valuable experience.

Jennifer Sacks

I am a Masters of Publishing student completing my final semester of study. I have long had a passion for reading and editing, and have worked as an English tutor throughout university, which has allowed me to exercise some of my editing skills. I look at the anthology as a great opportunity to be exposed to editing different text types, and hope to one day be a fiction editor!

Isla Scott

I have adored reading, writing, and having strong opinions since a young age, so pursuing a career in editing seemed like a perfect fit. I am currently in the final semester of my Master of Publishing degree, and spend my spare time lamenting the state of current affairs, drinking tea, and idolising my next-door-neighbour's cat.

Emily Smith

I am a postgraduate publishing student and bookseller with a passion for storytelling. I have a background in film and television, having studied communications for my undergraduate degree, but my love for reading and writing ultimately led me to the book publishing industry. I love reading fantasy, sci-fi and magical realism books (if it's dark, gritty and has well-written villains or anti-heroes, I'm guaranteed to love it!) and I am particularly obsessed with characters and stories that push the boundaries of the 'norm'.

Melissa Snook

I am a publishing graduate, working towards becoming a freelance editor. I have previously worked on the *Diversity* (USYD Anthology 2020), with this year contributing my own photographic and non-fiction works. I love reading books and collecting books (which are *definitely* two different hobbies), buying way more books than I could ever read. I also spend way too much time gaming and on Discord chatting with fellow gamers.

Mary Stanley

Being a lover of all things science-fiction and horror, I am hard-wired to finding and nurturing stories packed with adrenaline and conflict. Some of my favourite stories include *The Road*, *Marianne*, and *Roadside Picnic*. As an editor, it's my goal to cultivate and publish speculative fiction that forever changes a reader's perspective on the world around them.